Security in Post-Conflict Africa

The Role of Nonstate Policing

Advances in Police Theory and Practice Series

Series Editor: Dilip K. Das

Policing Organized Crime: Intelligence Strategy Implementation
Petter Gottschalk

Security in Post-Conflict Africa: The Role of Nonstate Policing
Bruce Baker

Community Policing and Peacekeeping
Peter Grabosky

Community Policing: International Patterns and Comparative Perspectives
Dominique Wisler and Ihekwoaba D. Onwudiwe

Police Corruption: Preventing Misconduct and Maintaining Integrity
Tim Prenzler

Security in Post-Conflict Africa

The Role of Nonstate Policing

Bruce Baker

CRC Press
Taylor & Francis Group
Boca Raton London New York

CRC Press is an imprint of the
Taylor & Francis Group, an **informa** business

CRC Press
Taylor & Francis Group
6000 Broken Sound Parkway NW, Suite 300
Boca Raton, FL 33487-2742

First issued in paperback 2017

ISBN 13: 978-1-138-11229-2 (pbk)
ISBN 13: 978-1-4200-9193-9 (hbk)

Library of Congress Cataloging-in-Publication Data

Baker, Bruce.
    Security in post-conflict Africa : the role of nonstate policing / Bruce Baker.
        p. cm. -- (Advances in police theory and practice)
    Includes bibliographical references and index.
    ISBN-13: 978-1-4200-9193-9 (alk. paper)
    ISBN-10: 1-4200-9193-X (alk. paper)
    1. Police--Africa. 2. National security--Africa. I. Title.

HV8267.A2B354 2010
363.28--dc22   2009005323

Visit the Taylor & Francis Web site at
http://www.taylorandfrancis.com

and the CRC Press Web site at
http://www.crcpress.com

Table of Contents

Series Preface

While the literature on police and allied subjects is growing exponentially, its impact upon day-to-day policing remains small. The two worlds of research and practice of policing remain disconnected even though cooperation between the two is growing. A major reason is that the two groups speak in different languages. The research work is published in hard-to-access journals and presented in a manner that is difficult to comprehend for a lay person. On the other hand the police practitioners tend not to mix with researchers and remain secretive about their work. Consequently, there is little dialogue between the two and almost no attempt to learn from one another. Dialog across the globe, amongst researchers and practitioners situated in different continents, are of course even more limited.

I attempted to address this problem by starting the IPES, www.ipes.info, where a common platform has brought the two together. IPES is now in its 15th year. The annual meetings which constitute most major annual event of the organization have been hosted in all parts of the world. Several publications have come out of these deliberations and a new collaborative community of scholars and police officers has been created whose membership runs into several hundreds.

Another attempt was to begin a new journal, aptly called *Police Practice and Research: An International Journal*, PPR, that has opened the gate to practitioners to share their work and experiences. The journal has attempted to focus upon issues that help bring the two on a single platform. PPR is completing its 10 years in 2009. It is certainly an evidence of growing collaboration between police research and practice that PPR which began with four issues a year, expanded into five issues in its fourth year and, now, it is issued six times a year.

Clearly, these attempts, despite their success, remain limited. Conferences and journal publications do help create a body of knowledge and an association of police activists but cannot address substantial issues in depth. The limitations of time and space preclude larger discussions and more authoritative expositions that can provide stronger and broader linkages between the two worlds.

It is this realization of the increasing dialogue between police research and practice that has encouraged many of us—my close colleagues and myself connected closely with IPES and PPR across the world—to conceive and implement a new attempt in this direction. I have now embarked on a book series, Advances in Police Theory and Practice, that seeks to attract writers from all parts of the world. Further, the attempt is to find practitioner contributors. The objective is to make the series a serious contribution to our knowledge of the police as well as to improve police practices. The focus is not only in work that describes the best and successful police practices but also one that challenges current paradigms and breaks new ground to prepare a police for the twenty-first century. The series seeks for comparative analysis that highlights achievements in distant parts of the world as well as one that encourages an in-depth examination of specific problems confronting a particular police force.

This third book in the series, *Security in Post-Conflict Africa: The Role of Nonstate Policing*, demonstrates that donors and governments are increasingly acknowledging that the post-conflict state in Africa lacks the capacity to provide an efficient and an equitable policing, to coordinate security agencies and to ensure human rights compliance. In this context the need becomes ever more apparent for partnerships with those actually providing policing services on the ground, which are invariably nonstate actors. Yet donors and states are nervous about the sustainability, reliability, human rights adherence and accountability of nonstate actors. They are also unsure how to support and collaborate with a sector so diverse, complex and mutable. Even when it is recognised that these are the dominant actors in the security sector and the preferred providers of everyday policing by most Africans in most circumstances, it is unclear to policy makers how support for such a group would be programmable. This is the first book to provide a comprehensive account of who these nonstate actors are in post-conflict Africa, what services they offer, how well they do it, what levels of local support and legitimacy they enjoy, and what are their accountability mechanisms. In doing so it challenges many of the negative stereotypes. Based on nine years field work in eight post-conflict countries, it honestly addresses the hazards of working with such actors and the potential. It also suggests ways in which programmes can be developed to enhance nonstate provision and to establish partnerships with the state police for the benefit of the citizens. It advocates a multi-layered approach that is supporting not just the state, but commercial and community-based policing groups as well. The urgent need is for a security model where the emphasis rests on the quality and efficacy of the services received by the end user, regardless of who delivers that service. This book takes us in this direction.

It is hoped that through this series it will be possible to accelerate the process of building knowledge about policing and help bridge the gap between the two worlds—the world of police research and police practice. This is an invitation to police scholars and practitioners across the world to come and join in this venture.

Dilip K. Das Ph.D.
Founding President, *International Police Executive Symposium*, IPES, www.ipes.info
Founding Editor-in-Chief, *Police Practice and Research: An International Journal*,
PPR, www.tandf.co.uk/journals

Preface

This book grew out of research projects I have undertaken in Africa since 2000. I can still remember the day in Grahamstown, South Africa, 2000, when my state-centric mind finally digested the fact, self-evident to all Africans, that policing is not just done by the police. Faced with car guard cooperatives, armed response private security, street committees, vigilantes, and community paid-for additional police patrols, I had to rethink how security was provided for the average African and whether it mattered that the state was such a small player. The following nine years took me over east, west, and southern Africa asking people who it was they looked to for protection from crime and, when crime occurred, to whom they looked for response. The voices of those in cities and the countryside were almost universal: primarily they did not look to the state for either protection or response but to a whole range of nonstate actors. Initially, I was surprised by the choice on offer for most Africans most of the time and how they negotiated their security in different settings and circumstances according to their norms, experience, and financial abilities. Eventually, however, I had to face the policy implications of multichoice policing. Why was the reality of actual provision so removed from the world as seen by those engaged in security policy and reform? Why was nonstate policing judged by standards that, if applied to the state police, might lead to the withdrawal of donor funding? Over time, I came to bring my own research findings up against current policy and came to adopt a multilayered approach of support for policing providers, although not without meeting considerable skepticism.

Nine years ago, it was hard to gain a hearing, but now there are many voices calling for an approach to security provision in post-conflict Africa that are determined by the realities on the ground in terms of available and sustainable resources rather than by imitations of Western methods. Yet even those, like me, who call for a reevaluation of the delivery of security to Africans do not pretend that they have all the answers. The awful tragedy of conflict welded to structural economic poverty is a combination none would want to start from as a foundation for building security.

This book therefore is only a beginning of the long process needed to rethink policing. It tries above all to put before the reader the perspective of Africans themselves—how they perceive their security needs and how they evaluate those who offer security to them. To understand what is happening on the ground seems a good place to begin before plans to "do people good" are announced by ministers of state. This account, as it unfolds, challenges several prevailing conceptions about policing, the state police, nonstate actors, vigilantes, customary practices, community policing, private/public distinctions, and state building. The most effective challenge is always that which is empirically based; it is hoped that this book provides some evidence for its claims, even if the limitations of my research allow no definitive statements.

In the final analysis, I will be content if all the hundreds of interviews and hours spent traveling on wretched roads produces a book that challenges the current understanding of post-conflict policing in Africa and stimulates thought about the way states and donors might proceed in the future in those restricted circumstances and faced with those desperate needs.

Bruce Baker
Coventry

Acknowledgments

This book is based largely on my research since 2000. In all the countries I have worked, I have been assisted by dedicated and able colleagues, including Amadu Sidi Bah in Sierra Leone, Cecil Griffith and Roosevelt Sackor in Liberia, and Peter Andrews in Rwanda. Funding for the research has come from generous grants from the ESRC, British Academy, and Coventry University: British Academy grant, "The Impact of Policing in Mozambique on Democratic Institutions," 2002; ESRC research fellow, "Multilateral Policing in Africa: Its Nature and Socio-Political Impact in Uganda and Sierra Leone," 2003–2005, award reference R000271293; ESRC research grant, "Multichoice Policing Resources for Post-Conflict Situations: Rwanda and Liberia," 2006–2007, award reference RES-000-23-1102; British Academy grant, "An Evaluation of the Effectiveness of Police Local Partnership Boards in Sierra Leone," 2006.

About the Author

 Bruce Baker is professor of African security and director of the African Studies Centre at Coventry University, United Kingdom. His published articles and books cover policing, security sector reform, popular justice, informal justice, African democratization, and governance. His last book was *Multi-choice Policing in Africa* (Nordic African Institute, 2007). He has conducted fieldwork in Zimbabwe, Mozambique, South Africa, Rwanda, Uganda, The Gambia, Sierra Leone, Cape Verde, Seychelles, Liberia, southern Sudan, and Comoros. He runs the Africa Policing Web site at www.africanpolicing.org.

Africa and the Post-Conflict Security Environment

1

Defining Terms

Like the alluring words on an exotic image of a holiday advertisement, the title "Security in Post-Conflict Africa" makes use of big but ambiguous terms. The ad's promises are uncertain until the small print is examined. What, then, is this book offering when it speaks of Africa, security, post-conflict, nonstate, and policing?

Africa

First, as to the geographical scope, the Africa with which this book is concerned is sub-Saharan Africa; that is, the forty-seven countries that are fully or partially located south of the Sahara.[1] In limiting the study to one subcontinent, I am not arguing for African exceptionalism. Many of the features on policing, particularly nonstate policing, have been recorded in other continents and in economies richer than those of African states. I am also not arguing that any subcontinent, let alone nation, can isolate itself from transnational security, whether interstate organizations, commercial multinationals, or informal cross-border raids and networks. Insecurity that overlaps state borders has generated security that ignores borders as well. The study is therefore a roughly torn page from a bigger book that I hope you will be encouraged to read.

Security

In a "securitized" world (Buzan, Waever, and de Wilde 1998), security fills our anxious horizon from questions of "Is it safe to let our children play outside?" and "Should this tree be lopped lest a branch fall on a passerby?" to "Can we stave off another terrorist attack?" But, the security that is the subject of this book is personal or citizen security; that is, security from crime and disorder (Call 2007). Put positively, it is the security that assures people that all in the community of which they are part (including the rulers and the powerful) live by the agreed rules governing relationships. Not that this relatively narrow perspective of security can be totally divorced from "nontraditional" security issues such as threats of floods, droughts, famine, global

1

warming, ozone depletion, infectious diseases, and many more (Commission on Human Security 2003; Axworthy 2001). Surprisingly, it was only in the early 1990s that it was first explicitly argued that the objective of security policy should be the security of *individuals*, not the state, and that this security was more than military threats but anything that threatened people's safety, rights, and access to resources necessary for life (United Nations Development Programme [UNDP] 1994). Such an apparently self-evident truth had sadly been buried under the state-centered focus of security.

These wider security issues can intensify traditional insecurity because insecurity is a web of threats. The understanding of the interrelatedness of causes of tension and conflict has promoted in the last ten years an integrated approach, captured by the concept of "human security" (Canada 2000; MacRae and Hubert 2001; Thomas 2000; UNDP 1999). From this perspective, there is no human security until people can

> Live in freedom, peace and safety, participate fully in the governance of their countries, enjoy the protection of fundamental rights, have access to resources and the basic necessities of life and inhabit an environment which is not detrimental to their health and well-being. (Organization for Economic Cooperation and Development [OECD] 2000)

The focus of this book on the protection of people's lives and property, the resolution of their disputes, and the maintenance of the social order is therefore only a corner of a wide canvas. Yet, it is a crucial element because it is foundational to human security. Without it, access to other key services and rights will be restricted. For this reason, personal security is a central concern of poor people. Many local communities in the World Bank's Voices of the Poor research identified physical insecurity as their major barrier to development (Deepa et al. 2000). This view was reinforced by the Development Ministers of the OECD:

> Security matters to the poor and other vulnerable groups, especially women and children, because bad policing, weak justice and penal systems and corrupt militaries mean that they suffer disproportionately from crime, insecurity and fear. They are consequently less likely to be able to access government services, invest in improving their own futures and escape from poverty. (2005a, 11)

Just how individuals in post-conflict Africa are actually provided with security will unfold in the course of this book. All that need be said now is that internal security or policing in Africa is not a monopoly of the state. Nonstate policing is embedded in every community. It is ubiquitous to the point that few in Africa challenge its legitimacy, even if they criticize some of its practices. Such is the current low priority given by state police to the protection of property that few, including the state police themselves, would deny that nonstate policing of whatever hue is seen as the best-available deterrent and the fastest responder in time of emergency. Notice that I used the phrase *state police* rather than *public police* here and throughout the book. This is because I have found very little understanding among the police of post-conflict countries that they in any sense belong to the public or are accountable to the public and local independent public authorities. The overriding view is that they are employed by the state and serve the state and its central government.

Conflict

Conflict in this book is used in the sense of collective violence. Previously, authors have worked within the construct of *armed conflict*, defined in terms of the participation of a state as one of the warring parties, a political objective, and the exchange of violence in battles. However, examining the conflicts that have marred the African Continent since 1980, it is apparent that they normally involve fighting between nonstate actors; the objectives of the conflict are as much economic as ideological or political, and the violence deliberately targets unarmed civilians (Brzoska 2007). In these circumstances, the broader definition of conflict is preferred.

The frequency and distribution of the conflicts across the continent of Africa are much greater than those relying on Western media reports might imagine. Many are scarcely reported, although to the people on the ground they are real enough. Since 1980, at least twenty-six states have endured the suffering and destruction of conflict over all or part of their territory (see Table 1.1 and Table 1.2) and, for some states, the slow dawn of reconstruction. They include Angola; Burundi; Central African Republic (CAR);

Table 1.1   Current (2008) Conflicts

Angola	Cabinda secessionists	1975 ff
DRC	Congo War	1998 ff
Côte d'Ivoire	Civil war	2002 ff
Namibia	Caprivi Strip secessionists	1966 ff
Somalia	Insurgency	1991 ff
Sudan (Darfur)	Insurgency	1983 ff
Chad	Insurgency	2008 ff
Kenya/Uganda	Armed pastoralist conflict	1980s ff
Niger/Mali	Tuareg rebellion	2007 ff

ff = & following

Table 1.2   Main Conflicts Since 1980

Angola	Civil war	1975–1992
Angola	Civil war	1992–2002
Burundi	Ethnic strife	1984–1989
Burundi	Ethnic strife	1990–1994
Burundi	Civil conflict	1993–2005
Central African Republic	Civil war	1990s
Comoros	Coups	1980s and 1990s
Comoros (Anjouan)	Secession	1997–2008
Congo (Brazzaville)	Civil conflict	1997–1999
DRC	Kabila rebellion	1996–1997
Eritrea	Independence war	1958–1991
Ethiopia	Civil war	1978–1991
Ethiopia	Second war with Somalia	1998–1999
Ethiopia	Eritrea war	1998–2000
Guinea	Mano River war	2000–2001
Guinea-Bissau	Civil war	1998–1999
Liberia	Civil war	1999–2003
Liberia	Civil war	1989–1997
Madagascar	Civil violence	1975–1992
Mozambique	Civil war	1970s–1992
Namibia	Independence war	1966–1990
Niger/Mali	Tuareg rebellion	1990–1995
Rwanda	Civil war and genocide	1991–1996
Senegal	Cassamance rebellion	1982–2004
Sierra Leone	Civil war	1990–2002
Somalia	Period of terror	1986–1990
South Africa	Civil conflict	1985–1994
Southern Sudan	Second civil war	1983–2004
Uganda	Civil war	1980–1985
Northern Uganda	LRA rebellion	1980–2008

Chad; Comoros; Côte d'Ivoire; Democratic Republic of the Congo (DRC); Eritrea; Ethiopia; Guinea; Guinea-Bissau; Kenya; Liberia; Madagascar; Mali; Mozambique; Namibia; Niger; Republic of Congo (Brazzaville); Rwanda; Senegal; Sierra Leone; Somalia; South Africa; southern Sudan; and Uganda.[2] And, several of these states have endured multiple conflicts.

Understanding the post-conflict context for security necessitates understanding the sort of conflict that has gone on before. What was the conflict over, who was involved and affected, and what were the consequences? Some believe that since 2000 there has been an increase in conflict in Africa that revives and reflects divisions over ethnicities, regionalisms, and religions (Mbabazi, MacLean, and Shaw 2002). Others emphasize that at their heart conflicts concern the desire to exploit economic resources for profit (the so-called political economy of violence thesis: Collier and Hoeffler 2001; Forcese 2001; Smillie, Gberie, and Hazelton 2000; Duffield 2001; Berdal and Malone 2000; Howe 2001). Still others see conflict as the product of poor governance. In their view, economies have been impoverished by a mixture of bad management, imposed economic liberalization policies, and global markets. The resulting intensified inequality thus fuels conflicts to secure resources or a fairer distribution of them. As Reno (2000a, 2000b) argued, when weak African states begin to lose control throughout their territory, conflicts multiply over the shrinking national cake. Effective authority for "governance" comes to reside elsewhere, leading to an inability to contain either the causes or the consequences of conflict.

The conflicts in Africa must be differentiated not only in terms of their central dispute but also in terms of the nature of the protagonists. Was the conflict between states, between states and internal rebels, between rebel groups, or with and between what can only be called "criminal gangs," although they may have adopted more attractive titles?

Conflict, then, covers a broad landscape. Only as we understand the contours of the conflict can we understand the security needs and responses of the people in the post-conflict era.

Post-Conflict

The end of conflict may be a pivotal and defining moment in the life of people, but determining the point at which a conflict ends is not as simple as recording the date of the peace agreement.

> There are few truly post-conflict situations. Conflicts become more or less violent, more or less manifest or latent, but they seldom stop altogether. ... [According to the World Bank in 2004,] in 44 per cent of all post-conflict situations, war resumes in the first five years after the violence has stopped, and about 50 per cent of the post conflict countries revert back to war in the first decade of peace. (Junne and Verkoren 2005, 1)

Think of the repeated failure of peace agreements in Angola; Burundi; CAR; Chad; Comoros (Anjouan); Côte d'Ivoire; DRC; Eritrea; Ethiopia; Guinea-Bissau; Liberia; Mozambique; Namibia; Republic of Congo (Brazzaville); Senegal (Casamance); Sierra Leone; Somalia; southern Sudan; and northern Uganda. In fact, it is not uncommon to have a situation that can only be described as "no war/no peace." For instance, in 2008 this would apply to Angola (Cabinda), Burundi, Côte d'Ivoire, Chad, eastern DRC, Senegal (Casamance), Somalia, and Kenya/Uganda (pastoralists). For this reason, it is preferable to conceptualize the presumed final phase of conflict as one "emerging from conflict," rather than as "post-conflict," or simply "post-settlement."

Peace does not necessarily preclude a lingering rebel rump or ex-combatants with weapons turning to violence or new discontents emerging who, having received nothing from the peace, return to war. Could conflict even be endemic in pastoral lands on the Uganda, Kenyan, Ethiopian borders, where the very limited resources are never distributed equitably? And, there is always the "lucrative lure of perpetual violence" for certain entrepreneurs (Salomons 2005, 21). The conflict therefore will end at different times for different people. The conventional portrayal of conflict as a deviation from "normal" life fails to comprehend situations where conflict splutters, re-ignites and is rarely settled by "peace" agreements (Luckham et al. 2001).

The term *post-conflict* is used in much current security literature in a quite technical and short-term sense. It denotes that relatively brief period when peacemaking and state reconstruction missions set about the task of pacification, stabilization, reconstruction of damaged institutions, and reform of those institutions that have proved unfit for their purpose. It is often preoccupied in the initial stages with disarmament of combatants, confiscation of weaponry, mine action, reintegration of former rebel armies into the state security forces or civilian life, and child soldier demobilization and their return to their families and communities. The World Bank has defined *post-conflict* as a "situation where a conflict which prevented a return to a functioning peace-time economy without international assistance ... has subsided to a degree to which ... international assistance is both possible and sustainable" (quoted in African Development Bank [ADB] Group 2004, 11). Other institutions defined post-conflict as when "normality" returns or when "routine national development" is under way (United Nations Development Assistance Framework [UNDAF] 2005). This emphasis on a short period between the end of hostilities and the reestablishment of peacetime services, political and socioeconomic "normality," and when there is a degree of handover of security back to the elected authorities of the country concerned is largely measured in terms of the state. Indeed, the period is often called *state building* (Fukuyama 2004) or establishing legitimate government (Orr 2002).

However, in keeping with my people-centered perspective, I have chosen to take a longer view of post-conflict. I apply the term to the generation that has to put together its lives after the suffering, loss, damage, and mutilation. This certainly lives on beyond the return of control to the central authorities of the country. Like Wallensteen, I agree that "even under the optimal circumstances, peacebuilding is likely to be a concerted process for ten or fifteen years" (2006, 10). Making allowance for the blurred nature of war's end, most commentators would conclude that the *post*-conflict countries of Africa since 1985 would include Angola; Burundi; Comoros; Eritrea; Ethiopia; Guinea; Guinea-Bissau; Liberia; Madagascar; Mauritania; Mozambique; Namibia; Niger; Republic of Congo; Rwanda; Sierra Leone; South Africa; southern Sudan; and Uganda (except the north). Yet, even as I write there are serious doubts about some of these. Nevertheless, in the following chapters these eighteen countries are the main source of concern, and particularly those where I have done fieldwork: Comoros, Liberia, Mozambique, Rwanda, Sierra Leone, South Africa, southern Sudan, and Uganda.[3]

Even when it is fairly clear that the conflict is ended, it is difficult to measure the exact nature of the damage done and of the scale of human and physical wreckage. If the provision of internal security is difficult everywhere and particularly where states have limited capacity, then how much harder it is to provide in a post-conflict environment. Uncertainty prevails about security requirements and resources. No one knows how many lives have been lost (although it may be several million in Africa since 1985); how many people have migrated or been displaced (possibly 10 to 16 million African refugees and internally displaced persons [IDPs] since 1985); what human capital has been dissipated; by how much poverty has been increased (it is estimated that armed conflict in Africa 1990–2005 cost the continent's development nearly $300 billion; IANSA, Oxfam, and Saferworld 2007); how long it will take for government services and economic activity to recover; how many small arms and light weapons are left uncollected (estimated in the millions); how many people are resorting to crime to survive or taking advantage of the general insecurity; how many women and children are left without husbands and fathers to protect them; how many people have become inured to perpetrating human rights abuses; how many people are scarred and traumatized for life. And, how are we to describe the condition of the security and law-and-order institutions? Mani suggested that they could be "corrupt and dysfunctional," "devastated and dysfunctional," or "illegitimate but functional" (Mani 2002). One can also differentiate between post-conflict situations in which policing has to be reconstructed and those in which it has to be built from scratch, as if in a new country. Given all these possible scenarios and the indeterminate nature of the measurements, it is difficult to plan effectively for the future.

Although "post-conflict" is an elusive date on the local-level calendar, that does not mean it is a valueless concept. Whether the break between pre- and post-conflict is ragged, blurred, or sharp, there is no doubt that the two worlds are very different in terms of security provision. The violence and disruption of war will have eroded the pre-conflict structures of law and order, both state and nonstate. Customary chiefs with their court and policing systems may have been driven out or fled, and state police may well have been targeted as defenders of the regime under attack. The social control of family, neighbors, and clan is likely to have dissolved in the anarchy of displacement and bereavement. Hence, crime is frequently a major feature of postconflict societies and is frequently said to rise dramatically at such times. Thus, Interpol heads were told in 2007: "Evidence seems to suggest that as society opens up during and after a transition, local crime emerges from severely constrained ghettoes and is exacerbated by international opportunism" (Graham 2007, unnumbered). The ready supply of arms enables banditry and revenge killings to proliferate. Distracted and weakened security forces allow systematic theft of the incoming aid and reconstruction material. Factions and groups that perceive a threat to their gains from the end of conflict or who resent the faction now in power may express their resentment through violence. In the frenzy to find employment and support for impoverished families, corruption, nepotism, and black markets will flourish. For organized gangs, the opportunities abound to exploit the weak surveillance or even to penetrate state institutions.

Conflict not only disturbs the old order, but also provides the opportunity to bring in a new order and a new way of regulating that order (Call 2002; Call and Barnett 1999). If during the conflict the regime policing fell with its autocratic rulers, new democratic doctrines of civilian policing and community involvement may gain entry after the conflict. Donor reconstruction programs may bring a state policing agenda that includes new styles of policing, new skills in management, new institutions to crack down on endemic corruption, and new capital resources. Reconstruction may also bring economic liberalization and with it the growth of commercial security.

Just how fast and effective the change takes place will be a security issue in itself. It may well be that post-conflict regime change is slow, and there may be an initial security vacuum in the time gap between the discrediting and dismantling of old forms of social control and policing and the introduction of new substitutes. How this law enforcement vacuum is filled could be crucial for policing in the foreseeable future.

There must obviously come a point in a country's history when it is no longer appropriate to call it post-conflict or postwar. In this book, I intend to take the figure of half a generation. Biological anthropologist Agnar Helgason and fellow researchers recommended estimating female generational line intervals at 30 years and male generational intervals at 35 years based on the Quebec and Iceland studies (Helgason et al. 2006). Similarly, sociologist Nancy Howell calculated average generational intervals among present-day members of the !Kung, contemporary hunter-gatherer people of Botswana and Namibia, as 25.5 years per female generation and 31 to 38 years per male generation (Howell 2000). I shall take the post-conflict era therefore to be roughly 18 years.

Nonstate Policing

One of the novel features of this book is the focus on nonstate policing in the context of seeking security for post-conflict societies in Africa. Outside South Africa, little research into this area has been undertaken in the last twenty years, with the exception of customary structures. Too often, such policing groups are dismissed as "vigilantes," with the assumption that they are violent and criminal and have no part to play in assisting the internal security of the new post-conflict era. Such views are a caricature. Many nonstate policing groups are civic minded, locally supported, and concerned for the security of their neighborhoods. This raises, then, the question of what is meant by policing. *Policing*, as understood in this book, is any organized activity that seeks to ensure the maintenance of communal order, security, and peace through elements of prevention, deterrence, investigation of breaches, resolution, and punishment. As such, it can be authorized and provided by local communities and groups as well as the state. Some will be uncomfortable with this wide definition of policing, but in its defense it can be said that it is undeniable that that there is an interconnectedness between different agencies' activities. For example, improved detection affects arrests, which in turn have an impact on prosecution services, courts and jails, or community service. Together, the activities of prevention, deterrence, investigation of breaches, resolution, and punishment constitute a concerted effort to preserve or restore order. Certainly, governments and donors see the value of better coordination across the internal security (or law-and-order) sector to ensure an effective and cohesive strategy and with it the increased likelihood of an enabling environment for development. Ball, Biesheuval, and Olanisakin said of the security sector:

> All key security services, the justice system, and security and justice management and oversight bodies are part of the sector, as are informal and traditional providers of security and justice where these exist ... [This view sees] security and justice as indivisible at the strategic level. (2007, ix)

In similar fashion, the United Nation's (UN's) Bureau for Crisis Prevention and Recovery (BCPR) has developed the concept of justice and security sector reform (JSSR) to emphasize that the justice and the security sectors are inextricably linked. My definition of policing also takes into account the increasing recognition that internal security is more than national security institutions. Beyond the public is not simply the private, but rather an array of community collectives with shared objectives and concerns regarding security (Shearing and Wood 2003). Increasingly, a holistic approach that recognizes the reality of nonstate actors is seen as "particularly relevant in postconflict contexts" (Hänggi and Scherrer 2008, 6).

The term *nonstate policing* can be applied to a wide range of policing agencies. Chapter 2 looks more closely at the definition, but for now it should be noted that these agencies may be provided by customary leaders, religious organizations, ethnic associations, youth groups, work-based associations, community police forums, conflict resolution nongovernmental organizations (NGOs), the lowest or informal levels of local government, and entrepreneurs. Given their diversity, it is not surprising that they have their authorization from a wide spectrum that includes economic interests (legal and illegal), residential communities, cultural communities, religious authorities, individuals, and governments (national and local) themselves.

In fact, they are often linked in some way to the state police, which makes "nonstate" a less-than-adequate conceptualization. The breadth of links often goes unrecognized. I have come across examples of the state police in post-conflict African states: taking offenders to nonstate customary and ethnic courts; asking nonstate groups for help (e.g., concerning suspects); receiving details of suspects from nonstate groups; sitting in nonstate headquarters; using nonstate groups for traffic control, vehicle inspection, and motoring offenses; patrolling with nonstate groups; training nonstate agents to police their neighborhoods/work community; turning to nonstate groups for crime prevention advice and initiatives; and receiving from nonstate groups the cases they cannot or will not handle. In other words, the one (and perhaps the only) thing that nonstate groups have in common is that they are *not* the state police. In the next chapter, it is also suggested that there are other distinctive features, such as that they frequently seek to enforce a different moral and social order and for the most part (with the obvious exception of commercial security) they are based on voluntarism and call on civic, tribal, religious, or union responsibility and personal sacrifice for the well-being of the community.

Conceptual Framework and Argument of the Book

People Centered

This book is focused on people's experience of security in post-conflict Africa; of what works and does not work for them; of what they value and do not value in their local context. It is concerned with how security is provided for them. It assumes that they are the best judge of the security they want and of how well that security is provided by the different providers. It is analyzed as subjectively perceived and objectively measured. To achieve this, hundreds of interviews were held with those authorizing and providing policing (state police, customary structures, commercial security, work-based security associations, local authority security providers, other state security organs);

users of policing (from urban and rural environments and of both gender); and other professionals with insights into internal security and crime (government administration, commercial, jurists, human rights and survivors organizations, and donors). The overall aim of my research since 2000 has been to capture the security experience of villagers and city dwellers.[4] This people-centered approach, as opposed to a state-centric approach, is in line with the human security perspective. It also incorporates the insight that security is something subjective and imagined. It is the product of a "securitization" process by which an issue is turned into a "security issue" when a threat claim is promoted and that claim is widely accepted (Buzan, Waever, and de Wilde 1998, 34). The process is, of course, often contested. Those who identify a new "threat" may be resisted strongly by others who see "it" as a long-standing practice, a gross exaggeration, or a prejudiced point of view. Indeed, the process can be seen as a power struggle to convince or resist assessments of threat and risk (Dupont 2006; Bigo 2000).

Identifying security might even be called a moral struggle, because the fragmentation of policing is not essentially about a dispute over the effectiveness of state policing. It is a dispute over the moral and social order being enforced by others. Policing has at its heart not just a political ambition to control others (the weak, the marginal, the different, and the radical) or a determination to uphold the status quo of power (the "specific order"; Marenin 1982). It is also about the perpetual striving for the elusive "good community"—good as defined by those who authorize the policing agency. It is a moral project in its ambition to improve, cleanse, and protect from evil. Yet, there are competing moral visions of what and how to police. Local leaders and customary chiefs, for instance, uphold local ("customary") law and values. This applies to the definition of crime, the appropriate method of investigation, and what is deemed an appropriate response or punishment. All three areas have the potential to clash with a liberal democratic moral order as incorporated in state constitutions or at times to be even more liberal. More detail is given in the ensuing chapters, but the point I want to make here is that policing practice is shaped by how people imagine security and how they view the ideal moral order.

Nodal Security

The very diversity of how people imagine security, how they view the ideal moral order, and how they wish to control others suggests that it is helpful to conceptualize security as nodal. That is, there exists a multiplicity of authorizers and providers of policing "that co-exist in multiple ways to produce diverse security outcomes" (Wood and Shearing 2007, 13). The authorizers and providers span the state, international corporations, local business, and customary and local/community-based groups. They may be formal (legally recognized) or informal, but they have "sufficient stability and structure to enable the mobilization of resources, mentalities and technologies over time" (Burris 2004, 341). The actual nature of their individual activity, their relationships, and their overall coordination must be determined empirically. I do not assume that the state is the dominant provider; that the nodes are all linked in a security network; that links that do exist are always formal; that nodes cooperate rather than compete; that constitutions and legislation describe reality on the ground; or that consistency exists within security groups over time, space, and grade levels. I have found a wide range of security patterns in the course of my research; therefore, the looseness and variability allowed by the nodal governance framework (and the corresponding social network analysis that determines its specific nature in a particular organizational field) is for me the most fitting for my work (Wasserman and Faust 1994; Dupont 2006). In Chapter 2, I speak more about the degree to which relationships exist that can be called security networks.

Normative Agnosticism

Regarding who *should* be providing security, this book takes an agnostic position. It does not privilege the state and its capacity building ahead of the provision of safety and security. Its focus is on security provision as experienced by people on the ground—on who is actually delivering security at the local level. My emphasis rests on people receiving the best quality of policing regardless of who authorizes and delivers that service. I make no assumption that the state makes a better or worse security provider than nonstate or that the state is more legitimate, more accountable, or more compliant with human rights. It may be; only empirical research can reveal that. I have no normative commitment to privilege the state as a deliverer of security services. I privilege those providers who are the most effective and just that are available. For ninety years, Max Weber has had his description of the state turned into a normative prescription. He wrote:

> A state is a human community that (successfully) claims *monopoly of the legitimate use of physical force* within a given territory. Note that "territory" is one of the characteristics of the state. Specifically, at the present time, the right to use physical force is ascribed to other institutions or individuals only to the extent which the state permits it. The state is considered the sole source of the "right" to use violence. (Weber 1948, 78; italics in the original)

Whatever was true of Europe when he wrote, it is not an accurate description of Africa today. Indeed, it never was true in Africa. The state has never had a monopoly of coercion. The African state's use of force has more often than not been the source of its illegitimacy, whereas others who have used physical force, as customary chiefs, have often (if not always) had communal if not legislative legitimacy. And, as an authorizer of violence the state has many competitors. It has never been strong enough to secure a monopoly of the rights to or the use of violence. It still does not have the capacity. It will not have it in my lifetime.

The Role of the State

Aware that the state cannot provide all services, security or otherwise, some have promoted in Africa the neoliberal vision (hinted at in Weber's 1948 quotation in the preceding section) of the slimmed-down state whose prime role is to oversee and supervise the service provision of others. The regulator-state "steers" not "rows" (Osborne and Gaebler 1992). Loader and Walker (2006) speak of pluralism "anchored in the state." Yet, where in post-conflict Africa is a state that can adequately oversee its own police force, let alone the diversity that constitutes policing within its territory? We cannot, as Paris pointed out, take the existence of functioning states as a given: "War-shattered states typically lack even the most rudimentary governmental institutions" (2004, 46). The problem is not just that the state cannot do all the rowing; it also does not have the capacity to steer. It does not have the capacity to ensure the quality, efficacy, and accountability of all policing agencies to license, vet, monitor, and regulate the delivery of security services; to ensure that effective policing is equally accessible to all; to protect and preserve civil rights and human rights; and to establish the parameters within which nonstate security is provided (Meagher 2005, 7). In these circumstances, it is still unproven that the African state has "a viable and justifiable role to play in the delivery or governance of security" in a pluralized world of policing (Loader and Walker 2001, 11).

For all that its security services are heavily subsidized by donor training and equipment, the reality is that the African state is one of many security actors and rarely provides the majority of the everyday elements of that service. It is but one node. Some may regret that, but nothing is gained by putting our blind eye to the telescope. That is why it is important to evaluate policing and not just the police; to eschew pejorative terms and narrative that make straw men of nonstate policing agencies to damn them. The task of objective analysis is not helped if we adopt double standards. We may well criticize nonstate policing for its poor accountability, its susceptibility to political manipulation, its weak human rights record, its discrimination against women and the poor, its inadequate record-keeping, and the like. Such critique is welcome as long as it is remembered that such concerns apply to the state police as well, perhaps more so (in the light of recent assessments of the police).

Many set security construction within an overall framework of state building. This is a conscious effort

> to increase the importance of state actors, structures and processes in governance systems: to shift *governance* towards *government*. It is the attempt to reform, build and support government institutions, making them more effective in generating the above mentioned public goods. (Nixon 2008, 3; italics in original)

The same OECD report that recommended the need to work with local forms of security governance still cannot see beyond state primacy: "The rule of law—both in the broad sense of accountable governance, but also in the specific sense of a strong judicial sector, including police—is a core process for developing resilient states" (2008, 38). Hence, it unquestioningly set security within the state-building context so that "supporting the long-term development of legitimate state security structures should be a core goal of state-building policy" (2008, 24; see Scheye unpublished manuscript). This is a political project. If the object of security reform is state building, then there is a case for concentrating efforts on the state police. However, if the object is security building, then, I argue, reform all reformable groups currently providing a security service in post-conflict Africa.

Chapter Outline

In summary, this book is empirically based in its analysis, nodal in its conceptual framework, and user centered in its approach to policy. *The primary thesis of this book is that nonstate policing is a significant security service provider in post-conflict Africa. It is in fact nonstate policing to which people turn first for their everyday security. It is the principal provider for most Africans most of the time. Those who use it may not approve of every aspect of it, but they prefer it to the police, whom they would turn to normally as a last resort. Nonstate policing is the dominant and preferred form of policing in post-conflict Africa.*

Chapter 2 therefore explains how nonstate policing is defined and outlines the reasons for its dominance and the significant changes that have taken place in the nonstate sector since 1990. It also examines the links that exist between state and nonstate policing that blur the boundaries and make an already-diverse field even more complex. The following chapters seek to describe and analyze the main types of nonstate policing found in post-conflict Africa. Chapters 3 and 4 look at policing the city; Chapter 5 at policing the village; Chapter 6 at policing the workplace; and Chapter 7 at policing women. The final chapter examines where nonstate policing fits into security sector reform and considers the policy implications of the dominance and popular preference for nonstate policing. Having evaluated the strengths and weaknesses of nonstate policing, it offers a multilayered approach to policing programming. The argument is that where the "layer" of nonstate policing is making a positive contribution, it should be supported as much as the layer of the state police. State-centric security policy and practice in post-conflict societies contradict its self-avowed "people-centered, locally owned" principles. They assume the post-conflict state is capable of delivering justice and security to a majority of its population and is the main actor in security provision. Yet, in the majority of cases where research has been undertaken, in Africa and elsewhere, these assumptions have been found to be untrue. It is argued that the prime issue for security programs is to concentrate on questions of service delivery by implementing a multilayered strategy based on an audit of who is actually providing safety and security. This is not to deny the clear inadequacies of current nonstate security actors, but it is to recognize that they are no more beyond reform than state security systems. One of the priorities for post-conflict Africa is the development of unique partnerships and networks between security nodes, state or nonstate.

The Post-Conflict Environment

In the remainder of this chapter, I outline some of the features and actors shaping security in the post-conflict environment. Understanding the legacy of conflict and the doors it opens for national governments and external intervention provides the context for appreciating the security provision that has arisen post-conflict.

Post-conflict countries, from a Western state-centric perspective, are commonly regarded as one category of fragile states; that is, "those failing to provide basic services to poor people because they are unwilling or unable to do so" (OECD 2006, 147). Their political instability, extreme poverty, and conflict-damaged economy and social fabric make security crucial and, at the same time, elusive. Even though the provision of the public good of safety is the foundation (with justice) on which all other human rights are grounded and the foundation of economic reconstruction and development, both the quality *and* quantity of human resources available in post-conflict states are insufficient to meet even basic requirements.

The Centrality of Security

Even when conflict ends, insecurity is still prevalent because countries are left with a disrupted social order, a severely depleted state police, and decimated (and possibly discredited) customary or local security systems. After the pain of insecurity, a priority of state and people is security. But, this is more than a desire for life to return to "normal"; it is also a desire to resolve what was wrong with security before the conflict. Indeed, security has often been at the heart of the grievances that have sparked conflict. Pre-conflict state security agencies often not only failed to provide protection but also were agents themselves of abuse, predation, and insecurity.

Take, for instance, southern Sudan. The northern National Islamic Front (NIF) regime dismissed hundreds of judges and police in the south "in the public interest"; military and special courts were set up for the trial of political opponents; and security agencies were given arbitrary powers of arrest, detention, and torture. As part of the Islamization policy, new judges were appointed in the south who had been trained in Sharia, and public order courts dealt with non-Islamic behavior from drink to dress (Johnson 2003). Provocation by state security forces was also a feature of Uganda. The Obote regime saw state-initiated (or -condoned) murder, torture, looting, rape, terrorism, and imprisonment of opponents. This only increased during the course of the civil war (Hansen and Twaddle 1994; Kanyeihamba 2002). The security forces were above the law, and the police "could not bring suspects to justice for fear of victimization" (Kabwegyere 1995, 228). Things were no better in Sierra Leone. The Truth and Reconciliation Commission described the pre–civil war Sierra Leone Police as "incompetent," "corrupt," "a ready tool for the perpetuation of state terror against political opponents," and as engaged in "extortion of money" and "the violation of basic human rights" (Sierra Leone Truth and Reconciliation Commission 2004, 77). Meek characterized the police's history as "a litany of oppressive policing, nepotism and corruption" (2003, 1).

In the course of conflict, also, abuse by state security agents has been egregious. During the civil war in Mozambique, state policing simply ceased to exist over large areas, but where it did continue, the police imagined that they had a license to act with brutality against enemies of the state and to use torture to secure information that would preserve state security (Hanlon 1991; Amnesty International 1998). Under the one-party state, they were agents of the ruling party, Frelimo, rather than of civilians and had no grasp of the concept of being accountable to the public rather than to the state.

With the state security forces creating such insecurity, it is hardly surprising, therefore, that in southern Sudan, Uganda, Sierra Leone, and Mozambique rebels targeted police and police stations in their attacks.[4] Because one of the causes of conflict was this failure of the state (and other) security agencies, the post-conflict era is invariably seen as the time for a "new" start for security. Yet, whether the newness should be a reform of the old structures or the construction of a police service radically different has been a perennial question. Further, there has commonly been a debate over whether nonstate groups should play a role alongside the state in the new security provision, filling the many security gaps that exist in the post-conflict era.

The response of post-conflict regimes to those questions of security architecture and security provision has not been identical. It has depended in large part on the background and ideology of the new regime. New regimes may comprise the successful rebels (Uganda, Rwanda, DRC, Chad, Eritrea, Ethiopia, southern Sudan, and Namibia) or be the successful existing state (Sierra Leone, Comoros, and Angola). In other words, the ruling elite have either a military past or a civilian past. In terms of ideology, some regimes have socialist aspirations and with them thoughts of popular justice and local participation in policing. Other regimes are more capitalist/liberal in outlook and are more ready to adopt state-centric international policing approaches.

Whatever the aspirations of the new regimes, similar constraints face them all. The security sector may have collapsed or may have fragmented into competing jurisdictions. Much of the security infrastructure is likely to have been destroyed. Local elites, compromised by their role in the hostilities, may still be in opposition. There is little evidence of the rule of law and no democracy. There may be continuing resistance to efforts to establish nationwide state control of security (Law 2006, 4). The regime's available resources for service provision will be seriously limited. Conflict typically reduces the number of state police officers and destroys many of their buildings, vehicles, equipment, and records. Following the African Union (AU) invasion of Nzwani (Anjouan) to regain federal control of the secessionist island of the Comoros in 2008, there were no police left as the island's gendarmerie fled and dispersed with the fall of the island president's regime. In Liberia in 2003, there were very few officers left in the Liberia National Police (LNP); most of the police stations were abandoned (in two provincial towns, Buchanan and Gbamga, rebel groups managed the police stations). Efforts to locate former LNP officers proved difficult, and most of those who were located were deemed to be too old or undereducated or to have unacceptable human rights records. When the process was over, Liberia had only 786 police officers, and the authorities were forced to call for volunteers. In the case of Rwanda, its police and security agents had been largely swept into the Congo forests. A UNDP report concluded the following:

> The material resources available to both [police] forces have been almost totally destroyed during the civil strife. In terms of both quality and quantity, the human resources available to these agencies do not suffice to meet even basic requirements. At the present time, the Government of Rwanda does not have available to it the financial means necessary to furnish minimal material resources. (1995)

It is from such low baselines that states seek to rebuild the internal security that they know is a key to their country's future.

The rebuilding process of post-conflict security commonly goes through three distinct but overlapping phases. The first is in the immediate aftermath of the political settlement. It is the international peacekeeping phase. This is followed by a donor-supported security sector reform phase. As the donor support slowly diminishes, there emerges the final stage of a national leadership with its own national security policy, although it is usually still dependent in some measure on donor support in training and equipment. Understanding where a post-conflict society is in this continuum or how it has departed from this pattern is important in evaluating its security provision.

The International Peacekeeping Phase

The security help in the immediate aftermath of conflict may be sought (or imposed) by peacekeeping missions, conducted by the United Nations or AU (or even the European Union [EU] in DRC). In the first few years when the embers of conflict still glow and could burst into flame at any provocation, the presence of international peacekeeping troops with international policing components is invariably welcome by insecure and nervous new regimes. An international peacekeeping force's prime role is to stabilize security in the country. "Just getting the random violence under control is usually the first step" (Salomons 2005, 19). Next, they must "strive to replace a culture of violence and impunity with systems of rule observance" (Plunkett 2005, 75). It is said that it is easier to lose the rule of law than it is to resurrect it, but in fact in many post-conflict African states it is not resurrection but creation that is called for since the rule of (state) law even before the conflict failed to encompass not only large areas of territory but also large sections of the powerful in society.

When first begun, most UN operations focused on monitoring the military forces of opposing states. Hence, for these "first-generation" peacekeeping operations only UN military troops were deployed, and any police duties had to be undertaken by them. Only two UN peacekeeping operations before 1989 contained UN civilian police components: Congo (1960–64) and Cyprus (1964 to the present; where the term UN CivPol for UN civilian police was first used). Since 1990, however, a CivPol component has become an integral part of UN operations (Broer and Emery 1998) as states and international agencies have all come to see the foundational role of internal security and rule of law to achieving human security, human rights, good governance, economic development, and international investment (Carothers 1998).

Mandates of UN CivPol have varied widely but have included monitoring the performance, vetting and training, and patrolling with the local police; overseeing security at elections; reforming police management and operations; and investigating alleged violations of human rights perpetrated during the conflict. The pattern followed by most missions has been to "draw experienced police officers from Member States, deploy them to troubled areas," and require them to create "the law and order conditions necessary for lasting peace" (Broer and Emery 1998). The role of police who are part of the peacekeeping mission is similar to standard national policing, with the exception that they normally have no law enforcement powers. This is taken to be the responsibility of the national government. Yet, since the state police in post-conflict situations are usually in a very weakened and disrupted state, local populations tend to expect UN CivPol to do everything they think their own police force should do.

The first large-scale CivPol deployment by the United Nations in Africa was in 1989 in Namibia. The CivPol element of UNTAG (United Nations Transition Assistance Group) drew fifteen hundred police from twenty-five countries. Since then, there have been CivPol missions in fourteen other African states.[5] In the "second-generation" UN operations that prevail today, with their focus on security within borders, "nation building" and peace enforcement have been the prime activities. This has brought a sharp rise in the presence and responsibilities of CivPol. In practice, however, CivPol have not always fulfilled their aims. Many of their problems have been those faced by most large multinational groups rapidly deployed to an unfamiliar environment. There have been difficulties in recruiting suitable police officers from member countries whose police forces are already overstretched and from forces that have different standards (Holm and Eide 2000; Oakley, Dziedzic, and Goldberg 1998; Day and Freeman 2005). Tensions are inevitable when mixing police from many different cultures. "Often there have been as many as 15 to 20 different nationalities working in the same station, bringing with them differing policing traditions, religious belief systems, working ethics, hygiene standards, eating habits, and agendas" (Broer and Emery 1998). Even the basic CivPol officer requirement that participants in the mission should be able to speak the language of the mission (normally English or French), be literate, and be able to drive have not always been met. Further, preparatory planning for the CivPol missions has often been poor, and there have not been adequate resources and powers assigned for CivPol to achieve mandates. Even the United Nations itself has recognized there is a problem (Brahimi 2005; Annan 2005).

Once in the post-conflict arena, CivPol quickly has to determine by what standards—whether international, regional, or local—it will recruit, monitor, and train local police forces. The criteria for those in the country (re)applying to join a reformed police service are always a contentious issue. Post-conflict regimes inherit police forces "contaminated" by past human rights abuses, extortion, and nepotism. Yet, to disband them is costly and leaves a vacuum before new forces can be created. In the case of Sierra Leone, it was decided not to disband the Sierra Leone Police (SLP) but to restructure it totally, to retrain the executive management team, and to undertake a recruitment campaign. A screening exercise of the 8,000 Uganda Police in 1986 declared that only 3,000 were qualified to be retained. In the reconstruction of the service, such a large number of officers at the level of assistant inspector and above left their posts that it had to be augmented by contracting 2,000 retired Ugandan police officers (Hills 2000, 95). Even at 5,000 personnel, this force was too small to maintain law and order. Thus, Uganda's National Resistance Army (NRA) had to assume responsibility for internal security until 1989. A vetting process in Liberia was equally harsh on former members of the police. By February 2007, UN CivPol had vetted 6,281. Just 2,079 (33 percent) of those vetted qualified for the new service. The rest were disqualified on the grounds of having abused their office, being underqualified, having served for more than twenty-five years, or of being older than fifty-five years.

Donor-Supported Security Sector Reform Phase

Once security has been stabilized in the post-conflict country, international peacekeeping missions withdraw. The next phase, which normally overlaps with the peacekeeping phase, involves donor programs aimed at the security sector or law-and-order sector but which, in terms of policing, seeks to restructure, modernize, professionalize, and democratize the state police (Ball, Biesheuval, and Olanisakin 2007; Department for International Development [DFID] 2002, 2006; OECD 2004, 2005b, 2007). The intention is to seize the reform opportunities opened up by the disruption of state police services through death, displacement, and severance. With the reform, it is hoped, will come a legitimacy and efficiency that the state police may never have known before. Beyond that is the aim (or possibly dream) of creating a self-sustaining system of policing.

The focus of the programs of the donor agencies has been on police management, especially the training of senior personnel in strategic and operational planning (OECD 2005b, 2007). There have been concerted efforts to improve accountability, coordination, and effectiveness. The reforms typically involve institutional change with the introduction of research and planning departments, inspectorates, community affairs departments; human rights desks; women's units; and complaints departments.

In and of themselves, the donor-assembled international police advisers can only offer a short-term and limited impact on the daily security of those living in post-conflict societies. There are increasing doubts about how well implemented are the training courses they give to the police, how sustainable are the management systems they put in place, and even if we assume the very best outcomes, how the majority of citizens are going to benefit from a mission focused entirely on strengthening state security systems (Peake, Scheye, and Hills 2006; Bayley 2001). No one doubts that changing police culture and practices is not an easy or a short-term program anywhere in the world, particularly in post-conflict states (Marenin 1996; Bayley 1997).

For all the effort that has gone into recruiting, training, equipping, and institution building in post-conflict police forces in Africa, they still remain incompetent and predatory (and often brutal; Amnesty International 2007a, 2008b) forces. Etannibi Alemika, professor of criminology and sociology of law at Jos University in Nigeria, said the evidence demonstrates that the police forces in most African countries are "significantly brutal, corrupt, inefficient, unresponsive and unaccountable to the generality of the population" (IDASA 2007). Above all, they remain small in numbers. For instance, even by 2005, at thirteen years after the conflict, the number of police in Maputo was 3,574. When the desk officers, those who are disabled, those who are chronically ill, and those who are studying were subtracted, there were 2,352 police (men and women) to patrol the entire city.[6] The low numbers do not tell the whole story. Assessing the appropriate staffing levels of a police service must take into account demographic data, transportation systems, geographic terrain, economic information, education levels, available skills, and crime statistics. Overall, police deployment in Africa is thin, and police personnel are rarely found beyond the tarmac road. Policing is focused on the commercial centers of the main towns and disproportionately on crimes that affect the wealthy and that disrupt a male-defined order. For some, the answer to low numbers is simply that security reform "may have to be accompanied by increases in the costs of at least some types of uniformed forces" (Brzoska and Heinemann-Gruber 2004, 10). Yet, even if, as a result of donor-funded reforms, state police officers are increased in numbers, trained to new levels, and serviced by sustainable equipment, it is still impossible to imagine that such services will be sustainable, well managed, or able to provide crime protection and crime investigation for all citizens.

Both donors and governments recognize that in the post-conflict situation they face a tension between short-term achievements and long-term development. The urgent priority to establish basic security can lead to a strong emphasis on short-term initiatives to strengthen the capacity of security providers. Yet, these initiatives invariably result in unsustainable programs for those government agencies. A recent study suggested that sectorwide approaches to justice and security programs were not yet achievable in any fragile state, partly due to serious shortfalls of human capital (Stone 2005). Further, shortfalls in public revenues raise questions regarding whether post-conflict countries can sustain security reform after donor money ceases (Sedra 2007). Finally, it may well prove impossible to sustain donor-supported security reform programs when the values embedded in them are not compatible with the local cultural value systems and historical legacies.

Another set of tensions arises from the state-building focus of security programs. Strengthening governance and creating an effective centralized, coordinated, state-provided security may appeal to the local political elite and can be justified by donors in terms of equality of service. However, it sits uncomfortably with responsiveness to local needs and local ownership (Scheye and Peake 2005). It is also not in harmony with the limited capacity, legitimacy, and even territorial penetration of the post-conflict state. The fact is, many countries "have artificial and imposed borders, heterogeneous and divided populations and privatized and personalized structures, where traditional notions of kinship, religion and community matter more than modern ideas of citizenship and nationality" (Anderson 2007, 7). It is not easy to pursue centralization without ignoring local needs, which are often better served by local security systems.

Security reform that is promoted by donors too often miscalculates the resources available to the fragile state. By definition, fragile post-conflict states lack the capacity to deliver core functions, such as safety and security provision, in an effective and accountable manner. Their finances are overcommitted and dependent on uncertain revenue streams. In addition, they face severe shortages of human skills, and training facilities and the basic infrastructure (physical, constitutional, legal, and administrative) required for effective service provision are often lacking. Further, the African state is in "transition towards both down-sizing and redefinition, given two decades of neo-liberal conditionalities" (MacLean and Shaw 2001, 22). The diminished African state is not in a strong position to maintain large expensive services. The question of what to do, given that the post-conflict state is unable in the short and intermediate term to provide an adequate security service, cannot be avoided. It is at this juncture that nonstate policing achieves its popular appeal and must be addressed by security policy makers. It may be that the policy makers turn their backs on its possibilities and insist that there must be more investment in rebuilding police systems (Luckham et al. 2001), or perhaps they might explore more radical alternatives to this "bottomless pit" approach (Baker and Scheye 2007).

Notes

1. Angola; Benin; Botswana; Burkina Faso; Burundi; Cameroon; CAR; Chad; Comoros; Côte d'Ivoire; DRC; Djibouti; Equatorial Guinea; Eritrea; Ethiopia; Gabon; Ghana; Guinea; Guinea-Bissau; Kenya; Lesotho; Liberia; Madagascar; Malawi; Mali; Mauritania; Mauritius; Mozambique; Namibia; Niger; Nigeria; Republic of Congo; Rwanda; São Tomé e Príncipe; Senegal; Seychelles; Sierra Leone; Somalia; South Africa; Sudan; Swaziland; Tanzania; The Gambia; Togo; Uganda; Zambia; Zimbabwe.
2. A more extensive list of armed conflicts since 1980 in Africa would include the following:

2007

Ethiopia	Somalis and Oromo militants in Ogaden

2006

Chad	Communal fighting between Toroboro ("black" sedentary farmer) and Janjawid ("Arab" pastoralist) militias

2005

Chad	United Front for Democratic Change (FUC) rebels
CAR	Popular Army for Unity and Democracy (APRD) (northwest) and Union of Democratic Forces for Unity (UFDR) (northeast) rebels

2003

Sudan	Communal-separatist violence in Darfur

2002

Congo-Brazzaville	Civil violence (Ninja militants in Pool region)

2001

Rwanda	Ethnic war (attacks by Hutu guerillas)
CAR	Civil violence (attacks by Bozize loyalists; coup)
Nigeria	Ethnic violence (Christian-Muslim; Plateau, Kano regions)

2000

Guinea	Parrot's Beak clashes
Liberia	Civil violence (attacks by Liberians United for Reconciliation and Democracy [LURD] guerrillas)
Côte d'Ivoire	Civil war (north, south, and west divisions)
Rwanda	Ethnic war (attacks by Hutu guerillas)

1999

Ethiopia-Eritrea	Border War 1999–

1998

Ethiopia-Eritre	Border War
Sierra Leone	Revolutionary United Front (RUF) resistance–
DRC	Tutsi rebellion 1998–

1997

Comoros:	Anjouan and Moheli secession
Sierra Leone	Mutiny 1997; ECOWAS intervention: 1997–98

1996

Burundi	Hutu rebellion–
Burundi	Military coup
Liberia	Civil war 1996–97
Sierra Leone	Military coup

1995

Ghana	Tribal violence
Burundi	Hutu infiltration
Uganda	Lord's Resistance Army (LRA) insurgency 1995–

1994

Ghana	Ethnic violence 1994–95
Rwanda	Genocide

1993
Burundi	Civil war 1993–94
Somali	Clan warfare 1993–

1992
Comoros	Military coup
Chad	February coup
Chad	May coup

1991
Djibouti	Civil war 1991–94
Madagascar	Palace massacre
Sierra Leone	Civil War 1991–96

1990
Comoros	Mercenary uprising
Mali	Tuareg separatism 1990–96
Nigeria	Jukun-Tiv violence 1990–92
Niger	Tuareg separatism 1990–95
Somali	Revolution 1990–91
Rwanda	Tutsi insurgency 1990–91

1989
Senegal	Cassamance secession 1989–91
Comoros	Denard's coup
Madagascar	Election fraud
Somalia	Somali Patriotic Movement (SPM) insurgency 1989–90
Somalia	United Somali Congress (USC) insurgency 1989–90
Liberia	Civil war 1989–95
Namibia	Transition crisis
Senegal- Mauritania	Border war 1989–91

1988
Burundi	Pogrom

1987
Burkina Faso	Rebellion
Comoros	Presidential guard violence

1986
Uganda	Civil war 1986–95
Nigeria	Student protests

1985
Mali-Burkina Faso	Agacher Strip war
Comorios	Military revolt
Nigeria	Coup
Sudan	Military coup
Uganda	Military coup

1984
Cameroon	Army revolt

1983
Upper Volta	Military coup
Nigeria	Coup

Sudan	Revolt 1983–87
1982	
Ethiopia- Somali	Border clash
CAR	Military coup
Somalia	Somali National Movement (SNM) insurgency 1982–88
1981	
Chad	Libyan invasion
Comoros	Coup
Seychelles	Mercenary coup
Ghana	Military coup
Uganda	War in the Bush 1981–86
1980	
Liberia	Coup
Mozambique	Rebellion 1980–87

Sources: Global Conflict Trends, http://members.aol.com/cspmgm/warlist.htm; Wars of the World—Armed Conflict Event Data, http://www.onwar.com/aced/index.htm.

3. Since 2002, I have undertaken field research in policing in Mozambique, Uganda, Rwanda, Sierra Leone, Liberia, southern Sudan, and Comoros. I gratefully acknowledge funding from the Economic & Social Research Council (ESRC) (RES-000–23–1102; R000271293), the British Academy, and Coventry University to undertake this research.

4. Rebel groups have also singled out the state police for attack where they have been seen to be dominated by a particular ethnic group or because they presented an obstacle to ethnic cleansing or other wartime atrocities.

5. Current UN operations in Africa: MINURCAT Mission in the CAR and Chad, 2007; UNAMID Africa Union/UN Hybrid Operation in Darfur, 2007; UNMIS Mission in Sudan, 2005; UNOCI Operation in Côte d'Ivoire, 2004; UNMIL Mission in Liberia, 2003; MONUC UN Organization Mission in DRC, 1999; UNMEE Mission in Ethiopia and Eritrea, 2000.

   Past UN operations in Africa: MONUA Observer Mission in Angola, 1997–99; UNAVEM I Angola Verification Mission, 1988–91; UNAVEM II Angola Verification Mission, 1991–95; UNAVEM III Angola Verification Mission, 1995–97; ONUB Operation in Burundi, 2004–6; MINURCA Mission in the CAR, 1998–2000; ONUC Operation in Congo, 1960–64; UNOMIL Observer Mission in Liberia, 1993–97; ONUMOZ Operation in Mozambique, 1993–97; UNTAG (Namibia) Transition Assistance Group, 1989–90; UNAMIR Assistance Mission for Rwanda, 1993–96; UNOMSIL Observer Mission in Sierra Leone, 1998–99; UNAMSIL Mission in Sierra Leone, 1999–2005; UNOSOM I Operation in Somalia, 1992–93; UNOSOM II Operation in Somalia, 1993–95.

6. Mozambique News Agency AIM Reports No. 320, May 16, 2006, http://www.poptel.org.uk/mozambique-news/newsletter/aim320.html.

Nonstate Policing Explained

2

Introduction

The privatization of security in the last half century globally and in Africa, especially since the 1990s, has been the subject of many studies. The rise of private security at the expense of public-provided security is seen as the product of economic liberalization and government fiscal constraint. Certainly, there has been a mushrooming of private security companies, as Chapter 6 details, but nonstate policing is a much broader sector than that. In Africa today, there is great diversity in the community collectives providing everyday policing. Examples include the following:

- Private citizens organized on a voluntary, as-needed basis to combat local crime (Buur 2006; Heald 2006; Buur and Jensen 2004; Fourchard 2008; Last 2008; Pratten 2008). Although commonly known as vigilantes, with all the negative overtones that this term carries in the West, they often have the approval of local elders and are not all violent.
- Religious police (especially Islamic) organized by religious or sometimes political leaders in the community to oversee moral conduct (Peters 2001; Casey 2007; Adamu 2008).
- Ethnic defense forces, which can be protectors, providing security within their area of operation, as well as predators (Reno 2007).
- Anticrime groups that have grown into (semi)commercial operations (von Schnitzler et al. 2001; Ruteere and Pommerolle 2003).
- Security groups organized by and for the benefit of trading communities (Baker 2007c; Lund 2001).
- Informal (and largely autonomous) local government security structures that provide everyday policing (Baker 2007d).
- Customary chiefs, who intervene to prevent or resolve customary, civil, and often criminal cases (Kyed 2007; P. Jackson 2005; Fanthorpe 2006; Bennett 1985; Koyana and Bekker 1998). Their customary rules, often uncodified, are a mixture of norms and institutions drawn from precedent; mutations of inherited colonial practice; values and practice adapted in the course of interaction, immigration, and conflict; and state regulation.

- Restorative justice community-based organizations (CBOs) or peace committees (Massaquoi 1999; Wood and Shearing 2007).

Groups such as these are the primary providers of protection, deterrence, investigation, resolution, and punishment for most Africans in most circumstances. The Organization for Economic Cooperation and Development (OECD; 2007, 17) asserted that the evidence suggests that "in sub-Saharan Africa at least 80 percent of justice services are delivered by nonstate providers." In Africa as a whole, customary courts, often the dominant form of regulation and dispute resolution, are estimated to cover up to 90 percent of the population (Chirayath, Sage, and Woolcock 2005, 3). In recognition of their prevalence and their dominance of the justice and security sector, the UK Department for International Development (DFID) wrote a policy paper on how to support these nonstate networks (DFID 2004), and the United Nations Development Programme (UNDP) has argued that these networks "are the cornerstone of dispute resolution and access to justice for the majority of populations, especially the poor and disadvantaged in many countries, where informal justice systems usually resolve between 80 and 90 percent of disputes" (Wojkowska 2006). Similarly, the OECD (2007) published recommendations on how justice development practitioners can support their activities. Data from the national crime victimization survey in Nigeria (CLEEN Foundation 2005) showed that 50 percent of Nigerians patronize the services of informal policing systems for their protection from criminal attacks. Other research from Nigeria showed that in four of its federal states "a total of 16 types of informal policing structures [have been identified] that were established in their communities to deal with crime"; in two of the four states, these networks were the population's preferred choice of delivery 88.9 and 62.5 percent of the time; in one state where only 38.1 percent of the population availed themselves of the services of these local justice networks, 94.7 percent of the population approved of and supported their compatriots using their services (Alemika and Chukwuma 2004, 6). The evidence, therefore, is overwhelming that local or nonstate justice is a significant provider of services in Africa.

This chapter attempts to establish the key features of nonstate policing, explain the reasons for its dominance and review the changes in the nonstate security sector since 1990.

Characterizing Nonstate Policing

What is the value of a term that can be applied to security agencies run by customary chiefs, religious leaders, ethnic elders, "youth" groups, work-based associations, residential groups, conflict resolution nongovernmental organizations (NGOs), informal levels of local government, and entrepreneurs with commercial, political, and even criminal motives? In Chapter 1, I offered the facetious comment that the one (and perhaps the only) thing that nonstate policing groups have in common is that they are not the state police. If we can put on one side for the moment commercial security companies, then let me suggest some other common features concerning their objectives, personnel, boundaries, and mutability, although exceptions abound.

Their Objectives: Enforcing a Locally Defined Order

Nonstate policing is usually described in terms of filling the gap left by state policing. But as I understand it, it exists not just because the state police is seen as ineffective in enforcing order but because it is perceived as enforcing an alien or at least partly inappropriate or erroneous order. In other words, what is contested is the moral and social order being enforced by others (Carrier 1999; Nina and Scharf 2001; Buur 2006). It is for this reason that nonstate policing, which predates state policing, was never totally displaced by it because the two are not policing the same order. Independence in Africa did not bring about the "public good" as defined by the state. Rather, some disregarded the law of the state as being an alien element that required them to flout their own sense of right. They did not argue for the absence of "the rule of law" but only for freedom from (aspects of) state law. In other words, they desired that their own local rules and values still be observed as the rule of law (Woodman 1996, 4, 6). The overriding objective for most is to ensure that the community, whether geographical, economic, or ethnoreligious, has its prevailing values and standards of acceptable behavior upheld and restored when disrupted.

I say *prevailing* because it should be remembered that the values of the ruling group in the community (invariably older richer males) may or may not reflect the values of all the community. Communities are rarely homogeneous or egalitarian. For instance, in a Ugandan fishing village on the banks of Lake Victoria in 2004, the male leadership told me that the lowest level of local government that they were executive members of, the Local Council Level 1 (LC1), ensured "good manners," mediated disputes between husbands and wives, and protected property with a nightly patrol. There were occasional cases brought to their court of "fighting, after beer," "stealing from homes," and "stealing nets." Yet, according to them, so good was the order that they maintained that sometimes they went a month without a case. However, when twenty women from the same village were brought together, a very different view of order was portrayed: "Youth use vulgar language about women"; "There's a lot of alcoholism"; "The fishermen spend their earnings on women and alcohol"; "The men don't spend money on children and family"; "And only rarely take the children to school"; "Housewives' access to

LCs is difficult"; "The LC may listen more to someone who has money; [they] are cowardly before power and money. They are easily intimidated." Women clearly defined law and order not, as the men, in terms of the absence of fighting and theft but more in terms of responsible and moral behavior. Yet, even when sections of the community challenge the prevailing norms, it does not necessarily mean that the dominant class does not have their support. Ubink and others have found that people can simultaneously support institutions like chieftaincy and be highly critical of the performance of certain chiefs or certain tasks (Ubink 2007).

The prevailing local norms, however representative of all in the community, may very well coincide with those of the state. If they do not, the first priority of local policing is to the locally defined norms. It is these norms that determine what in the community is policed and how it is policed. Local leaders and customary chiefs, for instance, uphold local ("customary") law and values. This applies to the definition of crime, for example, whether it covers witchcraft, adultery, teenage pregnancy, use of drugs, disrespect to parents, and "unwarranted" hut evictions. It applies to the response to crime, for example, whether the investigation includes trial by ordeal and whether corporal punishment is permissible. Such conflict does not apply only to customary groups. Islamic religious police, using a code of morality based on the Koran, criminalize behavior that may be permitted by the state (e.g., male-female association, adultery, drinking alcohol, prostitution, female dress code, homosexuality, and games of chance). And, there are youth groups that simply make rough-and-ready rules that conform to their notions of the acceptable. For example, a youth group, whose "hangout" is on the beach at Krootown, Freetown, Sierra Leone, told me in 2005 that for them smoking marijuana is permissible. But, on the wall of their hut is the declaration that "being abusive" and "provocation" are unacceptable and liable to a fine. Such locally defined norms are often regarded by "enlightened elites" as reflecting religious intolerance, traditional conservatism, and male chauvinism. The alternative orders certainly have the potential to clash with the liberal democratic constitutions of many African states.

On the other hand, there can be nonstate groups that are *more* liberal or exacting than the state. For example, restorative justice CBOs may uphold codes more gender equal than state law (e.g., regarding divorce or inheritance). Work associations may demonstrate a specialist focus on transgression within their sphere of operation. Taxi drivers' associations, for instance, can have very distinctive views about what constitutes dangerous driving that exceed the legal requirements of the state (e.g., forbidding in Bo, Sierra Leone, the carrying of pregnant women on motorbikes).

It should be remembered that in much of post-conflict Africa, no single code expresses a general public will. There may be no general societal consensus or even a unified sense of belonging to the one collective of the state.

The very conflict may well have given expression to the contradictory views of how society should be ordered, but a military victory does not necessarily imply the victory of one set of ideas and values. Establishing security as a country emerges from conflict, therefore, is more than just establishing the rule of law in the sense of the rule of the state. As Rachel Belton observed: "While customs without institutions can manage to uphold some rule of law ends … institutions without customs are weak and easily circumvented by raw power" (2005, 22). Whether desired or not by the new regime, the best that can be hoped for in the short term is a security that upholds the rule of laws, that enforces the social order prevailing in the local community. Achieving the absence of a chaotic lawlessness is about restoring this locally defined order after its disruption. It is about protecting local people from what is defined in their communities (or by their leaders) as crimes, disorder, immorality, disrespect, or any other "unacceptable" behavior. And, for the enforcement of this locally defined moral and social order, there is only one available provider: nonstate policing.

Their Personnel: Volunteers

Nonstate policing is primarily based on voluntarism at the level of both authorizer and provider. The authorizers are mainly adult men who do it out of a mixture of civic responsibility, a desire to be seen as community leaders, and for some small (in most cases) financial gain. It is true that chiefs have been accused in some areas of excessive fines (Richards 2005), but this certainly does not apply to all. In Uganda in 2004, when a U.S. dollar was worth nearly 1,700 Ugandan shillings, the lowest level of local authority in Uganda, the LC1, received small monthly dues of typically 500 shillings from homes for the provision of patrols. An LC1 court charged 2,100 shillings for its services (100 were for the pen and book to record the case), and older people received them free. Taxi drivers pay small subscriptions to their work association, which will include its security work. Toro Bicycle Service, Fort Portal, asks each member to pay 10,000 shillings to join. Residential groups ask a small subscription from those who benefit from patrols and the enforcement of order. A crime prevention panel in Uganda charged a membership fee of 5,000 Uganda shillings. Few of these authorizers could be seen as making a large profit from the security they organized. The authorizers call on young men under their authority or influence to demonstrate their civic, tribal, religious, or union loyalty to provide security for the well-being of the community.

The providers, mainly men eighteen to thirty-five ("youth" in African parlance), respond to their leaders or take the initiative themselves out of a mixture of duty, the tradition of service by youth, and pressure from leaders and for a little financial gain. There may even be guilt and a desire for amends after the violence of the conflict. Explaining why he worked with a community policing forum, a young man in Makeni, Sierra Leone, replied: "We did what we did in the 10 years [of war] and now we want to find another way." The nature of the work is primarily part time or simple availability as and when needed. Often, the work is at night on patrols or lookout. Small amounts of money or food might change hands, but they cannot be construed as full payment for the service provided. A vigilante group that operated a night patrol in Gaye Town, Monrovia, in 2006 said that the local people "give us small things—coffee, a little money." Before the civil war in Sierra Leone, at least, native authority police who worked for the chiefs "hoped to keep some of the fines and taxes." The main motive, therefore, is rarely financial.

Communities following conflict may be particularly keen to fight against injustice and disorder and therefore willing to serve for no pay. It could well be, however, that such voluntarism is unsustainable. As a senator in Rwanda observed in 2006:

> To sustain voluntarism is a great challenge. The spirit of voluntarism is very high here now. But we are very worried about how to sustain it. So many have served their country for no pay—women, youth, but when they get married and both go out to work will it continue?

The volunteerism of nonstate policing may make it attractive in terms of running costs, but the issue of its sustainability on that basis needs to be evaluated.

Their Relationship Boundaries: Links with the State

What makes the term *nonstate* problematic is that state and nonstate are not always clearly separated and distinct, as noted in Chapter 1. There are plenty of examples of nonstate policing agencies acting autonomously with no reference to other policing groups. Yet, post-conflict Africa has many examples of policing activities that are shared across the state/nonstate boundary, formally or informally. Johnston (1992) talked of these relationships as "hybrid" policing. Some groups realize that there is much to gain from tapping into the knowledge, capacity, and resources of others to achieve their own agenda—none more so than the state police. It is no surprise that many instances can be found of state and nonstate actors carrying out joint patrols and operations or exchanging information about crime and criminals. Then, there are cases of vigilante groups working with state police in dividing the work according to whose modus operandi was best suited for the required task (Buur 2006). For example, youth groups on the Ugandan/Democratic Republic of the Congo (DRC) border, who themselves conducted criminal activity away from the border town, are willing to exchange information with the police about local and transborder criminals in exchange for immunity for themselves (Titeca 2006). The state may also equip nonstate police; for example, in Zinder, Niger, a local group established to protect local businesses was provided by the mayor with torchlights for night patrol and with a pair of handcuffs by the police commissioner (Lund 2001). And, the state may offer training to nonstate groups; as an example, Uganda police train some of the community police forums in law and law enforcement (Baker 2005a).

If the policing work is not shared across the state/nonstate border, it might be delegated to the other side. There are clear gains to be had for the state police in lessening the workload. Police take offenders to nonstate courts (e.g., to customary courts in southern Sudan and to ethnic elders courts in Nigerian cities). They commonly ask nonstate agents to undertake patrols from which they have withdrawn, to trace suspects, and to provide intelligence. They use nonstate agents for traffic control, monitoring motoring offenses, and running bus stations. They may even ask nonstate agents to devise anticrime action plans; for instance, violence in Sierra Leonean schools was addressed by Freetown community police forums. In Rwanda and Uganda, the state has authorized volunteers at the lowest level of local authority to undertake everyday policing. Elsewhere (e.g., Liberia, Sierra Leone, Mozambique and southern Sudan), the state "allows" customary chiefs to handle lesser criminal cases as well as civil and customary. And unofficially, state police may outsource their "dirty work" to nonstate agents that, as the police, they are not entitled to perform (e.g., in rural Mozambique) (Kyed unpublished manuscript).

Is nonstate policing, then, simply a case of the state ruling by other means? Is this a continuation of the bifurcated state of colonial times when there was a direct rule for the key economic interests and indirect rule for the rest (Mamdani 1996)? Is this a case of two forms of power under a common domination or what Menkhaus called in postcolonial times, the "mediated state" (Menkhaus 2007). It is not quite that simple. In most cases, the leaders of these nonstate policing groups are not state appointees, and state approval is not required (although in some areas chiefs are appointed and in Rwanda the informal local government levels are). And, the inconsistency, irregularity, and sometimes the informality of the relationship stretch the term *indirect rule*. Moreover, sometimes the enrollment is reversed, with nonstate policing enrolling the police. There will always be disputes that nonstate groups send to the police because they cannot or will not handle them themselves. But beyond that, there can be delegation, in which the motive is more a case of seeking legitimization than decreased workload; for example, customary courts in southern Sudan ask police officers to keep order in their courtrooms and to do the whipping of those found guilty. And, a taxi drivers' association in southern Sudan has authorized the police to sit in its headquarters to handle serious matters. If it is not legitimacy they seek, then it may be that they enlist the police to turn a blind eye. Vigilantes in South Africa and Uganda ask the police *not* to act—and as long as the nonstate groups recover the stolen goods and undertake any "discipline" of offenders before the crime becomes public, the police see nothing, happy to have their crime statistics improved (Buur 2006; Titeca 2006).

Yet, mutual enrollment does not capture the nature of the state/nonstate relationship in all cases. Lund saw value in recognizing policing organizations as resembling "twilight institutions" (Lund 2001) since both state and nonstate adopt elements of the other for their own organizational or individual purposes. For instance, nonstate groups may draw symbols, paraphernalia (e.g., uniforms), and legitimacy from mimicking the state and its procedures. On the other hand, as Jensen observed in northeastern Mpumalanga, South Africa, the state and especially its local representatives negotiate, appropriate, and sometimes even shed their "stateness." Thus, police officers "saw" violence as state employees but "saw nothing" as civilians participating in communal discipline of "criminals." He found that state representatives needed to negotiate danger (they lived in the area they patrolled) and notions of morality when they often agreed personally with the contraventions of the law (Jensen 2003).

Whether it is collaboration or imitation, in truth there is a large degree of shared attitudes and values among agents on both sides of the boundary. They are shared because policing authorizers and agents on both sides come from the same cultural milieu. Policing agents in Africa, whether state or nonstate, are typically sympathetic to male primacy, conservative sexual morality, and a denial of rights to the criminal for these are commonly the prevailing attitudes of their communities. Policing agents on both sides are not averse to using violence both as a punishment against suspects and for obtaining information (on extrajudicial killings by Kenya, Mozambique, Angola, and Nigeria police, see Kenya National Commission on Human Rights 2007; Amnesty International 2007a, 2008b; Human Rights Watch 2007b). State police training, so often mistaken for learning, has made only minimal inroads into these attitudes. It should come as no great surprise, therefore, that at other times state agents undertake nonstate policing (e.g., out of hours, police officers join vigilante groups) (Buur 2006; Baker 2002). And, there is a certain inevitability that security agents move from positions in state to nonstate and vice versa. State police have been recruited not only by private security firms but also by residential security organizations. In addition, community anticrime groups have been absorbed into the public police, as have local militias. This was true in Somaliland (Lewis 2004) and in Sudan, where "an estimated 5,000 Janjawiid have been absorbed into the Popular Defense Forces (PDF) and police, apparently representing the majority of the 'new' police dispatched to Darfur" (Justice Africa 2004). Again, youth in Zimbabwe serving in the Zimbabwe African National

Union-Patriotic Front (ZANU-PF) party militia have been incorporated into the police, further politicizing it (African Commission 2002). There has also been an absorption into the police of warring factions after civil wars. Members of the Southern Peoples Liberation Army (SPLA) have been taken into the police (and army) in southern Sudan, and initially the transitional government in Liberia absorbed military/rebel faction members into police and security forces.

In the mutual penetration and enrollment, some see policing "networks" that embrace state and nonstate providers. Yet, this conceptualization of the blurred boundary is not without its difficulties, even though it is possible statistically, following social network theory. The linkages between all the security nodes are invariably incomplete, and if they do occur are often too informal, ad hoc, and tenuous to be consistent. Further, it is common, where state/nonstate partnerships exist, for them to be so dominated by the state police that the relationship looks more like a hub linking nodes that have no connection among themselves. And, when the relationship is unidirectional, as is often the case with intelligence, for instance, then again it is less than is normally implied by the metaphor of a network relationship.

Perhaps most of the links, where they occur, are better seen as negotiated tactical alliances. Although for the state this may entail a loss of a centrally imposed normative and legal uniformity on the nonstate policing actors, its advantage is that it is less likely than direct control and incorporation to engender the opposition of nodes embedded in local support. It is also well suited to providing a degree of coordination among a diverse assortment of policing agencies. To this end, therefore, the state engages in enrolling techniques such as sponsorship, regulation, information inclusion, collaboration, and training. Or, it can be thought of as the organization of interoperability at different levels of integration: unified, combined, collaborative, cooperative, and independent (Clark and Moon 2001). The risk with loose tactical alliances between state and nonstate policing is that they tend to be associated with minimal centrally provided resources. This failure to provide more than token support risks the likelihood that nonstate policing groups will seek to loosen or break the alliances. The tribal militias of Karamoja, Uganda, were seen at first as a way of controlling cattle rustling more successfully than the police. However, when financial support faltered and finally stopped in 2001, the militias turned increasingly to road banditry (Mkutu 2008). Again, the community policing forums that were begun as a "partnership" in Freetown, Sierra Leone, have begun to break away and do their own patrols because of the inadequacy of police support and resources. For instance, one Community Policing Partnership Board in 2006 set up a "neighborhood watch" to undertake foot patrols "after," in their words, "the police were called out to a shop that was being burgled at night. By the time they came the shop was cleared out." The idea spread to the whole police division. With no incentives or funding from the police, partnership board members feared the partnership would collapse, but they were not overdespondent. One executive member told me: "We are 90 percent, the police are 10 percent."

While analysts might grapple with the difficulties of indistinct boundaries, and even policing providers debate the advantages of cooperation or competition, users of policing services are less perturbed. Indeed, the state/nonstate boundary is not one recognized by most African citizens as fundamental. Issues of effectiveness and accessibility trump concerns over the nature of the authorizer. In the course of a week, an individual may move from the arena of one security provider to another and from state to nonstate. In the village, the headman or maybe the imam is there to bring a settlement regarding "men-women problems." To settle the land dispute, there is the paramount chief, or there may be a restorative justice organization. On a visit to the town, a neighborhood committee will be on the watch for armed robbers; a commercial security guard will protect the entrance to the bank; and a taxi drivers' association (or a mob) will deal with any pickpocket at the bus station. Finally, if there is a serious crime and a "shedding of blood," there is the state police. The boundary, as it is experienced, is crossed without concern. The issue for the user is invariably pragmatic, not normative. It matters less who has authorized the security than how good the provider is at protecting them and their property.

Their Mutability: Changing Nature and Status

Security boundaries are radically disturbed by conflict due to loss of policing personnel, weakened societal bonds, undermined norms, and allegedly rising crime. In Liberia, for instance, the shrinking of public policing left a security vacuum in the immediate aftermath of war, filled in urban areas by private commercial security and partly by informal groups of youths. But, in Sierra Leone's rural areas the prime providers of policing, the customary chiefs, underwent a loss of respect (due to their humiliation by rebels or their flight; Baker 2005b) that made exercising authority after the war problematic. As the authority of chiefs has shrunk, young men in particular have filled their place. They have taken both sides of the legal/illegal boundary. Some have formed local vigilance and patrol groups:

> We know everybody and everything. There is no police post in the community of Yengema. ... We patrol at night. We respond if there is a problem. We harass anybody who brings drugs. We arrest them, destroy the drugs; we give them a beating. Solved! No more drugs!

For other youth groups, it meant working with the police for the first time:

> We did what we did in the 10 years [of war] and now we want to find another way. … We're helping the police because the security of this country is in our hands. We should play our role with the police as partners.

State policing changes also, but reform "tends to be superficial, localized and temporary in nature and effect" (Hills 2008, 217). With nonstate, this is less so. The terms *customary* and *traditional* structures suggest that these are systems that go back unaltered to before colonial times. In fact, they have changed more than most realize, and many chiefs are only too well aware that unless they "adapt to the times" they face extinction. Many I spoke to in southern Sudan, for instance, realized that they were vulnerable in a way that the state systems were not and that it was incumbent on them to take on board new ideas, such as treating women equally or having women chiefs.

Change in nonstate groups can be much more dramatic than any changes perceptible in customary structures. Neither their nature nor their legality is necessarily fixed. The character of nonstate policing can change for better or worse over quite short periods of time. Aided by businesspeople desiring an orderly commercial environment, Sharia courts in Mogadishu, Somalia, became in the 1990s the main judicial and social welfare provider. They ran schools, hospitals, and Islamic-oriented police services. They gained widespread public support and helped to reduce robberies, drug dealing, and prostitution. In 2000, the autonomous courts came together as the Union of Islamic Courts (UIC). By 2006, they had become a powerful political and military entity, in part due to Al Qaeda infiltration. Thereafter, they became locked in a war first with the Somali warlords and then with the transitional government and its Ethiopian allies. They now operate as an insurgent group. Another well-known case of mutation was the South African vigilante group People Against Gangsterism and Drugs (PAGAD). It began as a CBO to tackle local drug syndicates in the Cape Flats of Cape Town but slowly became more politicized until some regarded it as an Islamist movement with a terrorist agenda (Dixon and Johns 2001).

But, groups can also positively regenerate. The youth organization of eastern Sierra Leone known as the Movement of Concerned Kono Youth (MOCKY) is an example. Formed after the war mainly of Civil Defense Force members, it adopted a campaign against the influx of non-Kono alluvial diamond miners and was accused of human rights abuses. Later, they began holding informal courts to settle disputes among area residents not satisfied with the results of the formal judicial system. They now focus on development advocacy and work with the local Police Partnership Board

(Baker 2002). Change, then, is an inherent part of nonstate policing, and with it comes changes in their relationships with others.

In addition to changes in their practices, there may be changes in their legality. Boundaries between public and private, legal and illegal, state and nonstate are subject to ongoing power struggles and negotiation that result in change and reconstruction (Migdal and Schlichte 2005). Thus, for the most part, states since independence have been concerned to encroach on customary territory by reducing their authority and powers. With independence, many African states stripped customary chiefs of their judicial powers and placed their former powers in the hands of lay magistrates. The boundary now is moving the other way in some countries (e.g., Malawi and Mozambique). Or, take, for example, the case of vigilantes in Monrovia, Liberia, and the side of the legal/illegal boundary on which they lie. In 2006, the new minister of justice in Liberia spoke of the inability of the police "to decisively deal with this upsurge in criminal activities." Consequently, she asked "community dwellers to organize themselves into vigilante groups." Taking the minister at her word, young men in the high-density areas of Monrovia formed groups to tackle the daily fear of armed robbery in their neighborhoods. They registered with the police and began night patrols armed with "rubber guns" (catapults). The minister's remedy was not, however, well received by human rights groups, international aid agencies, the UN, or the police, the last seeing this as an encroachment on "their territory." All lobbied the minister to revoke her statement. The commissioner, UN Police (UNPOL), said: "We have to forget the word vigilante and focus on community policing forums that were created by the LNP [Liberia National Police] supported by UNMIL [UN Mission in Liberia]."[1] One Monrovian police chief superintendent told me: "People always like to take the law into their own hands. People want to see quick results and tend towards mob justice. ... They were wounding people." Another chief superintendent from Gbarnga told me: "I am not ready to accept community task forces and watch teams. They can be ex-fighters with other motives. Who empowers these groups?" Under this pressure, the minister did a U-turn and issued a statement that she had been misunderstood and that she had meant to convey that groups should work alongside the police. The police thus directed the groups to disband one year after they had formed. They were now criminalized again; the communities were extremely angry, and armed crime increased. Yet, in April 2008 there was another boundary shift. Public outcry against increasing armed robbery led to the president urging the police to establish, in consultation with community leaders in Monrovia, security zones and to organize "vigilante or watch groups" in the communities in each zone.[2] This account demonstrates the ebb and flow of the legal boundary according to the dominant policy: crime prevention as advocated by the minister of justice or police monopoly/dominance as advocated by the police and state-centric professionals.

Not subject to legal restraints or support, unencumbered by large organizational structures, and sustained largely by volunteers, nonstate policing groups are inherently mutable.

The Reasons for Their Dominance

Most of the policing in post-conflict states is not carried out by the state police and judiciary but by nonstate organizations. In the great majority of circumstances, people look first to nonstate agencies for crime protection and crime response. Some observers assume that nonstate policing is only popular because the state police are not available. In other words, if the police service could be expanded as people want, then nonstate policing would wither (Goldsmith 2003). That is not how I understand the current situation from the research I have conducted. Far from being a merely default position, large numbers of interviewees have expressed to me how they prefer the nonstate policing that is on offer over the police. The support for nonstate policing is due to a number of factors.

First, nonstate policing is accessible. For the most part, it is within walking distance. To get assistance takes as long as it takes to walk to the chief's dwelling, the forum chair's house, the market association committee's office, or the compound of the NGO. For people with a lot to do and only daylight to do it in, this is a huge advantage. In contrast, the nearest police station or police post will be perhaps a minibus drive to the nearest town or a cycle ride to another, larger village. Policing requires accessibility to be a useful service.

Take the example of Liberia. The complaints of so many Liberian villages in 2007 were "the police don't visit us," "they pass by on the main road," and "we call but they don't come." Likewise, in the poor townships of Liberia, they claimed: "The police do not go off the main street. There are no patrols here." Even where there are posts, it does not mean the police are accessible. Said a man in New Kru Town, Monrovia: "There is only one police [officer] at the station at night. He won't leave the station. Even if we run for help he won't do anything."

What of Liberia's emergency response telephone number, 911? For all the county of Montserrado, which includes Monrovia, the police communication center in 2007 was receiving seventy-five calls per day, of which they claimed "95 per cent are insults"; in other words, there were about eight genuine calls a day for police or fire service help. Why so few? The phone is not answered, or if it is, there is no response. As a barrister in Monrovia observed: "If you phone 911 you don't get a response. You need the number of a senior police officer to get them to come and then it may take an hour by which time the criminals have left." Most people in post-conflict Africa do not have access to the police, so they turn to those who are accessible.

Second, nonstate policing is understandable; that is, it is in the users' own language and does not use formal legal language or formal procedures. In fact, it may actually exclude the use of lawyers. Users of these services therefore perceive a great advantage in being able to understand and be understood, normally by the very people with whom they live and work. And, when, as many nonstate policing organizations do, there is an emphasis on restoration more than apportioning blame, the proceedings do not threaten relationships. This sits well with the widely held principle that, first of all, a person should try to resolve a dispute amicably "amongst the family" before escalating it to the level of the state criminal justice system.

The approach of "keep it in the local family" is firmly embedded in Rwanda, both among the volunteers that run the lowest informal levels of dispute resolution and by the judges of the formal state court system. Said a local leader: "I try to make relationships between me and the population and for them to see that we are one and are able to solve our problems together." According to another: "We prefer to sort out disputes amongst ourselves rather than forward them to outside." At the state formal level in Rwanda, the same benefits of the informal level are expressed. A Kigali judge told me: "The local courts bring two people together and bring about reconciliation that can be better than a judge sorting it out."

Third, nonstate policing is affordable. Many criticize nonstate policing in principle based on the assumption that when security is a commodity, it is only available to those who can pay and will therefore create a tiered society in terms of security provision.

> Some objections to privatized security stem from democratic principles—namely that privatized security often means only those who can afford it can get it. Thus security, which is often described as being a public good and a key responsibility and function of the state, becomes a commodity monopolised by the rich and powerful and is distributed unequally among the citizenry. (Caparini 2006, 270)
>
> Private security activity may be counter-productive if security comes at a price that only the rich can afford thus excluding a majority of the population from its benefits. Such developments risk undermining long-term development efforts as well as fundamental tenets of the human security paradigm. (Bearpark and Schulz 2007, 73)

This certainly applies to commercial security but is less relevant to noncommercial groups. It is true that payment in money or kind usually occurs, but the norm is that these are relatively small amounts and are affordable for the users (as noted in the first section of this chapter when discussing volunteers). It is also worth noting that state policing is rarely free to users in post-conflict Africa. To secure the interest, investigation, and prosecution of a criminal case by the police may well necessitate people offering bribes. Further, daily encounters with public policing at roadblocks and at roadside vending pitches is costly. A typical scene in the central area of Monrovia at 4 p.m. is of up to thirty police and new recruits moving through the main market area. Ostensibly, they are there to clear the streets of vendors using the pavement. In fact, they will be seizing goods they want or demanding typically $150 Liberian dollars to return goods they snatch from traders. Nearby, at a main traffic intersection, the officer in charge and his men and trainees are taking bribes from taxi drivers (who are stopping illegally while they load and unload passengers) or demanding goods from passing mobile traders. Thus, as Clapham pointed out, "public" policing fails to serve all freely and equally. Further:

> Many of the claims that are made for the provision of public security through states are actually little more than special pleading, designed to appropriate a veneer of legitimacy for attempts by people who control states to use them for their own interests. (Clapham 1999, 42)

In the light of this, the small payments required of nonstate policing look less problematic.

Fourth, nonstate policing is effective. Of course, not all problems are solved given the dependence on witnesses, and some groups, like women and children, may be less happy than older men at the outcomes. But, by and large people turn to nonstate policing because neighbor disputes are resolved; antisocial behavior is restrained; homes are protected at night; and stolen goods are returned, not lost in the criminal justice system after a thief is arrested. People would not part with their money or give their support or even time to systems that do not deliver the desired results. The advantage of all nonstate policing is that it has local knowledge. Its informant network quickly finds out the perpetrators; in close communities (and this applies as much to the high-density urban neighborhoods as villages), it is hard to hide illicit activities. Thus, the youth chair for Yengema, Kono, Sierra Leone, explained to me: "We know everybody and everything." A *nyumbakumi* (a local leader overseeing 10–15 households) in Kigali, Rwanda, in 2006 said: "I am responsible for 10 houses: seeing how people live, things they do. ... So I need to know what is happening between people." A *résponsable* (a local leader overseeing 500–1000 households), in Igihogwe, near Kigali, Rwanda, said: "The way we work is that the nyumbakumi get to know people; who went out and who went in. He keeps a visitors book for all who stayed over night. ... Then if there is insecurity in the area such as thieves, we look to see who has been staying to see if possibly it was them. ... The résponsable [also] has a book with people in it known for different trouble." The chair of the West Point Community Police Forum, Monrovia, Liberia, was asked in 2007 whether they ever found out who committed burglary: "It is not difficult to track down with teamwork. We know most of the people who do these things." The information that is available locally, however, is not always shared with the police. Thus, the head of the Central Investigations Department (CID), in Zone 1, Monrovia, Liberia, complained: "People are afraid to give information lest there be an attack. So co-operation is not much." A chief superintendent in Zone 6, Monrovia, added: "People are not too willing to give us information. They prefer hiding it. They don't inform us." Too often, the police from their distant station have no knowledge of what is available locally, hence their ineffectiveness compared with nonstate groups.

Finally, the local policing systems may accord more with the local view of justice. The aim of the state system of crime response to produce a winner and a loser may well be perceived as conducive to injustice. For example, in the case of a land dispute, a state court would determine the boundaries according to a strict interpretation of the law, with little consideration given to other circumstances. And, formal court decisions will be immediately enforceable. A customary court, on the other hand, might adjudicate on a basis deemed to be equitable to the disputants and the community concerned and give a longer time frame for implementing the decision.

Of course, popularity of usage does not mean necessarily popularity of service. Yet, it is striking how, when there is a choice, there is often a marked preference for local justice. For example, research in nine provinces of Burundi indicated that of all returnees who have sought outside assistance in disputes, over half have approached the *bashingantahe*, a customary dispute resolution institution. Almost half have approached the local administration, while 28 percent applied to the Tribunaux de Residence (the local court system). Instances of corruption have been reported in all these processes. In particular, the formal state justice system requires that plaintiffs have financial resources and often lacks local credibility (Huggins et al. 2005).

It is also true that some may accept or comply with such nonstate groups, feeling that they have no choice in the face of threatened violence or ostracism. Some may simply follow out of tradition or habit. But, there are many who, because of these features of accessibility, intelligibility, affordability, and effectiveness, along with the compliance of nonstate policing to the prevailing local values, give their support—support that many police services have not yet achieved.

Changes in the Nonstate Security Sector Since 1990

One of the most dramatic changes in nonstate security has been the rapid growth in formal commercial security in post-conflict Africa since 1990. Static guards dressed smartly and often armed are a ubiquitous feature outside the banks, hotels, government buildings, and embassies of the main cities and of the mines of the rural areas. The roots of the current growth can be traced to the conflict itself, when many businesses and wealthy individuals found that the police were no longer available to protect them. But, the expansion took place after the conflict when there was a weakening of traditional forms of social control, a perceived rise of crime (Adu-Mireku 2002), and a police service that was unable to address it and was itself undergoing transformation. In addition, there was a large demand for security from international agencies and organizations that entered the country as part of the peacekeeping and reconstruction effort. In this context, security firms seized the opportunity to offer guards for site protection, VIP protection, and rapid response to alarms and for the movement of cash, making use of the demobilized youth who had a degree of military training. The pattern of expansion therefore has had more to do with the post-conflict socioeconomic context than an economic liberalization with its shift from the public to the private.

Although the security businesses were originally local, there has been an increasing trend toward multinationals taking them over at the upper end of the market. In terms of personnel employed, the commercial security companies are big security players. Group4Securicor works in more than twenty African countries, employing 60,000 people. The number of private security guards now approaches or exceeds those of the state police. For example, there were more than eighty commercial security companies in Uganda in 2004, with the largest two employing some 2,000 guards between them (cf. police numbers of 13,000). In Sierra Leone in 2005, I found that the four largest companies employed 4,400 (cf. police numbers of 8,000). There were only five commercial security companies all told in Rwanda in 2006, but four of them employed 4,300 (cf. police numbers of 5,800). Just six companies in Liberia in 2007 employed 1,750 (cf. police numbers of 3,500).

The expansion seen in commercial policing has not been so obvious at the noncommercial end of nonstate policing. The security provided by customary chiefs and groups associated with residential or trading communities represents a long-term solution to the absence of state (colonial or postcolonial) security. It is not the privatization of the state that has produced choice in this sector but the absence of the state—its failure of provision. And, the reality of "shopping around" for security in a fragmented market has a long history (Baker 2007c; Bierschenk and Olivier de Sardan 2003).

Nevertheless, there have been some changes within the noncommercial sector of nonstate policing. First, the increased need for local security necessitated by Africa's conflicts when state protection has failed or been inadequate has obviously stimulated local response. The fear of both rebels or the state army led to the emergence of ethnic/clan militias (e.g., Somalia; Menkhaus 2007) and civil defense forces (e.g., Sierra Leone; Reno 2007). In addition, rebel groups called on local communities to organize their own security, often in line with socialist principles of popular justice (e.g., Uganda, Rwanda [Baker 2004] and Mozambique [Isaacman and Isaacman 1982]). These popular justice groups were explicit reactions to customary justice and its abuses. On the success of the rebels in seizing control of the state, the local popular justice was incorporated into a local government security structure (Baker 2005a, 2007b).

A second change in the sector is that the role of young men in security has become less tied to the elders and increasingly autonomous. This is a result of enlistment in military groups, internal displacement, urbanization, and the penetration of new ideas of authority and lifestyle. Where chiefs were noted for excessive punishments and forced labor or abandonment of their community in the time of conflict, as was the case in some parts of Sierra Leone (Richards 2005) and Liberia, young men became disillusioned. The result of these societal changes in the postwar societies is that youths have become more willing to take the initiative regarding security with or without the full approval of their elders and chiefs.

A third change has been the advent of restorative justice CBOs. These have adopted principles taken largely from Western mediation and reconciliation sources. Although they imitate, in part, customary approaches of conciliation and consensus, they have emphasized gender equality, the renunciation of violence, and minimal costs and are seen by some as a negative response to customary justice (Wood and Shearing 2007; Massaquoi 1999).

Fourth, there has been the development in some Islamic communities of Islamic policing enforcing Islamic law, especially regarding its attitude to women and alcohol (Peters 2001; Adamu 2008). Islamic law and its sanctions of corporal punishment have been applied both within solely Islamic communities and, more controversially, in mixed communities. They represent a concern not only because of the state police failure to curb crime but because of their disinterest in enforcing locally defined moral values. In the case of the UIC in Somalia (prior to their becoming a militia and briefly seizing power in Mogadishu in 2006), they began as a grassroots movement in the absence of any other legal order in the country. In Somalia (and northern Nigeria), many Muslims welcomed the establishment of some kind of legal order, even if they did not subscribe to all the courts' procedures or support the contacts that the leaders may have had with radical Islam abroad (Seesemann 2007).

It is not clear whether this moral policing is to be seen as part of a resurgence of Saudi Wahhabism that has accompanied significant investment of oil money in mosques and Islamic education in the last twenty years; as instigated by radicals with a political agenda; or whether it is a naturally occurring rediscovery of cultural roots in communities. Anderson has reported efforts by Islamic radicals from Algeria and Pakistan to attract supporters in Mali and to undermine traditional versions of the faith. She quoted one imam as saying:

> Their presence here has raised a kind of conflict with the people. Wahhabis come here from Saudi Arabia. They have means. They give money and build mosques and schools and buy books. If you don't have means, you cannot stop them. And if we don't pay attention, they will use the students against us. (Anderson 2004, unnumbered)

Anderson, however, argues that Mali's history of tolerant Islam is resilient enough to resist external fundamentalism.

The fifth and final change is that "community policing" has been widely adopted as a broad approach to police-public relations by police forces. This is largely due to its promotion by donors as a solution to the lack of police effectiveness and legitimacy. Typically, it has sought to mobilize local communities through police-sponsored community policing forums that develop anticrime strategies in partnership with the police (Brogden 2004; Brogden and Nijar 2005). It is still unclear whether the citizen-led committees will survive the initial enthusiasm or whether being without deep roots in the culture of the police service they will wither for lack of police support (Baker 2007a). For now, the committees engage a good number of "concerned" citizens in urban areas. (More is said on community policing in Chapter 4.)

Conclusion

There may have been additions to nonstate policing groups as a result of war and the penetration of new ideas, but the need for accessible, understandable, affordable, and effective policing predates conflict, as do many of the nonstate policing systems. Neither the change nor the continuity is captured by the concept of fragmentation. The changes described are not so much the state losing its monopoly as its failure to secure a monopoly. This is not a process of fragmentation but of nonaggregation.

For all the long-standing dominance and even growth of nonstate policing, states frequently speak and act as though they were hardly aware of it. Although they know that they have neither the capacity nor even at times the legitimacy to organize authoritatively the cooperation of all to deliver public goods easily and although they know that the social collectivity of choice for such goods is nonstate, they are in denial. States, their police, and their external advisers are constantly engaged in constructing an image of policing and its boundaries that does not correspond with reality. Public statements present an image of the state as the sole legitimate, effective, and accountable provider of nationwide policing, the rightful holder of the monopoly of force. For example, UN Secretary Ban Ki-moon (August 8, 2007) claimed that in Liberia, "Only the police prevent internal insecurity and anarchy."[2] If the state police is portrayed as fit for purpose, what is the image that the state creates of what lies beyond the boundary of the formal and legal? Nonstate policing is portrayed as poorly trained, abusive, unaccountable, and frequently illegal. Links across the public-private boundary are seen as problematic except in very limited circumstances. This chapter has argued that the case for state and nonstate policing being very distinct is imagined for political reasons but does not correspond with reality.

Notes

1. https://unmil.org/article.asp?10=1630, accessed December 10, 2007.
2. *The Analyst* (Monrovia), April 29, 2008, reported:

> Increased public outcry against the increase in armed robbery in Monrovia in recent weeks has forced the police to begin holding strategic dialogue with community leaders across the city. A community-police strategy meeting involving some 20 communities in Monrovia and its environs agreed to pool their efforts in order to end the wave of armed robbery by proffering intelligence information, reporting criminal incidents and movements, and organizing vigilante and community-watch groups. ... [Among other things] the meeting agreed to set up a task force with the mandate of demarcating Monrovia into five security zones and organizing vigilante or watch groups in the within communities in each zone.

Policing the City
Neighborhood and
Customary Responses

3

The City Context

It is of course true that the separation between city and countryside is not clear-cut. Physically, African cities merge into the surrounding countryside, and most city dwellers maintain regular contact with the villages that they came from or where family members still remain. It is not true that the distinction between urban and rural is one of values and lifestyle. It is surprising how much village life continues in the townships of the cities and how evidences of Western lifestyle are to be found in villages. People are very often composites of both the rural and urban, and the difference between urban and rural is essentially situational. Far from being absolute, the differences are a matter of degree. Yet, with these provisos, there is value in considering the city as distinct from the village in terms of policing. The very scale of the population of cities creates a different dynamic to crime and disorder and demands particular policing methods for challenging it.

Right across the continent there has been rapid urban growth since the 1960s. Although Africa is still less urbanized than other continents, urbanization is occurring rapidly, with figures of 4–5 percent growth per annum typical. The urbanization has been the result of both the growth of existing urban populations and migration to urban centers. The perceived prospects of employment, improved security, and available welfare amenities have been "pull" factors, while rural poverty and civil conflict have been push factors. The urban population of Sierra Leone grew from 21.4 percent of the population prewar to 38.1 percent in 2002, with 2015 projection of 47.6 percent.[1] In Monrovia, Liberia, the population was 250,000 in 1987. By 2007, with many having fled to the city for safety during the course of the war, it was over one million. Some of Africa's fastest-growing cities (over 750,000) are in countries that are experiencing or have recently experienced conflict, such as Mbuji-Mayi, Democratic Republic of the Congo (DRC; average annual growth, 4.6 percent); N'Djamena, Chad (4.5 percent); Lubumbashi, DRC (4.1 percent); Luanda, Angola (4 percent); Kinshasa, DRC (3.9 percent); and Mogadishu, Somalia (3.52 percent). They also are large in absolute numbers. It is estimated that Lubumbashi has 2 million; Abidjan, Luanda, and Maputo are verging on 3 million people; Khartoum and Addis Ababa have roughly 4 million; and Kinshasa has anywhere from 6 to 7 million.

These rapidly growing cities are sometimes weakly industrialized, with corresponding unemployment, poverty, and homelessness. Further, public services, such as piped water, electricity, sanitation, and waste disposal, are minimal, especially where there is illegal occupation on unplanned, over-crowded sites. In sub-Saharan Africa, the proportion of urban residents in high-density areas is the highest in the world at 71.9 percent (United Nations Human Settlements Programme [UN-HABITAT] 2003). A 2007 survey of Maputo's barrios asked inhabitants what they saw as their main problem. They answered unemployment (35.8 percent); crime (23.3 percent); water (9.2 percent); sanitation (5.8 percent); education (3.3 percent); and housing (1.7 percent) (Paulo, Rosário, and Tvedten 2007). With the steep rise of global food prices from 2008, even access to most staple food products has severely hit the cities, produced widespread rioting, and led to people reducing the number of meals they eat to one or two a day, eating fewer foods and smaller quantities at each meal. With the urban poor now typically spending up to 80 percent of their household income procuring food, it leaves little for other basic necessities, such as health care, transport, water, or education fees. In some areas, the food price rises have led to a rise in robbery and prostitution (Egal, Valstar, and Meershoek 2003).

Urban migration brings people from across the country who may reside as minority ethnic groups in discrete urban territories, creating a city that resembles a cluster of ethnic villages. These minorities may experience a breakdown in social support structures, such as family and the community. They may also be subject to discrimination by the surrounding dominant group and to neglect by the city authorities. The "detribalization" effect that has been thought to be associated with urbanization is far from automatic. Rather than being zones of transition, the enclaves are often becoming per-manent zones of minorities.

The Post-Conflict City

Not all the conflicts of Africa reached the main cities. During civil wars, cities tended to be government strongholds, although that in itself does not mean that their troops and the influx of refugees from the countryside do not do considerable damage to the fabric of the city. The military may comman-deer factories that never recover their functions postwar, while states neglect essential maintenance. Further, many of the migrants stay on in what were to be only temporary shelters because their village homes have been destroyed.

Yet, for Freetown in Sierra Leone and Monrovia in Liberia, civil war did penetrate the suburbs, causing death and the destruction of homes. As the civil war came to an end in Liberia, there were at least 150,000 displaced persons living in Monrovia, taxing food and shelter resources. More than 60,000 residents of Monrovia were sheltering in sports stadiums and in schools waiting for relief supplies. In addition, there was a large influx of returnees from neighboring Côte d'Ivoire, causing further instability. Crime was reportedly high, with theft and assault prevalent, particularly at night. Residents of the high-density suburbs reported armed robberies and incidents of rape committed at night by armed men. Unfortunately, the police were ill-equipped to provide effective protection.

A young man in Monrovia reported the following in 2006, three years after the war ended:

> I am a 28 years old Liberian, resident of Monrovia. The capital was badly damaged during the civil war. Monrovia remains a city of one million plus people with no piped water or mains electricity. Everyone is running to bigger cities for survival because of lack of employment. The electricity supply network was destroyed in 1990 at the start of the civil war, so the entire country now depends on private generators. Every hospital, school and public building has been stripped bare by wartime looting. The port of Monrovia is choked with wrecks and has been ransacked to the point that it barely functions. A whole generation of youngsters from whom I am not excluded has been brought up without education. They have only known violence and warfare, often as fighters in the conflict themselves.[2]

Even when war and conflict do not directly damage the physical structure of the cities, it has an impact on their economic and welfare activities. The Rwandan genocide saw in Kigali, as elsewhere in the country, the hunting down and murder of Tutsi people by Hutu militias. The resulting effect is captured in a World Bank report of 1995:

> The country's institutional memory and project implementation capacity have been all but wiped out by the killings and disappearance of personnel, destruction of files, and theft of computers and equipment. The crisis caused a sharp drop in the delivery of social services; particularly hard hit were health and education. A sizable part of the services personnel in both sectors was killed or fled. Medical supplies, essential medicines and vehicles were stolen, medical centers were damaged and normal distribution channels broke down. Equally, educational infrastructure and equipment were stolen or vandalized. Nevertheless, some primary schools had restarted activities by mid-September 1994, albeit with greatly reduced resources: student/teacher ratios, already high before the crisis (57 primary pupils per teacher) have greatly deteriorated; school buildings have been damaged and basic equipment and essential learning materials (textbooks, notebooks, pencils, etc.) are lacking. (World Bank 1995)

Concerning the degree of insecurity, crime, and disorder, the African post-conflict city is similar to any African city but to a greater degree. The pre-conflict policing and criminal justice system that resided largely in the cities may not only have lost much of its infrastructure and personnel but also will face a

> violent political culture and a traumatised and highly divided society. ... In addition a shadow or criminalized economy is likely to be entrenched and there is likely to be widespread access to small arms reflected in a high level of violence. (Samuels 2006, 6–7)

Some believe that crime is particularly prevalent in postwar situations where a political transition is also taking place. The link would appear to be that internal security practices employed by authoritarian states to maintain control over the political opposition may also have reduced ordinary crime. Although liberalizing governments may abandon these practices, they are slow at developing effective alternatives. Hence, although the police are told to shun the old coercive methods, they are not given new skills and resources. As a result, crime flourishes.

Crime in the City

Cities everywhere have higher crime rates, particularly of theft and robbery, than rural areas (United Nations Interregional Crime and Justice Research Institute [UNICRI] 2003). With poverty and wealth living in close proximity, yet in a space where state policing is minimal, crime is readily generated. As has long been observed, it is the poor of the cities, not the rich, who are the most vulnerable. They are likely to be victimized since they are less able to protect themselves with alarms and substantial locks and perimeter walls and live in areas of no street lighting (Louw et al. 1998).

Simone believed crime may well be related to the changes taking place in the global economy:

> In an era of trade liberalization, where many new commodities are entering urban markets and many new channels are opened up to acquire them, a whole range of illicit business, protection rackets, smuggling, money laundering have become available. A climate of insecurity has been used to control competition, promote hoarding, mask clandestine import/export channels. Insecurity reduces the amount of scrutiny the general public can apply to both governmental operations and those of the private sector. (2002, 62)

It may even be, as he suggested, that the "convergence of insecurity with economic accumulation" is producing a new urban understanding of effective practices of livelihood formation. The path to success may now be perceived as less to do with education and hard work than to do with criminality, illicit deals, and trickery.

All post-conflict countries are only too well aware of the priority of security, not only for reconstruction and development but also for their existence. As a Rwandan security company manager explained to me in 2006: "We know what evil is and it is important to work together to fight against it." If there is only limited freedom from crime and disorder, there can be no sustainable building of political institutions, no economic growth, and no social reconciliation. Policing is central to post-conflict reconstruction (Call 2002; Center for Strategic and International Studies [CSIS] and the Association of the United States Army [AUSA] 2002; Plunkett 2005; Washington Office on Latin America [WOLA] 2002; Woodrow Wilson School of Public and International Affairs, 2003; Baker 2006, 2007c; Baker and Scheye 2007, 2009).

Yet, how safe are the cities once the conflict is proclaimed over by the politicians? Is there, as many claim, a crime epidemic following conflict when arms are easily available? How are security and order created in the shattered life of a city whose physical infrastructure, such as it was, has been ruined; whose families have been disrupted by death, injury, displacement, and the loss of their possessions; and whose state services, including policing, are too decimated and underequipped to offer very much? How is a city turned around, where for the length of the conflict there has been a disregard for the rule of law and respect for human rights and where some of the worst abusers have been the very security agents of the state? These are the perplexing questions facing the new regimes.

Unknown is just how great the level of criminal activity in African cities is. Accurate statistics of crime rates are sparse. Inevitably, there are problems of underreporting to the police because of lack of access; alternative policing and resolution systems; a desire for speedy justice; the intimidation of complainants by criminals; and shame or fear to report crimes such as sexual abuse. There is also a fear of or lack of confidence in the police. In Mozambique, a victimization survey found that only 26 percent of burglaries were reported. "Citizens very often indicated that the police could do or would do nothing about what happened" (UNICRI 2003, 16). In addition, there is the problem of police not being able or willing to collect crime statistics seriously. The Sierra Leone Police (SLP) admits that most police officers "have yet to grasp the importance of crime statistics. ... Some crime officers do not send accurate crime figures" to police headquarters (SLP 2005). In Liberia, the UNPOL (UN Police) Crime Analysis Team is attempting to ensure that all Liberia National Police (LNP) officers record the details of reported crime, and that the data are sent to the UNPOL statistics office. Nevertheless, as one UNPOL officer regretted in 2007:

> If you ask the LNP what is the crime rate you can't get an answer. ... Though they do have reports on crime, they still can't be found, for there is a lack of systematic recording and different agencies are collecting their own data but not sharing it.

As a result, Liberia is "a country where there are no authoritative statistics to measure crime trends over time" (Malan 2008, 52). In southern Sudan, there was an additional logistical problem of collecting data. With little or no communication between police stations and district headquarters, officers are forced to travel by public transport with their brief station crime reports in their pockets.

Although crime data based on reported and recorded crime are not therefore reliable, the evidence of victimization surveys suggests that many country crime rates have increased rapidly since 1990, especially in post-conflict states. The surveys suggest that Africa is currently the most violent continent (Zvekic and Alvazzi del Frate 1995; UN-HABITAT 1996). According to one survey of cities in Uganda, South Africa, and Tanzania, three of every four had been victims of violence in 1991–1995 (UN-HABITAT 1996). A survey nine years after the war ended in Mozambique disclosed that robbery was very frequent, with very high rates in the main cities. Of the robberies, 37 percent were committed using a weapon (UNICRI 2003). In 1999, a South African survey revealed that 47 percent "felt unsafe or very unsafe" (Humphries 2000, 1). A crime perception survey in Sierra Leone, three years after the conflict, revealed that in urban populations in Sierra Leone, 58 percent felt unsafe in their community (SLP 2004). My own research in Uganda in 2004, eighteen years after the end of the civil war, showed that of thirty-eight shopkeepers (twenty-two men, sixteen women) interviewed in central Kampala, 30 percent (thirteen) felt unsafe at times or always and 18 percent (seven) had been a victim of physical assault in the last twelve months or had known someone who had been (Baker 2005a). Yet, a survey conducted in urban Liberia two years after the war in 2005 found that, regarding personal safety, 25 percent felt "very safe," and 43.7 percent felt "it's OK" (Basedau, Mehler, and Smith-Hoehn 2007, 88). This was, however, largely attributed to the continuing presence of UNMIL, which has subsequently left. Since then, the UN and Liberian police officials in Monrovia have confirmed that crime has been steadily increasing. In one week in July 2008, Liberia was reported to have been hit by a wave of 160 armed robberies that not only had left inhabitants fearful but also had the government admitting the security situation was deteriorating. One woman reported the following: "When they came they kicked the door open, put the entire family under gun point and began to demand money. When they could not get what they expected, they decided to beat my husband with machetes."[3] Anecdotal evidence from police officers interviewed suggests that gender-based crimes, such as sexual assault and

domestic violence, are high in all post-conflict countries. Although sensitization programs have encouraged higher reporting of these crimes, officers in
South Africa, Sierra Leone, Rwanda, Uganda, Liberia, and southern Sudan
have all expressed concern to me over the scale and apparent growth of the
problem. This is covered in more detail in Chapter 7 on policing of women.

Even using the underrecorded crime figures of the police, violence is
clearly a widespread feature of life in African cities. For instance, Uganda
police statistics showed increased numbers of reported violent crime in
urban areas, with Kampala 2002–2003 (sixteen to seventeen years after the
conflict) seeing those shot dead rising from 24 to 80 and a rise from 311
to 647 in aggravated assault cases.[4] Similarly, South African police figures
for 2002–2003 showed sixty murders a day. In 2007, the LNP spoke of the
growth of violent crimes as unchecked: "So far, [security forces'] operations
have been minimally successful as many communities remain vulnerable
with desperate marauding criminals still having the upper hand."[5] And, in
April 2008, the head of UNPOL in Liberia admitted that in the first four
months of the year, "We have already noted 47 cases of armed robbery in the
country and this has to be dealt with."[6] Again, the general commander of the
Maputo police revealed that for the first six months in 2005 and 2006 there
were respectively recorded 59 and 31 murders; 20 and 26 attempted murders;
1,257 and 1,509 robberies; 970 and 883 thefts; and 55 and 56 rapes (Amoproc
2006). In Sierra Leone in 2004 there were 4,183 cases nationwide of "wounding with intent" and 91 for "robbery with violence."

Police in all post-conflict African countries perceive urban crime in
remarkably similar ways. According to SLP commanders, the top four urban
crimes in 2005 were assault, larceny, money fraud, and wounding with intent
(Baker 2005b). In Kigali, the main reported crime in 2006, according to the
Rwanda National Police, was "beating with injury." There was widespread
agreement among the LNP commanders in 2007 that the main urban crimes
were theft, aggravated assault, armed robbery, rape, domestic violence, and
drug trafficking (Baker 2008). It should also be added that the police particularly target activities of the poor that have been criminalized by the state,
such as street trading (Wacquant 2001; Benit-Gbaffou 2008, 104).

Compare this police perspective of urban crime with that of the poor in
Maputo, Mozambique. A survey revealed that the main conflicts were related
to theft and assaults, but these were followed by alcoholic drinking, conflicts
over water, and conflicts over land (Paulo, Rosário, and Tvedten 2007, 47).
In Monrovia, when a nongovernmental organization (NGO) that offers an
advisory and mediation service was asked what were the main problems that
were brought to them, representatives from Foundation for International
Dignity (FIND) told me: "In Monrovia it is labour disputes—no payment
and unfair treatment: and the level of police brutality. Then there is gender violence such as rape. Then there are family disputes over inheritance,

which is always difficult in a polygamous environment." This was very similar to the responses of those interviewed in poor districts of Monrovia (see Baker 2008). They regularly mentioned theft, violent robbery, drugs, rape, and domestic violence. Yet, they also added intimidation of those who would report crime. Children have their own distinctive experience of crime according to Monrovian schoolteachers; these crimes include abuse by parents, whether sending them out to sell at the expense of their education or violent beating. Crime then is wider than the police perspective and police statistics indicate.

Living with Crime in the City

What escapes the reported crime statistics and victimization surveys is the fear of crime. Research in eastern DRC in 2008 examined the percentage of interviewees who felt safe or very safe in the following situations: going to nearest market, 58.9; going to the field, fetch wood, or water, 52.7; going to nearest town/village, 50.1; sleeping at night, 49; meeting a policeman, 45.4; meeting people from another ethnic group, 45.3; meeting strangers, 39.4; walking at night in village, 38.4 (Vinck et al. 2008). "We are frightened of armed robbers at night," three women shopkeepers in their twenties from Red Light, Monrovia, told me: "We can't protect our homes. Gangs of 20 bust the doors. Our only protection is to put pots behind the door. We don't go out at night. We don't go on the road after 8 p.m." And, three women in their thirties from New Kru Town, Monrovia, explained: "We are frightened of thieves breaking into our homes and stealing and raping us. We put all the dishes behind the door so we can hear if any break as someone tries to enter. We are abandoned." It was no different for men in the same area of Monrovia. One man said: "We have a very terrible situation. We have got to be careful at night. Nothing comes of going to the police if you are wounded by a criminal." President Johnson-Sirleaf admitted on radio that the security situation in the capital had deteriorated. She even said that some of the crimes were carried out by police officers assigned to protect the population: "The general security situation is bad. The reason is that our own security for several reasons has not been effective. Certain police officers have just been arrested as the result of their own participation in some of these crimes."[7] "It has become a serious nightmare. We don't close our eyes any more during the night," said one resident of Paynesville, Monrovia.[8] Unofficial curfews prevail after dark in most urban areas in Liberia.

Some criminologists argue that crime is a young person's behavior (Agnew 1990; Brantingham and Brantingham 1984, 1993; Kennedy and Forde 1990; Igbinovia 2000). Certainly, the deputy director of the Central Investigations Department (CID), SLP, confirmed in 2005 that "those who commit crimes are mainly youths between the ages of 18 and 30-something."[9] Yet, their records also show that youths are the victims of most crimes. In addition, they face unemployment, inadequate education, health issues such as AIDS, lack of socialization within the family, political marginalization, and the ongoing trauma of having been directly involved with the fighting forces in the war as combatants or sex slaves. The most recurring factors among the social causes of youth crime are all too familiar in post-conflict Africa. Even before the conflict, things were hard in Sierra Leone. The Truth and Reconciliation Commission (2004, Vol. 3b, Ch. 5, Para. 46) claimed: "By the eve of the fighting most urban youth had lost all hope. They had sunk into an abyss of unemployment and disillusionment. In this state, fighting the war seemed like a viable alternative." After the war, it was even harder. They lacked not only employment, but also the education to obtain the few jobs available. A 23-year-old man from the town of Makeni, Sierra Leone, said in 2005:

> Life is very rough because we are even suffering for food. I know many friends, they were jailed because they sell "brown-brown" [cannabis]—drugs you inhale. They say they have no regrets—that is how they make a living. But I don't want that. ... The war was a disaster. My father was killed. Twenty-three stabs. His property was destroyed. My mother also died soon after. I left school because I could not pay the 100,000 Leones [US$33] school fees or mend the properties.

The widespread reporting by citizens of Africa's post-conflict cities that they have been victims of crime demonstrates that, by and large, they are not being protected from crime by the state policing agencies. The failure of the police is a product of the difficult environment, lack of resources, and its traditional disinterest in the poor. Even though the state police are largely located in the cities, they face in the post-conflict urban context a tough environment. It is one in which mechanisms of social order have been undermined, poverty has been exacerbated, and there is a surfeit of weapons and unemployed ex-combatants (Schärf 2001; Mondelane 2000). Yet, although these circumstances call for additional policing, the police are likely to be less able to respond. The conflict will have reduced available resources and personnel and may well have further eroded respect for human rights as a result of police being drawn into paramilitary activities in the war. When these factors are added to the previous history of state police neglect, abuse, and impunity, it is little wonder that city dwellers have a wariness and lack of confidence in the police. As Paulo reported of the people of Maputo, they complained that most cases taken to the police "are not followed up by court prosecutions and convictions, which is often explained by corruption or the lack of an effective legal system from community courts upwards" (Paulo,

Rosário, and Tvedten 2007, 47). They are not persuaded by government promises of a new era of policing. They are acutely aware of their post-conflict government's inability to finance the new start that promises police availability, accountability, integrity, effectiveness, and community partnership.

The skepticism concerning change and the past disillusionment with the police explains the urban public's continued reliance on its own efforts for policing. Few believe that the time has come for alternative policing methods to be abandoned. What are the nonstate policing alternatives available in urban post-conflict Africa? Both the rest of this chapter and the next give some examples from the main categories and, at the end of each chapter, discuss some of the wider issues concerned with the nonstate policing that has been described. The remainder of this chapter examines and discusses mob justice, anticrime groups, and urban customary structures.

Mob Justice

Mob justice, or the violent response of an uncontrolled crowd to perceived criminals and violators of local norms, thrives in African cities, especially where crime is perceived to be on the rise and therefore "out of control" and the police are seen as ineffective. Despite the entry of Burundi's main armed political group (the CNDD-FDD, National Council for the Defence of Democracy-Forces for the Defence of Democracy) into government in 2003, Amnesty International reported: "Communities around Burundi are increasingly resorting to mob justice, including lynching, apparently because they do not believe in the justice sector's ability to render justice impartially."[10] Mob justice is a common event. Uganda's inspector general of police estimated that more than 1,000 persons had been killed by mob violence in the ten years 1991–2001.[11] Lynching frequently occurred in Maputo in the early to mid-1990s, following the end of Mozambique's civil war when crime flourished. Yet another wave of public lynching began in Maputo in 2006–2007, when at least twenty suspected criminals were murdered. It was apparently associated with anger at police failure to arrest criminals and the apparent police complicity with criminals in renting out their guns and even participating in crimes. The Mozambique press carried reports of citizens catching criminals and handing them in to the police, only to have the alleged wrongdoers released and harassing or murdering those who took them to police stations in the first place.[12] The chairperson of the League of Human Rights (LDH) claimed in 2006: "Everything indicates that the authorities have lost control of the situation. Citizens no longer believe that the existing powers can guarantee people's security and punish all offenders."[13] An attorney with the LDH explained in 2007: "What normally happens is, people drag criminals to the police, but the police don't do anything. The criminals pay off the police and the police let them go: it's a question of corruption."[14] Carlos Serra, a sociologist researching Maputo's vigilantes, spoke of lynching as demonstrating "a profound dissatisfaction with the state." In other words, lynching is not so much a manifestation of disorder; it is a protest against disorder.[15]

Even the claim that someone has stolen or raped quickly translates into immediate beatings or killing of the accused. It is normally perceived as spontaneous, but individual instigators and agitators are not uncommon. As might be expected, it is associated with the crime and disorder of the street, such as theft, women in sexually provocative clothing, witchcraft, or racist hatred. It is also frequently associated with misunderstanding of police bail, which can appear as if the police are simply releasing criminals that the public have arrested—a situation that seems both unjust and potentially threatening should the accused turn on their accusers.

To its perpetrators, mob justice is seen as a swifter justice than waiting for slow courts and, in the case of theft, offers the benefit of returning stolen property. As a town councilor in Sierra Leone put it to me: "Where I live we give thieves a good hiding; we don't take them to the police for we won't get the exhibit [the stolen property] back." Typically, crowds of local people (mainly, although not exclusively, young males) engage in stoning, beating, machete attacks, and burning alive or stripping suspects of their clothes and parading them through the streets.

Mob justice highlights the acute difference between the illegal and the illegitimate. It may be banned by statutory law and yet have widespread support, not only from the victims of crime, but also, as the following shows, from the public, the police, and international peacekeepers:

> In Liberia, nine suspected criminals linked with armed robberies in Monrovia's commercial suburban district of Paynesville, were mobbed to death and their bodies set ablaze in the full glare of Liberian police officers, UNMIL (UN Mission in Liberia) forces as well as petty traders and other onlookers who clapped in an apparent approval of the action.[16]

The fact that much of the driving force behind mob justice is frustration with the security forces explains why often it is the very security forces themselves who are the object of mob violence. In the Central African Republic, when a Chadian member of the presidential guard stabbed a Central African Republic policeman in an attempt to steal his car, he was attacked by youths and stoned to death. His body was burned in the street.[17]

Again, in November 2007, violent riots broke out in Huambo, Angola, after a policeman shot and killed a taxi driver, reportedly for his refusing to pay a bribe. Angry witnesses attacked and severely beat the police officer (U.S. Department of State, Country Report 2007). By 2005, mob justice in South Africa was declining from its levels in the late 1990s. Nevertheless, in just one weekend in October 2005, for instance, it was reported that mob justice had left four people dead and three injured. In just one incident, "residents of Olievenhoutbosch, in Tshwane, assaulted three men accused of robbing and raping a woman."[18] A striking feature of the murders was that those responsible appeared not to be violent gangs of the unemployed youths but concerned citizens who were members of the neighborhood watch that had formed to help the police combat crime. One of the committee members defended the actions: "The judicial system that is not delivering. ... People are overwhelmed by [anger and frustration] and the need for a proper process to be followed in identifying the person, so innocents are not victimized, goes out the window."[19]

Anticrime Groups

In essence, the anticrime groups are organized informal responses by sections of a neighborhood to tackle crime and maintain order as defined by local dominant norms. Their usual activities are patrols and punishment. Sometimes, their aim is to make their quarters "no-go" areas for anyone not affiliated with their own particular social or political grouping.

Some groups, however, are violent and vengeful (Harris 2001), in which case they tend to be called *vigilantes*. Harris listed the characteristics of contemporary South African vigilantes as those who are public; have a pervasive use or threat of violence; generate fear through repression; and follow an instant, retributive justice model. Besides the violent punishments of beatings, mutilation, and murder, they may also use financial punishments to "meet their costs" and to pay for compensation for the complainant. In neighborhoods where people are poor and cannot afford lengthy delays in justice and have no insurance, there is a powerful attraction to a system that offers rapid resolution through punishment of the guilty, compensation, and the return of any goods stolen. In other words, it is not just a self-help response in the context of state failure or absence (Abrahams 2007; Schärf and Nina 2001) but an alternative approach to crime deterrence and crime response that is being followed. Anticrime groups have less to do with the condemnation of the state for its failure to uphold the rule of law as condemnation of the state's law. In the case of postapartheid South Africa, Buur (2006) argues that the resurgence of vigilante groups since 1994 is related not so much to the inability of the police to curtail the crime wave as it is to the attempt by government "to enshrine human rights as an all-encompassing foundational value." Specifically, the government was seen, in the townships of Port Elizabeth where he was researching, as creating rights for children, youth, and women that undermined the sociocultural order and mechanisms of control of the township. With the granting of legal entitlements to women, children, and youth, local people perceived them as being given the right to flaunt social norms and established hierarchies with state legal protection. For example, they complained that children could now challenge a parent's right to beat them; women and girls could challenge the right of husbands and parents to control their sexual behavior or drug use; or anyone could challenge the right of elders to demand respect. State law, in their eyes, threatened the order they desired.

This use of violence to maintain local order is not something confined to the turmoil of transition post-conflict, as is sometimes suggested. These violent local security provisions predate the independent state, the post-conflict and political transition crime waves, and the privatization of security in a liberalized economy (Fourchard 2008). As Leach argues, they should be seen within a range of "longstanding ethics and practices concerned with the protection of their communities" (2004, quoted in Pratten and Sen 2007, 6).

Some violent anticrime groups are barely distinguishable from crime protection rackets or the violent enforcers of the will of local politicians and people of influence. For instance, an elected assembly member in DRC runs Bundu dia Kongo, which, apart from its violent political campaign to promote the restoration of the kingdom of Kongo, has also set up its own tribunal system and a vigilante group called the Makesa, who are armed with whips.[20] Menkhaus gave a Somali example. He described internally displaced person (IDP) camps in Mogadishu where "camp managers" offered protection in exchange for a proportion of the aid or wages that the IDPs received. Yet, although openly predatory, he found that many IDPs in fact found the arrangement better than exposure to unrestricted plunder (Menkhaus 2007, 87). And, of course, the anticrime groups have been used by the state itself to undermine opposition (as the apartheid regime of South Africa; the Côte d'Ivoire regime of Gbagbo; or the Mengistu regime of Ethiopia) or to provide a cheap alternative to the police for combating crime (as in the case of Liberia in 2008, mentioned in Chapter 2, Note 2).

It is not just the public who are frustrated by the slowness of the criminal justice system and of the ability of criminals to bribe their way to freedom or to intimidate witnesses into silence. The police themselves, acting unofficially, have been known to resort to violent forms of extralegal anticrime practices. The rise in violent crime in Maputo, Mozambique, and the associated lynching of 2007 led the interior minister to place his officers on a "war footing." This, in practice, encouraged the police to undertake their own form of vigilantism in extrajudicial killings of suspected criminals. In the first six months of 2007, seven criminals were found shot in the head at close range next to a police station near Maputo's beach. Three detectives were later charged.[21] In Rwanda in late 2006, there were several highly publicized killings of survivors of the 1994 genocide who had been witnesses in the gacaca courts[22] that were prosecuting those accused of genocide. There followed the death of at least twenty persons held in police custody from November 2006 to May 2007. It was said by the authorities that police officers shot and killed them as they attempted to escape or to take weapons from police officers. Most of the victims were said to be "of extreme criminal character ready to die for their genocide ideology." Human Rights Watch, however, suggested that there appears to be a case for examining whether these were not in fact extrajudicial killings by some police officers who "may have interpreted official exhortations as a license to abuse detainees, particularly but not exclusively those accused of crimes against survivors or persons involved in the gacaca process" (2007b).

Yet, not all anticrime groups deserve the violent, hateful, criminal image. Some groups are much more civic minded and concerned to maintain and restore social order as they understand it. These are less inclined to violence and likely to be supported by many of the local inhabitants, including the leaders and even the local police commander. As was argued in Chapter 2, the boundary between state and community-based responses to crime can be blurred in practice and subject to ongoing power struggles and negotiation. In the case of these anticrime groups, there is contestation over what is illegal behavior and what is the proper way of responding to it.

The popular image of unemployed ex-combatant "youth" as criminals at worst or untrustworthy at best is widespread. Some no doubt deserve this characterization, but it is surprising how many young people in post-conflict societies perceive themselves as "guardians of security." I have listened to unemployed youths in Makeni, Sierra Leone, in 2005, who, while they acknowledged that they were "still struggling to gain acceptance" from the local communities, nevertheless asserted that after the years of committing violence they now wanted to put something positive into their communities. Far from being criminal, many feel that in the absence of the police they have a duty to their communities to provide security. Besides, their service often provides a little income as well.[23]

Throughout post-conflict Africa, youth in the cities are not just serving in, but initiating, vigilante groups and night patrols (and community policing forums, peace committees, and taxi association task forces). This move from causing insecurity to providing security, however, is not welcomed by all. A paramount chief in Sierra Leone told me he feared that if they were given a role in security there would be a return to political militias, and the youth would "make a living out of it." And, an SLP commander felt that the neighborhood watch in his district was not effective because the youth representatives on it were "criminals."

Sometimes, the "security" role of youths is informal and marginal. In Monrovia, Liberia, vigilante groups sprung up after the war in 2003 until closed down by the police in 2007. One such group operated in Gaye Town, a large high-density area on the edge of Monrovia comprising perhaps 80,000 people. The population grew rapidly during the war. The group consisted of twenty-seven young men under the leadership of a local hospital dentist. By their account, the group began in 2006 "because when there was robbery the LNP [Liberian National Police] didn't get there soon. The police stop on the main road"; "because we were threatened"; "we wanted to go to bed soundly." As for the police, they were perceived as not having changed despite the reforms: "It is the same people, same police"; "They still take bribes." Using a household tax, they equipped themselves with flashlights, rubber guns (catapults), and whistles and began night patrols from 12:30 a.m. to 6 a.m. in groups of three to five. Often, there were violent confrontations with the men with AK47s, but overall, in their view, they succeeded in reducing robbery and made five arrests. An account by an IRIN reporter said the following:

> Every night Gibson Karchold and his neighbours pick up their machetes and nail-studded sticks and go out on patrol, trying to protect their homes in a run-down area of the Liberian capital, Monrovia. "Criminals come around to hijack you while you are in bed. They take your generator and then wake you up and take your mattress," he explained. "It's really the police's job but you could be killed before the police arrive. They are far away from where the action is." In response, vigilante gangs have sprung up around the capital. ... In Jacob's Town, another group had cornered a suspected robber. They held him more than half an hour—the time it took police to reach the remote area. This suspect was handed over, unharmed, and taken to the local police station. But there have been other instances, where no such restraint has been shown. The body of Magic D, described by locals as a notorious armed robber, lay on a rubbish dump in the Fiamah neighbourhood for days after residents tired of his repeated offences and took matters into their own hands, beating him to death.[24]

Adjoining Freetown's port, in Krootown, Camp Divas Youth claimed in 2005 to maintain a measure of order, especially among the youth. They fined cases of fighting and abusive language and "flogged" those who failed to pay the fine. Thieves, they said, were taken to the police. A local tribal headman concurred that youths often intervened to stop fighting when the police failed to respond, although on the negative side, he also noted that they stoned a police station when a suspect they wanted was taken there. Outside a police divisional headquarters in Freetown, I watched forty youths demonstrating loudly for compensation for a cow they had "arrested" wandering down the main road. Inside the station, the commander negotiated with the youths and the cow's owner until a financial settlement was reached, and the crowd left in jubilation. In the east of Sierra Leone, in the town of Yengema, the town chief claimed that the area was "depending on youths to take care of us at night," though he added that, "youths are not always reliable." The young men stay alert at night and respond to fights and other manifestations of disorder such as the sale of drugs: "We harass anybody who brings drugs. ... We arrest them, destroy drugs and give them a beating." In their view, the drug problem "is solved; no more drugs," said their leader.

In this section, I have argued that such groups would find it hard to exist without a degree of local support, but at the same time I have noted that there is a certain ambivalence among some. For them, it may be the only available option; nevertheless, they are seen as a flawed option. This may explain the results of a survey of perceptions of violent actors in urban Liberia. It found that although 62.9 percent regarded vigilantes, area teams, and neighborhood watch as "somewhat or very important for personal security," 17.2 percent saw them as a large or slight threat to personal security (Mehler and Smith-Hoehn 2007, 59).

Customary Groups

Customary is of course a problematic term. All societies come under outside influences. There are "no clear-cut boundaries between the realm of the exogenous 'modern' and the endogenous 'customary'" (Boege et al. 2008, 6). Instead, there are processes of assimilation, transformation, and adoption at the interface of the global/exogenous and local/indigenous. The customary structures are not unchangeable and static. They are in a constant flux and adapt to new circumstances and external influences. This fluidity and adaptability of custom allows customary and external approaches to be combined so that a hybrid is formed. For all the accommodation of the external into the indigenous, they still nevertheless retain a pattern that does not belong to the realm of conventional institutions originating in the West.

Customary leaders are not confined to rural areas. Whereas the state courts and police stations are invariably heavily damaged in war and the criminal justice system is severely undermined, the chiefdom system, where it existed (as in Liberia, Sierra Leone, Burundi, and southern Sudan), survived. Yet, even they did not always come out unscarred. Conflict often undermined respect for authority, and youths overthrew the leadership of their elders, or rebels enforced their own appointees as chiefs (e.g., in some cases in southern Sudan). According to one Liberian paramount chief in 2007: "Way back they respected us. But now people do their own thing. We have just got to bear it—it is our home."

The urban customary chiefs often have less authority than those in rural areas or at least less chance to get away with handling more than minor cases. Nevertheless, they are widely used. In terms of their importance in the urban setting, Mozambique's Supreme Court chief justice complained in August 1999 that only 25 percent of citizens had access to the official judicial system, while the rest had to look to local customary courts (U.S. Department of State, 2001). In Liberia and Sierra Leone, customary chiefs operate as dispute settlers within their own ethnic community in the urban areas. This means dealing with debt, street fighting, landlord-tenant problems, and "men-women" problems. Elsewhere, as in southern Sudan, they handle, often in a mixed ethnic panel, a wide range of customary and criminal issues, whatever the ethnic group of the plaintive.

Where chiefs' jurisdictions are legally constrained, their frustration tends to be directed at the police for complicity with criminals, faulty use of bail, and lack of knowledge of law and legal procedures. A Liberian chief in Paynesville, Monrovia, complained to me in 2007:

> There are so many blotches in the police. It's better to have less police and have those who are, trained, than to have those who will not uphold the law and the Constitution. We have cases where the police mingle with criminals. … The police are connected with those who fought the war. The police are falling short of ethics. … The problem is when he [a criminal] is arrested, instead of being prosecuted, in 24 hours he is on the street! We blame those who release them. Criminals and the police are in connection. They are sharing the goods.

Similarly, a Sierra Leonean headman in Freetown expressed his frustration to me in 2005:

> We have problems with pickpockets and fights—sometimes these are lethal with knives. Three weeks ago a car hit a person—the driver was dragged out and beaten—in front of the police! They did nothing! But often the local youth will step in if the police fail to respond. … The trouble with the police is that they are in collusion with robbers.

Whatever the legalities, however, some chiefs still handle criminal cases rather than wait for the slow process of prosecution in the state courts. Said a chief in Bo, Sierra Leone:

> There is just one magistrates court in Bo, but two Native Authority courts. Cases are reported from the town chief to the section chief, then to the speaker then to the paramount chief. … People would not report directly to the SLP even if it was a criminal case such as wounding or theft cases. They come to the paramount chief first and they [the chiefs] give advice as to what to do. You see there is a general ignorance of legal matters.

In southern Sudan, with the state court system even more embryonic and where the government (officially) welcomes the role of customary chiefs, these chiefs are the leading actors in resolving disputes and bringing order in urban areas. Mixed court panels are typical of customary courts, reflecting the mixed tribal nature of the urban areas. This can confer advantages in intertribal cases. In Malakal, for instance, I have observed a panel consisting of Dinka, Shilluk, and Arab judges. Because of the presence of the Arab chief, the state magistrate court had referred a case of "fighting" between an "Arab northerner" and a "southern Sudanese" to it, apparently in the belief that, since the case was politically delicate and could provoke public disturbance, the customary court was a better place to resolve the conflict. Further, the prevailing view in the towns of Juba, Yei, and Malakal is that any chief can solve a problem between two people from different tribes. The argument is that all customary courts are similar, even if particular offenses would warrant differing punishments depending on the tribe.

Delegation of cases in southern Sudan from town magistrate to local customary courts is not infrequent and illustrates the point made in Chapter 2 that there are linkages between state and nonstate. Surprisingly, delegation even occurs when the case involves something strictly outside the jurisdiction of a customary court. The delegation reflects the fact that customary courts are to some degree integrated into the statutory state court system. Hence, customary courts act with state authority when they issue warrants, which, if not answered, entitle the customary court to imprison the nonresponsive recipient; court clerks of customary courts often receive salaries from their respective ministries of local government/administration; and customary courts share the fees and fines assessed and collected with the state local administration.

A relationship between customary chiefs and the police is also more apparent in southern Sudan than Liberia and Sierra Leone. The police often refer to the customary chiefs when attempting to find a person. The police not only frequently testify in customary courts but also may act as prosecutors and bring the case to the customary court. In fact, in all the Juba, Yei, and Malakal customary courts of southern Sudan that I have seen, police officers were present and performed essential functions. In the Juba Paramount Court, the police officer, although in uniform, was "working after hours" and received some sort of "incentive" from the customary court for maintaining order in the courthouse. In Yei and Malakal, however, the uniformed police officer preserved order in the court in his official capacity as a state employee. In Malakal and Juba, it was even a police officer who carried out a sentence of the court by "whipping" the convicted individual.

Discussion

Insecurity is a permanent feature of the post-conflict African city, yet it is not something that is being addressed thoroughly by the state police. Reduced state and municipal budgets, overstretched criminal justice systems, escalating urban impoverishment, and the weakening of local control structures all combine to make the post-conflict African cities insecure. As Simone noted,

"Such heightened insecurity deeply affects where people can go and what they can do." In addition, he argues that for many African cities, high levels of everyday insecurity [are] a relatively recent phenomenon," and that many regimes are withdrawing from areas of the city because

> It is easier for them to consolidate their ruling position by either conceding territory to a state of ungovernability or by using insecurity as a means to accumulate wealth and resources. Instead of attempting to police, regulate or exert control over certain sections of the city, national and/or local states simply withdraw. (2002, 62)

Yet the evidence, I would argue, is not one of state withdrawal but rather that they have *never* been interested in policing much beyond protecting the regime and the central business district, government buildings, and the wealthy suburbs. What is taking place in the poor majority areas of the cities is not so much a process of withdrawal as continuing low government priority. The response of people to provide their own security therefore is not new or even a growing phenomenon; it is a long-standing response to state disinterest and absence.

While states and donors do engage with urban insecurity, working with neighborhood and customary policing groups is far from straightforward. They are varied assemblages and can be conveyors of both justice and injustice. This makes a common approach, even within a single country, difficult. On the other hand, both neighborhood and customary policing share a significant attraction to those seeking to provide a nationwide security in a post-conflict situation. "If there is a structure functioning at the local level, it is logical to include them in providing governance at a local level" (Lutz and Linder 2004, 48). Their attraction is that they are existing security groups with local support and in place in the very areas where the state has little presence now or will have in the immediate future. In addition, they require very little expense. The customary chiefs may be paid a little by the state, as in Sierra Leone by the Ministry of Local Government, which appoints the chair of the court. However, both groups, for the most part, are content to take as remuneration some or all of the fines collected and fees owing. And, although both neighborhood and customary groups would desire improved accommodation and equipment, they can operate without any serious investment of money by the state or donors.

In one important respect, the neighborhood and customary groups differ: their level of permanence, which is a key factor when states and donors are considering support. Anticrime groups are inherently unstable, whereas customary groups are on the whole stable. Although both are subject to change, it is the anticrime group that can mutate quite dramatically, whereas the customary is subject to ongoing but more gradual change. For the young unemployed youth who is the typical member of the anticrime group, personal involvement is only until something more lucrative turns up and something more urgent demands attention. The anticrime group may well be unsustainable beyond the life or commitment of the leaders, but the chieftaincy is an institution that will outlive the individuals and in that sense is sustainable.

No one questions that both groups need reform to reach the standards that states and donors would expect of security providers that have their authorization. Yet, by definition a post-conflict state, which may well be going though transition from authoritarian to democratic rule, will not have ideal security institutions. It is precisely in this period that security sector reform programs are introduced to address the problems. If security authorizers are authoritarian, they will not want reform of security providers; if the security authorizers and providers are fully democratic, they will not need reforming. We should not expect, therefore, that in a post-conflict situation security groups, whether state or nonstate, will be fully compliant with international human rights standards.

A frequent accusation against nonstate justice (whether urban or rural) is that when courts are involved, as is the case with customary structures and local government structures, those acting as judges are not required to step down if they have a personal interest in or knowledge of or relationship to the disputants. Although it is true that this is counter to formal court principles, the defense surely has some merit: that personal knowledge can actually assist in reaching an informed judgment. Participants in an informal court would normally make a protestation if the relationship or knowledge was seen to be used unfairly, although whether this would be a successful protest might depend on other factors. Inadequate compliance with human rights standards certainly applies to both anticrime groups and customary structures. They are commonly criticized for corporal punishment, bias against women, dubious sponsors, and poor record keeping. Interviewing women in southern Sudan, it became clear that for all the support they gave customary structures in general, not all were satisfied with chiefs' practices regarding women in all cases (see Chapter 7 on policing of women). But, the issue is surely not whether security providers need reform but whether they are reformable. After all, the state police are regularly criticized for all the same abuses that are leveled at anticrime groups and customary chiefs; yet, states and donors do not say that they are not even going to try to reform them.

Determining whether a group is reformable is a subjective judgment, but certainly there is cause for encouragement that many chiefs appear willing to reform. I have met many town customary chiefs who understand the need to strengthen their performance and look to the international donors for the support to improve their safety and security provision. For instance, three customary chiefs from Malakal, southern Sudan, told me: "If we are not reformed, we will collapse and die." More specifically, many chiefs realize that they need to keep abreast of the changes occurring in southern Sudan and that includes paying greater attention to the needs of Sudan's youth and working out ways in which youth leaders can advise them in rendering decisions. The chiefs are also aware, for instance, of the key role of their court clerks, not just in preserving the files but in their knowledge of court decisions and precedents. Those chiefs to whom I spoke in 2007 were very open to the compilation of these precedents within topic areas to improve consistency of justice. Further, some have recognized the need for women chiefs, especially in cases involving issues directly relevant to women. This is in line with a state "administrative decree" that female customary judges should be 25 percent of the total. There are, then, indications of a system that, at least in certain places, is open to reform. It confirms the opinion of the head of the South Sudan Human Rights Commission who has told me that the customary chiefs need support and strengthening "as they are now" so that there will be "greater success in changing them" slowly and over time.

The difficulty with reforming anticrime groups is that, apart from other things, they are subject to change. Their mutability means that yesterday's activities are very different from the group's activities today. There are none in the official pay of the government (although pseudovigilantes may well exist where government personnel organize death squads), so that there is not the same leverage. Should a group be deemed reformable, however, then as with the chiefs, their difficulties can potentially be managed and their advantages can be appreciated.

The logical first step for governments wishing to engage with city customary structures and anticrime groups is to identify those worthy of support for all their weaknesses and to establish partnerships with them. Without their help, the government will not be able to offer the people of the cities the security that they want and will have less chance of establishing legitimacy. Even on the assumption that, in time, the state police will be able to offer a service for all, there is a clear need to utilize these groups in the interim. Yet, it needs to be a partnership that genuinely assists or even transforms local policing and arbitration structures to improve their standards. In addition, there needs to be some overarching framework of principles and supervision and an appeal process to reduce inconsistencies and poor performance.

Any reform of these local justice and policing groups, however, necessitates a corresponding reform of the state police and justice sector. People will not entertain partnerships with state agencies regarded as violent, corrupt, incompetent, and at times complicit with criminal activity. Inadequacy of the state provision will only further entrench the view that state actors are illegitimate. The apparent bias in the criminalization of the activities of the poor also needs addressing. Simone made a good point when he argued

The selective and often arbitrary criminalization of informal economic activity often promotes a general sense that legality is an instrument used against citizens rather than supportive of them. Less policing effort should be directed toward regulating petty trade activity and more toward the public prosecution of economic crimes of scale. This would reassure urban residents that there is not a "sliding scale" of justice. With an urban public increasingly convinced that accumulation of substantial resources and economic capability is attributable to underhanded and illicit practices, everyday complicity—i.e. favor-seeking, goods purchase, petty extortion—with gangs, area boys, or wayward police is encouraged in thousands of small transactions. These transactions provide a platform on which, what are initially "small-time" criminal groups, gain prominence and up-scale criminal activities. (2002, 63)

For the state and donors to negotiate with urban customary and local anticrime groups would be a contentious policy. Both policing groups have bad reputations among human rights groups, women's groups, and donors. Likewise, the police themselves are likely to resist partnerships with such as potentially threatening their claimed monopoly on official security provision. For all the potential benefits in terms of the control and response to crime and disorder, it would be politically dangerous for new and unestablished governments. It is probably other forms of informal law-and-order providers in which states and donors will be more interested, and it is these I look at in the next chapter.

Notes

1. http://www.usaid.gov.
2. http://profiles.takingitglobal.org/aaron15.
3. AFP July 14, 2008.
4. The Monitor (Kampala), January 6, 2004.
5. The *Analyst,* January 3, 2007, http://www.analystliberia.com/liberia_resolution_2008_jan03_08.html.
6. *The Analyst*, April 29, 2008.
7. AFP, July 14, 2008.
8. Ibid.
9. IRIN, December 22, 2005.
10. Amnesty International, http://asiapacific.amnesty.org/library/Index/ENGAFR 160012004?open&of=ENG-2F2.
11. *New Vision*, December 24, 2002.
12. Inter Press Service, Africa, November 7, 2006.
13. Ibid.
14. IRIN, April 2, 2004.
15. http://www.irinnews.org/report.aspx?ReportID=71234.
16. *Panapress*, August 12, 2008.
17. Reuters, December 8, 2006.

18. Mail and Guardian South Africa, October 13, 2005.
19. Ibid.
20. http://www.voanews.com.
21. http://www.irinnews.org/Reports.aspx?ReportID=73143.
22. Local courts, loosely based on customary courts, established by the government 1996–2006 to deal with the large number of cases of genocide and war crimes.
23. Simone made the following interesting observation:

> Residing in close proximity, urban residents often use their knowledge of each other—their comings and goings, domestic intrigues, acquisitions, and tendencies—as knowledge with which to eke out some kind of advantage, and often a kind of parasitism. What is there to steal; who is available to abuse or manipulate; whose coattails can be ridden? Just as knowledge has been elevated to the primary object of production at the highest levels of global capitalism, so too with the poor, does the appropriation of knowledge—whether it be impressions, rumors, or observations about those with whom they share residential and operating space—start to take precedence. (2002, 62)

24. IRIN, October 18, 2005.

Policing the City
Community Police Forums and Local Government Responses

4

Introduction

The last chapter looked at how individuals and groups in African towns organize themselves to prevent crime and to preserve order. This chapter moves from those local policing initiatives to state initiatives. It focuses on two state initiatives that seek to mobilize local populations in crime prevention partnerships, namely, community police forums (CPFs) and local government security structures. It examines the effectiveness or otherwise of policing organizations instigated and sponsored by the state outside the formal police and justice system for a specific purpose.

Community Police Forums

Community policing (sometimes known as policing in the community or community-oriented policing, COP) and, in particular, that institutional element of it known as community forums, is consistently recommended for the developing world by donors and police advisers as part of police reform in post-conflict countries (Brogden 2005; Finnegan, Hickson, and Rai 2008; Groenewald and Peake 2004; Head and Brigada 2006). It is part of the shift that has taken place in policing philosophy to the view that policing is no longer the sole responsibility of the police—it is "everybody's business." The focus of community policing is on state police and communities working together in partnership so that policing reflects local needs. The intention is that both sides will design local responses to crime and disorder that are both proactive and reactive. The distinctive element, according to its proponents, is its focus on crime-producing conditions as the likely potential source for reducing crime. It is for this reason that the approach urges the police to turn to the local community to understand its needs and to avail itself of its local knowledge and resources. There is also a secondary agenda of "image enhancement" for the police, the hope being that contact and cooperation with local communities will go some way to overcoming the suspicion of and hostility toward the police built up over years of violent, corrupt, and indifferent policing. Authoritarian regimes nurtured police who saw themselves accountable to the state rather than to the public. As agents of the regime, they had grown accustomed to immunity from prosecution and to granting immunity to the powerful. As one forum chair in Freetown, Sierra Leone, in 2005, described it to me: "We started the committees because after the war people still regarded the police as enemies. ... There was no confidence." CPFs were intended to overcome this legacy of public mistrust.

A close connection between a society coming out of conflict and the perceived benefits of community forums is very apparent. In Uganda and Rwanda, the new regime's rebel experience had a profound impact on their approach. First, they saw their rebellion as aimed at transforming the corrupt institutions of state, which included, high on their lists, the police. Under Obote's regime in Uganda, for instance, the state initiated (or condoned) murder, torture, looting, rape, terrorism, and imprisonment of opponents. The security forces were above the law, while the judiciary were politicized and corrupted. The process inevitably contaminated the Uganda Police, who were too afraid to investigate for fear of victimization (Kabwegyere 1995, 228). And, as for Rwanda, the police were not only complicit in the genocide, but also, as I was told in 2006 by the commissioner general of the Rwanda National Police (RNP) in the first postwar government: "The local police was locally recruited, locally managed—which brought in the other negative sentiments of sectarian recruitment and corruption." The victorious rebels also had a positive vision of policing born of their war experience. They saw their success in their civil wars as due to winning the hearts and minds of the local people to provide them with intelligence and support. As one former Rwandan Patriotic Army fighter put it:

> We began as a very small group. We were poorly equipped and had no logistical support. We had to rely on the support of "family members." ... And they gave us food and cover and information about the movements of the enemy. We knew the population's support was crucial. In fact we were doing community policing! And it continued after we seized power.

Uganda and Rwanda saw, therefore, the solution to transformation as the popular justice that they had introduced during the civil wars.

Elsewhere, although post-conflict countries invariably shared Uganda and Rwanda's concern to rehabilitate a police force that had become totally discredited in the eyes of the majority of citizens, the community policing model was chosen. South Africa's force, of course, had lost all legitimacy as a result of their violent policing in support of the apartheid regime. Even when the ban on liberation movements was removed in 1990, there was evidence of police collusion in the political violence that followed in KwaZulu-

Natal and the Transvaal (now Gauteng). Faced with a strong, armed, and hostile organization, members of the African National Congress (ANC) were acutely aware of the priority of transforming the police into a democratic and legitimate organization. Yet, in finding a solution they were more ambivalent about the popular justice history of the struggle than Uganda and Rwanda had been about their wartime rebel structures. The ANC had had little control over the peoples' courts and township justice (Seekings 2001), and most in the new government thought their excesses needed to be curbed. Their answer was the creation of CPFs. The National Peace Accord, signed by the ANC, Inkatha, and the government in 1991, promised that

> Police shall conduct themselves so as to secure and retain the respect and approval of the public. Through such accountability and friendly, effective and prompt service, the police shall endeavour to obtain the co-operation of the public whose partnership in the task of crime control and prevention is essential. (National Peace Accord 1991, Sections 3.1.1–3.1.4, in Gastrow 1995)

The Interim Constitution required legislation to "provide for the establishment of community-police forums in respect of police stations." These were to promote police accountability to and cooperation with local communities; monitor police effectiveness and efficiency; advise the police regarding local policing priorities; and evaluate the provision of visible policing services such as the staffing of police stations, the handling of complaints, the patrolling of residential and business areas, and the prosecution of offenders. The South African Police Service Act followed in 1995.

Other post-conflict countries in Africa have followed the community forum pattern. Although CPFs are a state initiative implemented by the police, the declared objective is to set up a network of autonomous forums of local citizens with whom the police meet regularly. Groups of citizens are usually free to approach the police if they wish to set up a new group. Typically, the forum executives are chaired by a civilian body that includes representatives of the significant interests in the locality, including chiefs, religious leaders, business persons, and youth groups. To facilitate the partnership, an officer (usually in the local police station) is charged with the responsibility of identifying and liaising with community leaders and disseminating security information between the community and the police. The local police commander and perhaps a liaison officer will sit on the executive of the local forum. At regular meetings, the forum executive and general public share information on local crime with the police, discuss issues of local concern, and consider solutions to current problems.

The degree to which local practice remains true to the original concept of "state-sponsored yet autonomous" forums varies. The police often have a very different view of what partnership means to the local group themselves, usually wanting to dominate them (Brogden 2005) and sometimes paying them scant attention even while they praise their work (Baker 2007a). Cawthra's view was that "as with many liaison forums the police are often unwilling (or unable because of organizational policy) to regard the views of the 'community representatives' as necessarily relevant or deserving of an organizational response" (1993, 85).

In the case of Freetown, Sierra Leone, it was apparent that in every forum (called police partnership boards), the board executive bore the main burden regarding effort, enthusiasm, and funding. While the police appreciated the facilitating of crime investigation and the supply of crime intelligence, there was in 2005 little concrete contribution on their part to enabling the partnership. In some cases, there were joint patrols, but even these were viewed by some police commanders as "unhelpful" (Baker 2005b, 2007c).

Despite the police preoccupation with other matters, the achievements of partnership boards were not inconsiderable in terms of reporting, investigating crime, and even resolving social disorder. In one area of Freetown, they had mapped, soon after their formation, the "ghettoes" (drug centers) with a view to the police using the information to make arrests and to demolish the premises. They were also going into schools to dissuade pupils against violence; running clubs in schools; and bringing headmasters, teachers, parents, youth organization leaders, and religious leaders together to develop a strategy to combat pupil violence at interschool football matches and in the street. Some partnership boards have also moved into dispute resolution to "sort things out rather than going to police or courts."

The boards, however, make minimal impact in the area of the development of a police strategy for the local areas. Officially, a prime aim of the boards is to give local communities a say in how they want to be policed. Yet, when I observed a new partnership board in February 2005 that was scheduled to meet to draw up the community action plan, members were handed a printed copy of the plan drawn up by the police beforehand. The board was simply required to confirm it. Overall, however, the partnership boards in Freetown do represent local concerns in their campaign against schoolchildren's violence, in their removal of "pirate ghettoes" by the harbor, in the creation of their own neighborhood watch patrols, and through securing extra resources for their own police divisions.

The South African Police Service Act of 1995 formally established the CPFs, requiring CPFs at all police stations. The South African government's *Community Policing Policy Framework and Guidelines* in 1997 spoke of the basic elements of community policing as being service orientation; partnership; problem solving; empowerment; and accountability. These were fine words, but given that in many South African communities the police were perceived in the apartheid period to have been oppressors without integrity, while in others the police had been supported, there were always going to be differences of approaches to partnership with the police. Altbeker and Rauch (1999, 2, quoted in Pelser 1999) observed the following:

> In communities in which levels of conflict with the police were high, there has been, for obvious reasons, more emphasis placed on the importance of overseeing the police and building relations, in other communities, emphasis within CPFs appears more focused on improving safety and security through assisting, and collaborating with, the police. This pattern has been reinforced by a difference between these communities in the role they accord the police in preventing crime, with black communities typically more concerned with ameliorating socio-economic causes of crime and white communities more concerned with keeping crime and criminals out of their areas.

The distinctions were not only racial but also economic. The wealthier communities were also in a position to contribute more to the assistance of their local police in terms of vehicles or even reservists, creating patterns of policing according to CPF wealth. The dependence on wealth and leadership was well illustrated from my own research in Grahamstown, Eastern Cape, in 2000. In one small area of four roads in a wealthy, largely white suburb, the CPF had initiated (or at least lent their approval to) an anticrime patrol after a spate of burglaries in which one burglar was shot dead. The scheme, also approved by the SAPS (South African Police Service), had its own "prowlers" or "bobbies on the beat." Four police reservists were employed (for 55 rand per month per participant in the scheme) by some of the residents to patrol their roads from 7 a.m. to 5 p.m. They wore the bibs of the former apartheid SAP (South African Police) and carried radios. A similar action was undertaken by the residents of another small private estate in Grahamstown, who paid for two private guards to patrol their area from 6 p.m. to 6 a.m. It was intended to hand this over to the CPF once it was up and running. Shaw and Louw's criticism, therefore, was that

> The poor, lacking resources and more likely to be intimidated by the police, are often not well placed to sustain CPFs. Indeed, CPFs often work best in (white and wealthy) areas which require them the least, and remain fragmented and weak in poorer areas. (1997)

Research conducted by the National Secretariat for Safety and Security (quoted by Pelser 1999) found other systemic problems. One was the lack of resources available for both police and CPF members. Another was that participants were not always sure regarding their roles and responsibilities or the role responsibilities of the CPF and, lacking educational opportunities, often felt unable to contribute in a meaningful manner to their CPF.

Since that research, the forums have been extended. From 2001, they have been restyled as Community Safety Forums. These seek to reduce local crime by bringing the public together not only with the police but also with all relevant agencies to improve safety and security. The early reports were that, in fact, establishing networking relationships with other government departments and nongovernmental and community-based organizations was proving difficult.

Like South Africa, Liberia saw CPFs as key building blocks in its post-conflict society. CPFs were introduced by the police in 2004, one year after the war. I was told, "They told us that we need to work with the police; if we were to deal with crime it had to be done with the people." Each of the seven police zones of Monrovia and the surrounding area established a forum, with subforums based around the police stations. Overall, there were fifty-one forums in greater Monrovia in 2007. The liaison officers, however, are based at police headquarters in Monrovia, not the local police stations, since only nine officers were available for "community policing" for the whole county.

The forum executives in Liberia are mainly young men in their twenties and thirties. The activities of their forums include "watch teams" (trained by the Liberia National Police [LNP] and UN Police [UNPOL] officers) that patrol every night, sometimes with the LNP. The Forums also do investigations: "It is not difficult to track down with teamwork. We know most of the people who do these things," they said.

The chair of the New Kru Town CPF in Monrovia in 2006, when asked what the forum had achieved, answered: "It has reduced crime such as burglary and armed robbery. Then it assists the police. It settles disputes in the community rather than people having to go to the police. And it gives intelligence to the police." However, he subsequently admitted that drug "dens" were not closed down by the police even when they had been reported to the police. "It is frustrating. Information is filtered down to the criminals. ... One of their [police] weaknesses is that they don't follow up, especially CID [Central Investigations Department]."

The Uganda Police introduced community policing in 1989, three years after the civil war. It established community liaison officers at every police station. Many of these have become redundant, but one area where there has been some success has been in urban-based crime prevention panels (Brogden and Nijar [2005] took an uncompromisingly negative view of the entire program). These have a rather different emphasis compared to the forums already mentioned. The focus is the police training of individuals to fight crime rather than discussion and practical assistance by members to the police to help *them* fight crime. The panels consist of local residents who are trained in crime prevention with a view not only to empowering people about crime prevention and the requirements of the law but also that citizens and communities will accept responsibility themselves for law and order in their locality. Some are based on training individuals in a geographical area, some on training employment groups. An example of the latter is the Kawempe

Crime Prevention Panel formed in 2000 in a poor district in Kampala. It singled out distinct employment groups and brought them together in associations. They included milk sellers, timber merchants, motorcycle taxis, disco and video halls, teachers, probation officers, special hire companies, bars and brothels, and religious leaders. In the process of meeting with these groups, patterns of crime that particularly affected each one were identified, and complaints by the public about any member's activities were directed to these associations. In time, as they began to see their role in policing their own members and community, association members volunteered to attend the crime preventers' course. Being empowered in terms of knowing what the law required, the local panels have reported cases of unlawful activity (including police officers demanding bribes) and made recommendations for curbing crime (Baker 2005a).

In 2002, the Ministry of Interior (MINT) in Mozambique, some ten years after the civil war, launched community policing (*policiamento comunitário*; PolCom), following the South African model. The return to citizen participation in policing followed the disappointing results of the postwar police professionalization program. Community policing councils (CPCs) debate local crime problems and solutions with the police and provide civic education and noncriminal conflict resolution of quarrels over land plots, disagreements between neighbors, and family disputes (Baker 2003). The emphasis, again, is on the forum supporting the police and not being a substitute to carry out its functions. The CPCs do not engage in criminal cases, but they do undertake patrols and make citizens' arrests. Their main focus is on finding crime solutions and disseminating knowledge to the community on safety, crime, and citizen responsibilities.

With the forums faced with threats by criminals and lack of practical support from government and the police, there has to be some question mark over how long the initial enthusiasm for forums by local people and local police liaison officers will last. Where the enthusiasm of those leading these initiatives fails, it is unlikely that there will be enough institutional momentum to maintain them.

Local Government Security Structures

The local government security structures of Uganda and Rwanda had their origin in Museveni's embrace of popular justice from his time in Mozambique. He, the National Resistance Army (NRA) leadership, and the young Kagame (who was to become president of Rwanda) were drawn to the possibilities of a justice whose language was accessible; whose proceedings involved active community participation; and whose judges were drawn from the people (Museveni 1997, 30). Popular justice, they believed, could become a school of self-governance that taught people the social habits of cooperation. The details of the form they followed vary between the two countries, but in both cases it is a nationwide network accessible to all urban (and rural) inhabitants. For a large proportion of everyday policing, the local government security structures successfully resolve disputes, investigate cases, and even implement appropriate punishment. Hence, they greatly relieve the public police and criminal justice system of Uganda and Rwanda of a large number of cases.

In Uganda, where customary courts were scrapped after the civil war, the local councils at the lowest level, known as Local Council 1 or simply LC1, play a key role in security. They had begun life as resistance committees in NRA-controlled areas (the Luwero triangle) during the war. All adults in Uganda automatically become members of their LC1 and directly elect a nine-person committee to administer local affairs. To prevent discrimination against women, at least one third of the executive committee were required to be women, and at least one woman was to sit on the court (the number increased to three in 1998). Among other things, LC1s have responsibility for the mobilization of the local community in law-and-order matters; the gathering of criminal data; the establishment of bylaws that reflect local needs; LC courts; and, until recently, law enforcement through the LC-funded local administrative police. The jurisdiction of the courts is limited to civil and customary matters, and they are placed within the jurisdiction of formal magistrates' courts and have an internal system of appeals and a special appellate procedure to the chief magistrates' courts. In other words, when it came to implementation, the National Resistance Movement (NRM) government moved from offering a new model of popular justice for all to offering an alternative justice route to the technical, less-accessible, and expensive formal court system.

My research in 2004 (Baker 2005a) found that people in urban zones (as much as the villages) look first and foremost to the LC1 for protection from and resolution of disorder and crime. They undertake mediation, courts, and night patrols during periods of insecurity. Typically, they handle domestic violence, fighting, theft, illegal buildings, and disputes between landlords and tenants. When asked where people go to solve a problem, 85 percent said the LC alone or first; likewise, in cases of breaches of law and order they turn first to the LC1 (Wunsch and Ottemoeller 2004, 188). The LC courts are popular because they offer accessible justice in the local language, from a body that respects local traditions and is in turn respected, since leaders have been chosen who are known, experienced, and stand for the new postwar values (Barya and Oloka-Onyango 1994). They offer justice through representative processes at the grassroots level, which is faster, affordable, and in tune with local understandings of justice.

Although at times LC courts exceed their authority by hearing criminal cases or handing out sentences that are beyond their powers, such as corporal punishment and banishment from the locality (Kanyeihamba 2002), for the most part they provide popular and effective local policing. And, appeals can always be made to LC2 and LC3 and then on to the magistrates' courts. Initially, there were problems stemming from members' ignorance of their exact role. For example, members of Mbiro Zone, a high-density area of Kampala, told me in 2004 that when the court began they were not fully aware of which cases came within their remit and which were the duties of the Uganda Police. Subsequent police training overcame most of the problems.

In Rwanda, also, the informal local government structure introduced after the war has become the policing agency of first choice for everyday policing. The director of operations of the Rwanda National Police told me the following in 2006: "We can't do anything without the community. We have to realize that it is their own policing. They are crucial." The lowest levels of local government have wide responsibility. This includes the mobilization and sensitization of the local community in law-and-order matters; night patrols; law enforcement; promoting the functioning of the local (*gacaca*) system of justice to deal with minor antisocial behavior, disputes, and crimes (or directing them upward); recording strangers to the neighborhood; reporting deviant behavior; punishment for misbehavior; the establishment of bylaws that reflect local needs; and the local militia (Local Defense Force, LDF). One informal local government provider of policing,[1] a *chef de zone* in Kigali, described his role in controlling crime: "We handle perhaps 70 percent of the incidents and the police 30 percent." The exact legal status of the lower informal ranks of local government, however, is unclear. Technically, it appears to be outside the state, and its activities, such as patrols and "courts," are informal. The local leaders have a large measure of autonomy, yet they have close links with the state.

Local leaders, namely, the elected *résponsable*, and the informal levels that they appoint below them (which until recently were the *nyumbakumi* and the *chef de zone*, although now the two have merged as the *umukuru*), are held responsible for small geographic areas. The *résponsable* is responsible (with a committee of seven and five militia) for about 500 to 1,000 households and the lower levels for smaller units. Local voluntary leaders take responsibility for the conduct of their areas. In 2006, a *nyumbakumi* from Kigali explained:

> Seeing how people live, things they do; to know what problems they meet with, if there are any disputes or conflicts between people, make sure people keep the area clean and tidy. So I need to know what is happening between people so there are no difficulties. I try to reconcile any problem.

And a *chef de zone* from Kigali spoke of trying

> to make relationships between me and the population and for them to see that
> we are one and are able to solve our problems together. A *chef de zone* makes sure
> that the population don't see him as a leader among them, but one who is there to
> solve their problems. Before they go to the police they come to us. Whenever they
> bring their problems we speak to them as family members not as the police.

Unlike the police forums, the local government structures of Uganda
and Rwanda, although state initiated and regulated, are regarded by local
people as institutions under their own control rather than that of the state.
In Uganda's case, they are indeed a replacement for the abolished local chief
system, a manifestation of local democracy. Hence, those who run the LC
patrols and courts are willing at times to deviate from rules set by a distant
state. Nyamu-Musembi (2003, 34) spoke of them deciding cases "in a flexible
manner without being constrained by procedural technicalities." In Rwanda's
case, the regime expects closer adherence to state guidelines.

Discussion

Anything that is dependent on volunteers, such as CPFs and local government security structures, has a tendency to be unreliable and in the long term
unsustainable. Finnegan, Hickson, and Rai were a little naïve to argue that
for community policing to be promoted,

> the concept of volunteering needs to be engendered in local communities. In
> contrast to the past, the public should be encouraged to provide information
> without payment; communities should be made to understand that the reward
> for providing information is a safer community. (2008, 25)

There may well be an enthusiasm shown by the post-conflict generations
to "rebuild" their nation, but as Rwanda and Uganda showed, the problem is
maintaining it. There are already in those two countries signs of a wilting of
voluntarism and of it not being transferred to the next generation (Baker 2005a,
2007b).

In Liberia, the voluntarism of its CPFs is under threat from two other
sources: threats by criminals and apparent lack of official support. Concerning
intimidation, one Monrovian CPF chair admitted in 2007 that their patrol
had reduced from thirty members to seventeen "owing to threats from criminals and because people are reluctant to do things voluntarily and assume
that the president is getting paid but not distributing it."

A long-term strategy of using volunteers almost inevitably raises the
thorny question of "incentives," financial or otherwise. When most of the

energy for the partnership is being supplied by the local community, there is a danger that voluntarism might fade without some external support. An executive member of a policing partnership board in Freetown, Sierra Leone, could still claim the following in 2006: "I am very proud of what we are doing. We will get tired eventually. But it is still close to the war." Yet, a Monrovian forum deputy chair interviewed in 2007 was already resentful:

> We embrace the idea of community policing to promote justice. Since the idea was introduced into Liberia, the government has showed no appreciation. They don't understand the language of forums. We know their importance. The police cannot do it all. We live in the community. We're doing the work of the police. But we have no office [they use a local council office]. I use my own house. We purchase our own stationery and pay for our typing. Why was the forum founded if the government won't support it? ... We just sacrifice but there is no appreciation. ... The UN brought this idea; the Bryant [transitional] government brought this idea. But to act on an idea is different.

Kyed (unpublished manuscript) reported that it has also been found in Mozambique that CPC members are becoming disillusioned due to lack of knowledge, capacity, and state police assistance to tackle criminals (FOMICRES 2008, 15). There also is discontent about lack of state remuneration, such that in some cases CPCs are resorting to fixed monthly community fees, contributions from businesses, or illegal fining of community residents (MINT 2005, 14; Academia de Ciências Policiais [ACIPOL] 2006, 14–15).

I have mentioned the Rwanda senator who regarded one of the biggest challenges of the government as being to "sustain voluntarism." The use of night patrols by the *nyumbakumi* of Rwanda illustrates the problem there because I received reports in 2006 from some areas that patrols had either ceased completely, had decreased with many failing to turn up, had finished early, or were only reenacted when an outbreak of thefts occurred (Baker 2007b).

For many forum executives, the commitment put into the partnership with the police is seen as unequal. The Partnership Boards of Sierra Leone felt it was they who were taking the initiative concerning starting school clubs; securing funding for workshops; lobbying the inspector general of police for extra resources for their local police divisions; doing sensitization among the community; and even doing patrols with (or without) the police. To some, it felt as if they were "alone" in fighting crime. One Partnership Board planned to start anticrime school clubs to promote crime awareness and to foster good attitudes regarding the police. The plans were approved by the police but never funded. An exasperated executive member told me: "We never get any funding. Everything comes from our own pocket." The lack of support was not confined to finance. One Monrovian forum complained in 2007 that the police no longer attended meetings on the grounds that there were not sufficient officers anymore. Such lack of support saps the enthusiasm of local people to undertake local policing sponsored by the police.

Interestingly, the same frustration was not found in Rwanda and Uganda. In all my interviews with members of the local government structures in Uganda and Rwanda that have a large degree of autonomy and saw little of the police, I have no record of a single complaint about a lack of resources provided to them. Here, the leaders of local government security structures did not expect the police to work with them in policing and only called on them for "serious" matters. The police in those situations were seen as backup rather than as partners, or in the case of Uganda, as trainers as well. With lower expectations, there is less reason for disappointment.

Both the police and the local government initiatives have sought to establish security organizations that can speak for and represent their communities. Yet, such local security groups are problematic in terms of the unit of organization and the nature of the representatives. In the case of the police forums, the unit of organization is an undefined "community." Commentators have rightly observed that the word implies commonality of values, perceived needs, and ambitions when in fact no homogeneity may exist (Pelser 1999). It also suggests a degree of close and reciprocal interpersonal relationships that urban areas, whether so-called communities or the local authority areas, may lack. In fact, both the areas served by police forums and by local government security groups tend to be fragmented according to gender, ethnicity, age, and class. The diversity can make representing policing priorities and determining solutions harder than appears initially.

Also problematic are those who act as representatives. Generally in post-conflict Africa, forums and local government security structures are dominated by educated, politically active, and locally influential people, often older men (although Liberia appears to be an exception). And, they may represent their family's personal and political interests more than community interests (Brogden 2004). The *umukuru* of Rwanda are appointed by elected council leaders who themselves were eased into place by the ruling party. There is a new emphasis on local leaders being educationally "qualified." In South Africa, there is clear evidence that the membership of the executives of many CPFs have been actively chosen and controlled by the local branch of the ANC (Buur 2005). This cooptation and "top-down regimentation" of community policing only confirms Bayley's point that "democratic reform abroad cannot be achieved through the mechanistic importation of practices" from the West, for institutions and practices that "support democracy in one country may not do so in ... authoritarian countries where it can be used for co-optation and top-down regimentation" (2001, 11). And, even though the executives of forums in Sierra Leone and Liberia are elected at public meetings, they are largely the local elite, as was always intended by the police when they first approached these same people to form the forum. There was no suggestion in the LC1s of Uganda that those elected should be any other than the local (normally male) leaders. Likewise, although the CPCs of Mozambique were meant to be voluntary and selected by local populations, the Ministry of Interior (MINT) made it plain that members should include community leaders and representatives of different sectors in society: economic agents, religious associations, NGOs, schools, private and public institutions, and "other important social actors" (2005, 10); the state-recognized community authorities, such as chiefs, have been made compulsory CPC members (2005, 8). By whatever means, the end result is that the local elite have taken control of the forums and local government security teams. It is perhaps not surprising that in both Freetown and Monrovia I found many who knew little or nothing about their local forum, and a Nationwide Perception Survey of the Sierra Leone Police in 2006 found that 65 percent (76 percent of women) did not know what community policing involved (Braima 2006). Some Partnership Boards had as few as twenty general members to speak for the community. Even the most active in Freetown in 2007 had only over 550 general members and 120 youth members from the thousands in their neighborhood.

I noted the criticism that in South Africa (Shaw and Louw 1997) CPFs work best in wealthy areas that require them the least and are weak in poorer areas. However, in the cases of Rwanda, Uganda, Liberia, and Sierra Leone, although some of the volunteers often had education or status, the security forums and local government security structures of the poorest areas of the towns appeared to function in much the same way as those in wealthier parts. The much more relevant issue is the difficulty for forums to express "local opinion" or to exercise informal social control over their locality when they are so unrepresentative (Lyons 1999; Crawford 1999).

Forums and local government security structures have the potential to offer people the advantages of local anticrime groups but with external state supervision that can restrain or eradicate the defects. They offer the possibility of empowering local people with a policing group that is accessible (in terms of language, procedures, finance) and yet is under obligation to conform to state-determined standards. In other words, it offers (in theory) the opportunity to be freed from the worst abuses of autonomous local policing groups, such as their use or threats of violence, their unequal treatment, and their summary justice. Yet, if the partnership with the state turns out in people's minds to be one of state control with few state resources, the terms of the partnership are unlikely to hold. People enter partnerships with the police to improve crime control in their localities. They do not want a partnership that is little more than an instrument for the state to, as Buur put it, "domesticate and defuse potential antagonisms in the justice field" (2005, 256).

It is common for politicians to promise to put the full backing of the state behind community–police partnerships. President Mbeki of South Africa, for instance, in his opening address to Parliament in 1999, promised to "strengthen the Community Police Fora to improve their capacity to mobilize the people against crime."[2] Such words have to be followed by actions. Yet, the initiatives in South Africa, Liberia, Sierra Leone, Uganda, and Rwanda have not fully bridged the different expectations of communities and the police (Pelser 1999; Schärf 2000; Brogden 2004). Local partnerships have proved willing to shoulder most of the burden of everyday policing, but they do expect some resources from the state. Even the Uganda Police themselves admit that little is provided for their crime prevention panels. As a liaison officer in Kampala in 2004 explained: "There is a logistics problem. There is not much government effort for this program. The panel members are volunteers. But there is no transport allowance for them." And at the very least, forums assume that the partnership will lead to better response times from the police. The reality in Freetown was that the police were just as slow to respond as before the forums were created. There must be doubts about the sustainability of forums when a partnership board member in Freetown in 2006 admitted:

> I feel shy when I tell people I'm associated with the police. Someone is suppressed—he makes a call—I know the integrity of the police, they want to do the job, but they can't—and people say, "police no better." I feel shy!

Indeed, the slow response had led to the formation in Partnership Boards in Freetown of self-styled "neighborhood watch groups." It was a case, as one executive member put it, of the neighborhood watch doing the real crime prevention work and the Partnership Board being simply a place to share information with the police. "The Partnership Board has reduced crime; not the police but Partnership Board. The only crime in my area now is assaults. But theft and armed robbery are gone because of the neighborhood watch and the Partnership Board." Without success, as measured by improved police support and service delivery, the state project "to domesticate" the autonomous anticrime groups (of Chapter 3) is unlikely to succeed.

Forums, if not local government security structures, are set up in such a way that they lead their members to anticipate having some input into setting the anticrime agenda in their localities and challenging police failures and corruption. The initial aims usually proclaim: "The oversight of policing at the local level." Yet, almost invariably the police resist this and try to steer the forums into being little more than an intelligence-gathering body for their benefit. At best, they regard the members of forums as amateurs; at worst, they are inclined to see them as spies. What are the Partnership Boards of Sierra Leone to make of police commanders who say: "They are not directing *us* how to do our policing. They are helping us. We are professionals. Many of us have been to Bramshill [UK Police Training College]. They can suggest— they cannot direct us"; or: "They will not direct *us* what to do. We will not be imposed on concerning policing matters." To succeed, the forums need more than the support of political leaders. The local police have to demonstrate that they also welcome the partnership. Clearly, many do, but there is a minority who feel threatened by outsiders getting too close to knowing what the police are doing. As one Crime Prevention Panel chair from Katwe, Kampala, admitted in 2004: "We work together with police and resolve problems. But bad police see us with a negative eye." And, an executive member of a crime prevention panel in Freetown observed the following in 2006:

> Twenty-five percent of the police have an interest. The rest think we are the watchdog of the IG [inspector general] because last year the LUC [local unit commander] was sacked. He allowed two police boys [young men] to go uncharged who had had sex with a suspect [held at the station]. That is a criminal offense, but they were not cautioned and were allowed to run away. We asked him to try them but he let them go. They are still in hiding. We complained to the IG, and the LUC was sacked.

The fact is that very few partnerships live up to their promises of community oversight over their local police. It is left to very weak national oversight bodies to discipline the police, leaving many African city dwellers disappointed at the abuses and corruption that continue unabated. Urban citizens are left with a dilemma. They appear to want the police forums to work but are unconvinced that they are achieving what was promised of them, not because of their own efforts but because of the weaknesses of the police themselves. Thus, in a perception survey in 2006 on the Sierra Leone Police, just 28 percent of people living in Freetown were "very satisfied" with community policing initiatives in 2004–2006 (a figure that dropped to 17 percent for females). Also, 51 percent claimed to work in collaboration with the police to make their community safe and secure (this included reporting offenses and providing information); the 49 percent who did not stated that the "police do not act on information quickly, protect criminals and sometimes behave in an unfriendly manner" (Braima 2006). Indeed, 49 percent reported corruption/malpractice by the police. It is difficult to see how partnerships can work when one side views the other side so negatively. The relationship is particularly problematic when it is realized the extent to which the police are satisfied with how the Partnership Boards are working. Of the one hundred police interviewed in Sierra Leone, ninety were satisfied with their efforts to get to know the community. Such police complacency in the light of the views of the public of Freetown highlights the difficulties of bringing police and communities together.

Notes

1. The three lowest levels are, from the bottom: *nyumbakumi*, *chef de zone*, and *résponsable*.
2. South African Government Information. www.info.gov.za/9906281018a1006. htm

Policing the Village

5

Introduction

The countryside in post-conflict Africa provides a very different context for policing from the urban areas. Here, policing by the state is even less evident. Before examining some of the responses by local people to their policing needs, I provide a brief overview of the rural context.

The Rural Context

For all the rapid migration to the cities, Africa's population, according to the United Nations Human Settlements Programme (UN-HABITAT), will not cease on current projections to be predominantly rural until 2030. The World Bank estimates that the percentage of the population living in poverty in sub-Saharan Africa was 50 percent in 2005. In absolute terms the number was nearly 390 million by 2005.[1] Most of those who are poorest live in the rural areas of Africa. In 2000, it was estimated that a third of those living on less than US$1 a day live in Africa, the majority in the rural areas.

Large numbers lack access to medical services; have no access to safe drinking water; have limited access to education; have serious diseases like malaria and AIDS; and suffer from undernourishment if not malnutrition. In post conflict economics, the rural situation is marked by severely disrupted and low-yielding agricultural production. Kofi Annan has said:

> Food insecurity in Africa has structural causes. Most African farmers cultivate small plots of land that do not produce enough to meet the needs of their families. The problem is compounded by the farmers' lack of bargaining power and lack of access to land, finance and technology.[2]

Farmers face multiple obstacles to food production. The rural population is poorly organized, often isolated, lacks access to credit, and is untouched by government services and poverty programs because of lack of resources and urban bias. Then, there is a lack of access to markets and appropriate technologies, high rates of illiteracy (especially among women), weak local institutions, poor integration with the national economy, unstable domestic and international agricultural markets, livestock disease, and the migration of rural youth to urban areas. Environmental factors further threaten livelihoods. In some parts, serious land degradation has resulted from extensive agriculture, deforestation, and overgrazing. Elsewhere, rural poverty has its roots in limited availability of good arable land and water and the impact of droughts or floods. Women, who account for the bulk of food production in Africa, are a particularly vulnerable rural group. They typically have fewer rights, longer hours of labor, and heavier work burdens than men. Yet, they are often discriminated against. Finally, there are the terrible effects of HIV/AIDS. About two thirds of the 34 million people in the world with HIV/AIDS live on the African continent. In many areas, it is seriously debilitating the rural labor force. HIV/AIDS puts an unbearable strain on poor rural households, where labor is the primary income-earning asset.

Most poverty measurement focuses on private consumption below an objective line that is defined in terms of an aspect of welfare. For example, poverty is often defined as insufficient consumption of calories or as dollar poverty. But, poverty has both physical and psychological dimensions. Poor people themselves strongly emphasize violence and crime, discrimination, insecurity and political repression, biased or brutal policing, and victimization by rude, neglectful, or corrupt public agencies (Narayan et al. 1999). Some may feel poor or be regarded as poor if they cannot afford what others in their community can. Although poor people report their condition largely in terms of material deprivation (not enough money, employment, food, clothing, and housing) combined with inadequate access to health services and clean water, they in fact also give weight to such nonmaterial factors as security, peace, and power over decisions affecting their lives (Robb 1999).

The distribution of rural poverty varies, but hardest hit are the countries that have known conflict. Conflict disrupts agriculture and aggravates poverty. In conflict-torn countries, the capacity of rural people to make a livelihood has been dramatically curtailed by warfare, and per capita food production has plummeted. The connection between conflict and ongoing poverty can be illustrated from the example of Angola, whose civil war ended in 2002 but war-induced poverty continues.[3]

Thirty years of war destroyed the rural economy of Angola and led to a large-scale exodus from rural to urban areas for safety. At the end of the war, about 4 million people (about one third of the population) were internally displaced, and nearly 500,000 had fled to neighboring countries. The war destroyed much of the country's infrastructure. Health and education systems broke down; damaged roads and bridges left rural areas isolated from essential services and markets; and irrigation systems previously used for commercial farming were not maintained. Inevitably, agricultural production plummeted, leaving widespread and severe poverty.

That poverty persists today. The rural economy has all but collapsed. In Angola's rural areas, an estimated 94 percent of households are poor. Few homes have electricity or sewage connections. More than 60 percent of rural households obtain their water from unsafe sources, and only 30 percent of rural areas have access to health services. Much of the damaged infrastructure has yet to be reconstructed; land mines and unexploded bombs litter the countryside; and farmers are short of seeds, fertilizer, tools, and work animals.

The Central Highlands of Angola was the region most affected by the war and now is the most vulnerable to food insecurity. Something like two thirds of the population lives there, most of them in extreme poverty. The high population density has led to widespread subsistence farming and environmental decline. The poor farming practices and competition for land only further diminish productivity and aggravate food insecurity.

Although women are widely treated as subordinate to men, they did gain some autonomy during the war because then they turned to trading as an alternative source of income. Male migration and war deaths have left many more women than men in Angola. About a third of households are headed by women, but these tend to be the poorest and most vulnerable. Women sustain a heavy work burden. Female-headed households, with no male labor to clear and plough land, not only have to attend to housework, caring for their families and fetching water and wood, but also have to engage in cultivation and in processing crops. Indeed, they now provide most of the agricultural labor force.

Unfortunately, the story of Angola is not dissimilar to that of other war-torn countries. In Mozambique, the vast majority of the rural population still live on less than US$1 a day and lack clean water supplies and access to health facilities and schools. More than 80 percent of poor households live in rural areas. According to the International Fund for Agricultural Development (IFAD) (2008b), two thirds of rural people have to walk more than an hour to reach the closest health unit; only 57 percent of the rural population have access to primary school education (82 percent for the urban population); and more than two thirds of rural Mozambicans are illiterate.

Security is of even greater concern to rural conflict and post-conflict societies than the economy. It was found in 2007 that the population of eastern Democratic Republic of the Congo (DRC) viewed the following as their priorities: peace (51 percent of respondents) and security (34 percent). They also saw those as the two priorities that the Congolese government should pursue. Only after peace and security come other concerns, such as money (27 percent), education (26 percent), food/water (26 percent), and health (23 percent) (Vinck et al. 2008).

Crime

For many Africans, the definition of peace is not so much when the belligerents sign an agreement as a vision of "good relationships well lived; health, absence of pressure and conflict, being strong and prosperous" (Rweyemamu 1989, 381). Peace is about maintaining harmony between the community, the individual, and the cosmic totality, namely, God, creation, the living, and the dead (Cutter 2009). Hence, having experienced violent crime as part of their conflict experience both during and in the immediate aftermath of the conflict, there is a concern to see law enforced and lawbreakers brought to justice. Without justice, peace has yet to arise. Put another way, justice produces peace. This concern with justice was shown in a 2007 survey in DRC among a sample population of 2,620 individuals in the Ituri District in Oriental Province and the provinces of North and South Kivu (Vinck et al. 2008). It showed that the majority of the population of eastern DRC (85 percent) believed it was important to hold those who committed war crimes accountable, and that accountability was necessary to secure peace (82 percent). The most important war crimes to address, in their opinion, were murders/killings (92 percent) and rape/sexual violence (70 percent) (Vinck et al. 2008).

The scale of the experience of crime to be addressed as a result of war is enormous. The same DRC survey showed that there had been widespread experience of human rights abuses, including sexual violence. Many respondents were interrogated or persecuted by armed groups (55 percent), forced to work or enslaved (53 percent), beaten by armed groups (46 percent), threatened with death (46 percent), or had been abducted for at least a week (34 percent). In eastern DRC, 23 percent witnessed an act of sexual violence, and 16 percent reported having experienced sexual violence. More about sexual violence and abuse against women in war is covered in Chapter 7 on policing of women.

Yet, it must not be thought that war crimes are the only problem facing post-conflict rural communities. Unfortunately, the familiar crimes of common assault, theft, sexual abuse, and neighbor disputes over money and property continue to afflict them on a daily basis, as does cattle rustling among the pastoralists. What is new is an apparent increase in certain crimes due to the increased poverty and unemployment, the ready availability of weapons and ex-combatants who know how to use them, and the disruption and distraction of the state police. Hence, according to many post-conflict police officers, there is a steep rise after conflict in armed robbery, child prostitution, and drug dealing. The exact figures are of course unknown, but certainly a perception of a post-conflict crime wave is common among the public. It goes along with an awareness that those in the state criminal justice system are not in a position to respond in any meaningful way because of their small numbers and the distance they are from most rural communities.

Banditry also is a widespread experience for rural communities. Perhaps the main threat to security in northern Central African Republic (CAR) is well-organized gangs of violent highway bandits. The *coupeurs de routes* (highwaymen) or *Zaraguina* kidnap for ransom and loot road convoys and villages. They are not only a product of poverty but also of conflict. The military coup that brought General François Bozize to power in 2003 was aided by mercenaries from Chad and other neighboring countries, who have now turned to banditry, feeling that Bozize failed to deliver on alleged promises of recompense. Little stands in their way. The CAR army (FACA, Central African Armed Forces) has only 5,000 troops, and only half of these are on active duty. General Antoine Gambi has admitted: "The *Zaraguinas* do as they like because they know that our forces aren't strong enough to provide security across the country. … They enjoy the complicity of local officials in some areas who are in their pay."[4] The bandits have been joined by antigovernment rebels making extra money; Chadian rebels making money before going back to Chad; Chadian army defectors doing the same; and bandits pushed out of Cameroon as a result of its aggressive anti-*Zaraguina* policy.

If conflict caused crime, crime has caused further conflict. The insecurity is said to be one of the reasons in the CAR for the formation of the People's Army for the Restoration of Democracy/Armée Populaire pour la Restauration de la Démocratie (APRD), a rebel group made up in part of self-defense units set up to protect villages from the *Zaraguinas* (Boggero 2008). Yet, the ARPD itself has been widely accused of committing human rights abuses, including kidnapping and looting (International Crisis Group [ICG] 2007).[5]

War severely damages the mechanisms of formal justice delivery in as much as they ever existed in rural areas. Where these mechanisms survive, they are dysfunctional, inaccessible, or lacking in credibility. In addition, family and community discourage the transfer of disputes from local rural processes to the anonymous and threatening mechanisms of the urban formal justice system. Should people persist in going to the police stations and courthouses in distant towns, they find few police and lawyers and judicial procedures that are technical. It is not likely that the police will come to them. The police, mainly because of their small numbers, are rarely in rural areas except when there is a serious crime. Table 5.1 shows the estimated ratios of police officers to population in some post-conflict countries.

Given their small size, limited mobility, and the poor roads, it is inevitable that police forces rarely venture beyond towns and the tarmac roads. In Liberia in 2007, I met a chief in a village just a five-minute drive along the main road from a county town. By his account:

**Table 5.1   Estimated Ratios of Police
Officer to Population (as of January 2007)**

Rwanda	1:1,380
Liberia	1:857
DRC	1:812
Nigeria	1:722
Sierra Leone	1:612

Source: Based on information provided by the relevant police forces.

The average ratio of population per police officer for
England and Wales in 2002 was 402:1.

We can have an accident on the road or fighting. We call the police but they
don't come or come maybe a whole day after the accident. Maybe they don't
even pick up the phone. We have to take the person to hospital ourselves or
break up the fights. Or take them to the police. ... The police are not active in
coming near to our cause when there is a problem.

The police are neither the main providers of safety and security nor first
responders to whom most of the rural populace looks for assistance when in
need. Even when police do seek a presence in the countryside, they are not always
welcome in the post-conflict situation, given their poor human rights record
in the conflict. Kyed (unpublished manuscript) reported that in Mozambique
the mistrust of the police after the war was so great in rural areas that people
actively resisted the reestablishment of state policing in some areas.

So, whom do the rural communities look to for policing? In Mozambique,
people preferred to trust the range of nonstate policing groups they had used
in the war, namely, "chiefs; Renamo soldiers now acting as local administra-
tors; remnants of the *mujhibas,* Renamo's local police during the war; and
healers (*wadzi-nyanga*)" (Kyed unpublished manuscript). Elsewhere, nonstate
policing includes customary structures; secret societies; anti-cattle rustling
vigilantes; nongovernmental organization (NGO) peace monitors; and variations of the local government responses and community policing forums
that are found in the towns. This chapter looks at customary structures, local
government responses, community policing groups, restorative justice committees, and antirustling vigilantes.

Customary Structures

In the absence of the police, it is customary structures that very often keep
and restore order in African villages, organize their protection from crime,

and investigate and seek to resolve disturbances and disputes. On a daily basis, they handle antisocial behavior, domestic disputes, land issues, debts, fights, theft, abusive language, and the like using customary law.

Typically, their settling of disputes does not follow simply the individual justice as commonly followed by the state; rather, a communal justice is sought by which everyone (or everyone of influence) benefits. Such policing is in widespread use in post-conflict rural Africa. In Burundi, for instance, the customary system is the de facto court of first instance for the vast majority of the population, with estimates claiming that up to 80 percent of Burundians take their cases to the *bashingantahe* (customary justice courts) as a first or sometimes only instance. The bashingantahe have long assisted in resolving quarrels over land and boundaries, and their contribution is valuable when land disputes are at the heart of conflict. It also relieves the state courts, for whom 70 percent of the cases are concerned with land. The land issue will only increase as refugees return post-conflict, requiring resettlement and sometimes finding squatters on land they formerly farmed themselves (Thorne 2005).

In southern Sudan, it was found that over 90 percent of day-to-day criminal and civil cases were executed under customary law (Leitch and Vandewint 2004). Chiefs normally have no official powers to handle criminal cases, but practice can vary. In the case of Sierra Leone, it was claimed in 2002 that "80 percent of the Sierra Leone population will only find judicial access and redress from the Customary Courts or from the informal (and presently illegal) alternative dispute resolution mechanisms operated by the paramount and lesser chiefs" (DFID 2002, 40). A chief in southern Sierra Leone 2005 told me, "People would not report directly to the SLP [police] even if it was a criminal case. ... They come to the paramount chief first." In Mozambique, some chiefs continue to flout the law and solve criminal cases in order not to risk losing popular legitimacy (Kyed 2007). Likewise, Local Councils Level 1 (LC1s) in Uganda "exercise more expansive jurisdiction" than that laid down by the law (UNOCHA 2006, 9), and chiefs in Liberia "routinely preside over criminal cases outside of their jurisdiction" (ICG 2006, 8).

Although some African states stripped customary chiefs of their judicial powers at independence and placed their former powers in the hands of lay magistrates, they still remain state sponsored or state allowed in many post-conflict states, such as Sierra Leone, Burundi, CAR, Chad, Comoros, Côte d'Ivoire, DRC, Eritrea, Ethiopia, Liberia, Mali, Madagascar, Mozambique, Namibia, Niger, Republic of Congo (Brazzaville), Senegal, Somalia, and southern Sudan. Frequently, the boundary between the formal and informal justice systems is vague, as in Guinea, where a case may be referred from the formal to the customary courts to ensure compliance by all parties, or if a case cannot be resolved to the satisfaction of all parties in the customary courts, it may be referred to the formal system.

I used the term *customary structures* in the heading because there is usually a hierarchy of levels of customary justice ranging from subheadmen, through headmen, subchiefs, and chiefs, to paramount chiefs or their equivalent. The system may or may not be linked to the state magistrates' courts via appeal.

Customary law is the expression of the local prevailing customs, beliefs, and practices. As noted in Chapter 2, the chiefs seek to uphold these local norms whether or not they conform to state law. It is these norms that determine what is regarded as crime and disorder. Customary law may well regard witchcraft,[6] adultery, teenage pregnancy, the use of drugs, disrespect to parents, and certain hut evictions as unacceptable behavior. Of course, there can be dozens of ethnic groups in a country, and most have customary law systems, reflecting individual ethnic identities. And, despite the name, *customary* does not mean resistant to change. In fact, change (although not necessarily in a Western liberal direction) is an ongoing process in local communities as a result of exposure to new ideas and opinions. Few chiefs would desire to freeze customary law.[7] Bennett expressed it succinctly when he said that custom, although legitimized by age, is always "up to date, because, ancient though it may seem, no custom is ever older than the memory of the oldest living person." This means that systems of oral customs "have the remarkable ability to allow forgotten rules to sink into oblivion, while simultaneously accepting new rules to take their place" (2004, 2).

During war, customary law is usually the principal source of social order in the countryside. Yet, that is not to say that the system of chiefs remained unaltered by war. War causes large-scale displacement of people, and formerly homogeneous areas can become ethnically heterogeneous, bringing their own conflicts of culture and customs. War can also greatly reduce the power and status of tribal chiefs. In southern Sudan and Sierra Leone, the wars undermined not only the formal state justice structures but also the customary structures as chiefs fled and courthouses were burned. Many chiefs in Sierra Leone had their authority undermined because of their failure to protect the people, and some lost their "mystique" when they were seen being tortured and killed by the rebels or queuing with the people for food handouts. Reestablishing system of chiefs can be problematic after war. Nevertheless, chiefs continue to have considerable support, particularly for interpersonal disputes (Sawyer 2008), for as Leitch and Vandewint argue:

> The basic tenet of customary law is reconciliation, a vital tool in conflict resolution. In the immediate post-conflict period, old disputes will resurface and new disputes are inevitable. Conflict resolution through customary law will be essential to a peaceful and fair society. (2004, 6)

Customary law is often discriminatory, particularly against women and the poor, a point explored further in Chapter 7 on policing of women.

In addition to gender discrimination, chiefs' courts are also accused of frequently abusing their powers. There have been cases of them illegally detaining persons, levying excessive fines for minor offenses (Richards 2005), demanding forced labor as retribution, and adjudicating criminal cases. Perhaps the greatest cause for concern regarding chiefs' abuse of their powers concerns land allocation. Land is frequently allocated informally by local chiefs and administered under customary law. Addressing land disputes in customary areas falls under the chiefs and the customary system. One major cause of rural land conflicts is the issuing of formal title deeds under statutory law to government-selected concession holders where communities claim the land is customary. In many rural areas, people have limited trust in the customary chief's ability to resolve disputes as some of them are considered to be implicated in irregular land transactions.

War only exacerbates land contestation. Returnees trying to resettle find that others are on their land; war widows claiming the land of their husbands meet inheritance obstacles; determining rightful land ownership is hindered because most land allocations by chiefs are not registered, and chiefs who know the entitlements may have fled. In regions like northern Uganda, twenty years of insurgency by the Lords Resistance Army rebels, during which the majority of the people lived in army-protected camps, have created disputes over ownership. A recent incident highlights the conflicting interests. An army general (who represents the army in Parliament) and a clan chief were almost lynched outside a court as they tried to formalize the soldier's acquisition of 10,000 hectares of land (on behalf of a Western sugar producer) in the district of Amuru. Residents accused the chief's family of fraudulently selling off their communal land to the general. A resident said: "From today onwards we have disowned [the clan chief]. We cannot trust him any more. He has betrayed us; what kind of a chief is he when he loves money like a hyena? He wants to sell off all our land."[8]

Measuring the extent of rural injustice is impossible without widespread surveys. However, interviews in three areas of southern Sudan revealed that most regarded the chiefs' courts as just, fair, and effective. Clearly, not everything is unjust. I observed a case in Yei, southern Sudan, in 2007 in which a customary Boma Court heard a fraud and embezzlement case in which one of the two owners of a business accused the other of "stealing" the monies in dispute. The three judges, including one woman, methodically questioned the two parties and examined documentary evidence. They asked the defendant to produce any evidence he could to indicate that he did not defraud his partner. When the judges' decision was rendered, the defendant publicly stated that he had received a fair and just trial. One women's leader told me, "If [the chiefs] were not just, there would be no peace." It would certainly undermine a chief's authority if he or she were not perceived as fair and equitable given that many are "elected" to their positions and therefore can be deselected. Speaking of southern Sudan, Golooba-Mutebi and Mapuor pointed out the following:

> Chiefs do not preside over trials and adjudications on their own, but are assisted by panels of advisors and lay members of the public. The variety of participants means that verdicts are not seen as those of the chief alone but in a sense, those of the community. This suggests that judgments are fair and just. During inter- views, almost all respondents, young and old, women and men, were unanimous in the view that judgments passed in chiefs' courts are generally fair and just. ... The possibility of blatant miscarriage of justice is obviated by the wide participa- tion in court proceedings by ordinary villagers and the real possibility of removal of a chief seen to act contrary to acceptable and accepted standards. (2005, 18)

Other researchers have found similar popular support. A four-county study in Liberia found that customary courts were not only the primary pro- vider of justice but also the one people preferred for resolving disputes (ICG 2006, 7). The apparent contradiction of severe local criticism and yet support suggests that people distinguish between support of *institutions* like chief- taincy and being highly critical of the *performance* of its officeholders such as chiefs (Ubink 2007).

Customary chiefs not only provide courts for dispute resolution but also make bylaws that they enforce. In a village in northern Sierra Leone in 2005, it was the following: "No beating of wives at night. For that it is a 4,000- leone fine [US$1.34 in 2005]." In a village off the main road near Kakata, Liberia, in 2007, it was "150 dollars [Liberian LRD; US$2.36, 2005] for fight- ing or abusing; when they don't help a cleanup campaign, 150 dollars." In a village near Monrovia, Liberia: "If there is fighting you pay money—we made a law. And if you profane LRD250," said the chief. Another village chief near Monrovia reported: "If a man is on the road and abusing [public insult], the fee is LRD250. We expect respect of elders. Fighting is LRD150. Spreading 'dissy' [rumors] that you can't prove is LRD200. If you don't pay, we will turn you over to the police, and they will put you in a cell."

Sometimes, they have chiefdom police to enforce order or, more often, rely on local youth to do patrols and arrest troublemakers. For instance, the Native Authority police in Sierra Leone are a shadow of their prewar condition, num- bering today just two to twenty-five per chiefdom. Kane reported that

> The extent to which these police are organized, equipped or even active varies considerably. So too do their roles (and presumably their understanding of their roles). Some are basically court messengers. Others play a role in com- munity safety and security. ... They play an important policing role in rural areas where in many cases they are the primary policing body. (Kane et al. 2002, 16)

In the absence of chiefdom police, it is the youth. When I asked a village head in northern Sierra Leone in 2005 who provided security in the village, he said: "Youths do some patrol. They safeguard the village. [They use] just torchlight, no weapons." Likewise, a chief in eastern Sierra Leone said: "Youth control things. They see things go on normally. They fill the gap [left] from the native chiefdom police."

Local Government Responses

In Uganda and Rwanda's villages, as in the towns, the lowest levels of local government have responsibility for the mobilization and sensitization of the local community in law-and-order matters; night patrols; law enforcement; the local court to deal with antisocial behavior, disputes, and crimes (or directing them upward); recording strangers to the neighborhood; and the establishment of bylaws that reflect local needs.

How do the views of the leaders compare with the villagers themselves? Take Cyabatanze, Rwanda, which lies a good hour away from Kigali and half an hour from the main road. The scattered inhabitants number some 500 adults. The *résponsable* (local government official) of the mountain valley in which it lies has held the position for twenty-one years and when interviewed in 2006 had just been reelected: "There were two candidates, and of 480 votes I got 438!" He saw his responsibilities as essentially "to come close to the people and talk about security in the area." That means writing reports for higher authorities about any troublemakers; warning those acting unacceptably, such as "wife beaters"; calling the local court (*gacaca*) of nine to "sort out land disputes for instance"; ensuring all those appointed under him, the *nyumbakumi*, (lowest level of local government), provide the patrol for a week when it is their turn on the rota. In his view, crime was low: "Theft is not common; but there is unauthorized local brew, which is prohibited, and building illegally [in an unapproved place or with unapproved materials]—without asking permission." Should a thief be caught, the punishment depends on the scale of the theft. "We may come across someone who is poor stealing bananas. Then we arrest them and keep them for a night. In the morning, we judge accordingly. But, if it is a cow that has been stolen, we forward it to the police."

The view of the thirty people interviewed in Cyabatanze was very similar: There was very little crime. They reported only occasional fighting; some cattle theft; cattle trampling of crops; and what was termed "borrowing of bananas" from the plantations by the poor. Many people could not report any experience of crime, and most had no fear at night. When a disturbance or conflict did occur, they respected the hierarchy by first going to the *nyumbakumi* to seek an "amicable solution" and appropriate compensation. If it

could not be resolved at that level, then they went to the *résponsable* and ultimately to the police. Cyabatanze might be a poor village in a poor country,
yet it was striking that they could phone the police if they wanted since "lots
of people around here have mobiles so we get in touch with the police." In
practice, the police only appeared when there was serious violence. The local
night patrols, in their view, were a little less regular and well supported than
the local government leaders made out. Yet, the overwhelming impression
was that the village felt that it could solve all but the most serious problems
in a just manner. When crime did occur, they were, of course, like virtually
the whole of Africa, dependent on witnesses because no forensic policing was
available. As one man complained: "Nobody is ever caught, and so there is
nothing that you can do. You need a witness in order to take the problem to
the authorities."

The local government system operating in Uganda's rural areas is similar
to Rwanda's. The lowest level, the LC1s are "in charge of good manners." The
members report petty theft of goats and bananas; "defilements" (the sexual
abuse of women, especially children); domestic violence; drinking that leads
to fighting and rape; theft; deceitful trading at the market ("We give them
three chances, and then they are expelled"); land issues such as inheritance
and property ("after a death, relations are coming and chasing away widows and mothers; they just want to sell the land"); and drugs and drunkenness by unemployed youth. They also do night patrols, armed with "pangas
[machetes] and sticks," or if they fail to do so, the LC3 (Local Council Level
3 of local government) may have a militia that covers a collection of villages.
The LC1 court meets perhaps every week, requiring only a small charge for
those who use it. Serious crimes are taken to the police.

One distinctive feature in Uganda is the presence of a woman's voice on
the rural LC1s. One LC1 women's secretary in a fishing village on the banks
of Lake Victoria told me that her goal was "to promote women and to see
what can be done as regards development and in home matters." In her view,
the presence of a women's secretary had improved things for women since
"women had no say before. All they could do was go to court," and of the
forty who had trained in the village as "crime preventers" (see Chapter 4)
through the community policing program, most were women. However, the
formal requirement of a women's secretary does not necessarily meet all the
perceived need of local women. In speaking to them, they told me that the
village suffered from drunkenness; fights; "men who do not buy food or look
after the children"; and promiscuity. All were not convinced of the value of
the LC1: "Housewives' access to LCs is difficult. Husbands might not listen
to you"; "LC may listen more to someone who has money at the expense of
power. They don't always care. The LC are cowardly before power and money.
They are easily intimidated." In this case, a woman's voice on the LC1 did not
mean full female representation.

Rural Community Policing

Community policing translated into the rural context either struggles to take root or takes on a very different form from that intended. The latter is in part because it is seen by the police as part of its project to reassert its authority lost in the war, especially in rebel-held territory. Ten years after the war in Mozambique, police still lacked the capacity and popular legitimacy to prevent and respond to crime. Outsourcing of policing to nonstate authorities and popular participation in security provisions were seen as a solution. In the rural areas from 2002, more than 4,000 traditional and other community leaders were formally drawn into assisting the state police with core policing functions. This coincided with the introduction of state-sponsored *vigilança do povo* (people's vigilance), by which each citizen was encouraged to assist the police in "inspecting, locating and providing information about trouble-makers" (Kyed 2007, 400). But, from 2004 community police forums, which had been used in the urban areas, were extended over Mozambique's rural areas as well.

Kyed describes how community policing (*policiamento comuni-tário;* PolCom) was introduced in one central rural area of Mozambique, Sussundenga. The process began with a disregard of the principle of volunteers chosen from the community. Instead, the police summoned chiefs and village secretaries and ordered them to select intelligent, trustworthy, and physically strong persons to be forum members. As a result, the members were usually either close male relatives of chiefs and their councilors; already existing chieftaincy police; those who had formerly been Renamo *mujhibas*; or those who had served the Frelimo-state military. Many chiefs and rural residents from Renamo areas, seeing community policing as another Frelimo-state project, resisted joining until the local police obligated them. The members' training emphasized that essentially they were members of the state police rather than a group serving the community. The police ordered each chief to provide two community policing members for twenty-four-hour weekly shifts at the police post, together with members residing close to the police post. As a result, police posts were provided with young men, equipped with batons and handcuffs, awaiting orders from the officer on duty. They would be sent to arrest suspects (other than for murder); to beat people under interrogation inside the police post; to clean the post; and to cook for the officers. At night, they were ordered to enforce the midnight to 4 a.m. curfew; to maintain peace around the bars; and to inspect vehicles for stolen or smuggled goods. As Kyed observes, the Police Force of the Republic of Mozambique (PRM):

> used PolCom [community policing] as a way of outsourcing to non-state actors, not simply the physical hard work of policing, but also those measures

that were now illegal for PRM officers. PolCom members did the "dirty work" of the police, but the extra-legal practices were, it should be noted, delegated to them and regulated by the PRM. ... This was not alone a state police capacity problem. State police authority was also at stake. Police officers repeatedly explained that PolCom not only helped reduce crime, but enabled the PRM to (re)assert control of crime and (dis)order. (Kyed unpublished manuscript)

Sensing their power, some young men of the community policing units have been accused of beating people even though they did not resist arrest, of forcing those arrested to pay money, and of threatening people on the street with arrest or beating if they do not pay money. In other words, the law enforcers are in danger of becoming lawbreakers, in part due to police policy.

Rather than creating forums for citizens' participation in crime prevention, rural community policing in Mozambique has become a means by which the state police, out of sight of supervision, draw young men and elderly leaders into using or threatening violence on local people. The people may well conclude that the state initiative is not a solution they want to pursue or an instrument of promoting unity between the police and the people. Rather, they will see it as a means of the state to control them because of their Renamo sympathies.

Restorative Justice Committees and Legal Aid NGOs

The NGOs promoting restorative justice mark a new approach. They reflect traditional justice values of the customary courts, particularly their emphasis on restoring relationships, but eschew gender discrimination and all forms of violent and inhumane punishment. They deal with disputes from strictly non-illegal matters, such as infidelity and insulting language, to serious domestic disputes. Negotiated outcomes may be an apology and a plan of action that might include a promise to return stolen goods, to help repair material damage, to repay money owed, or to desist from offending behavior. Usually, the process ends with some form of celebration. The restorative justice committees, in contrast to other informal justice systems, pledge to work within statutory law, to abstain from violence, and to follow procedures that are open for the community to see.

The committees can be the product of NGOs with state backing, or they can be spontaneous phenomena in the community. The former has been the case in townships and some small rural towns in South Africa. For instance, "peace committees" have been formed in some ten townships (Roche 2002; Johnston and Shearing 2003). In the informality of committee members' homes, they bring together the victim and offender, with their respective supporters, to attempt to negotiate on a consensual basis the resolution of the injustice. The peace committees work closely with the police so that when cases come in to the police station, the police either respond or refer them to the peace committees.

In Sierra Leone, they have extended out from urban areas to rural ones. Around Bo in the south, the Bo Peace and Reconciliation Movement (BPRM) is a coalition of eleven community groups working on peace building, reconciliation, and crime prevention in the Bo District. Its twenty local peace monitors have resolved many conflicts, such as family matters, fighting, land cases, and leadership issues, including some long-standing disputes (they handled 255 cases in 2004). The evidence is that their work has reduced community conflict and litigation in the local courts and helped many ex-combatants reintegrate into the communities. The BPRM's success has earned it the recognition of the provincial administration in Bo.

Further south, the Soro Gbema chiefdom, in Pujehun District, had a number of local problems, including disputes caused by the death of a paramount chief, lack of civil authority, and the usurpation of this authority by the CDF (Community Defense Forces; wartime militia) commanders. With help from the only community-based organization working in the chiefdom (the Sulima Fishing Community Development Project), the community developed a peace monitoring system that promoted peace building, development, and access to justice. Each section of the chiefdom was provided with a peace monitor for early intervention in conflicts. The community also established grievance committees. Local conflicts are brought to this committee for arbitration or mediation. The twelve peace monitors (mainly respected Koranic teachers) work for a small stipend ten days every month and cover ten to fifteen villages each (Baker 2005b).

When there are local grievances over property ownership, looting and unlawful claiming of property, drug abuse and trafficking, and disregard of traditions and customs, the people turn to the peace monitors in preference to court actions. Hence, one of the negative impacts of this alternative policing is that the district administration has been unable to generate revenue, and resentment among local officials and chiefs has been generated. A summons fee of 10,000 leones (US$4) is required by Native Authority courts, but the people prefer the free assistance of peace monitors to settle their conflicts and differences (Massaquoi 1999).

Often, NGOs working in peacemaking in rural areas also engage in legal aid. In northern Uganda, Oxfam and local Ugandan groups such as ACORD (Agency for Cooperation and Research in Development) have been providing financial and logistical support as well as capacity building geared toward strengthening community-based dispute resolution systems. The Foundation for International Dignity in Liberia, for instance, was aware that without money people were denied justice and therefore began providing legal aid. Paralegal officers begin the preliminaries, and if there are legal issues, they document them and assign them to a pro bono lawyer in Monrovia, according to resources available. Typically, they handle labor disputes (the failure to pay wages and unfair treatment); police brutality; land disputes; rape; and family disputes (always difficult in a polygamous environment) (Baker 2008).

Anti-Cattle Rustling Groups

Kenya is not normally described as a conflict or post-conflict state, yet for twenty years the conflict between the cattle herders of northwestern Kenya and the neighboring areas of northeastern Uganda, southern Sudan, and southern Ethiopia has not simply been traditional raids with spears for replenishing stocks and bride wealth. An influx of modern automatic weapons and men willing to use them ruthlessly for personal gain is now threatening the very existence of traditional cattle herding in these grasslands. Colonial and postcolonial governments have long marginalized the pastoral areas economically and politically and have continued to alienate land to ranchers and farmers and for game reserves. Through shrinking the land available for pastoralists, they have exacerbated the conflict for natural resources. An inevitable downward spiral follows of ever-shrinking land; conflict over grazing and access to water; stock reduction; young men unemployed and unable to pay the bride price but with access to AK47s from the 1990s; crime syndicates and growing violence; increasing counterviolence and a local arms race among the ethnic groups; and violent state interventions by armies and militias aimed at disarmament that produce a demand for weapons for groups to defend themselves (Mkutu 2008). The days of young men or warriors defending their homesteads and herds and of using small-scale posses to recapture the cattle and perhaps carry out the summary killing of those deemed responsible now seem to be over in the pastoral lands of the Kenya/Uganda border, even if they persist elsewhere (Heald 2006, 2007; Mirzeler and Young 2000). Ugandan and Kenyan armies, police, militias, and paramilitary proxies have all failed to prevent the raiding and have often been implicated in it. Much of it now appears to be on the bigger scale of large armed violent retaliatory raids on tribes and clans deemed to be guilty of the latest cattle theft.

Yet, even in this region where communities move in and out of conflict, some small informal policing has emerged. Some of it has been notably ineffective. Perhaps the most egregious is the "peace work," in which NGOs engage in bringing protagonists together to seek reconciliation and to discuss the causes of violence. The impact is marginal, and in the view of some, it is both exploitative (of donor funding) and exploited (by raiders attending meetings to spy out the land for future raids). Eaton dismissed peace work "as big business ... which has not produced any major successes during the post-colonial period ... [it is characterized by] widespread corruption and financial mismanagement" (Eaton 2008, 257). More encouraging, but still only small scale, are the community-state partnerships that have emerged. Mkutu described two communities, Seku and Ilngwesi, that decided to form a joint security system:

> With the help of some NGOs and in collaboration with the local Member of Parliament and other leaders, they selected a commandant and an assistant and resolved to hire five Kenya Police Reservists. ... [Donors provided] a jeep, uniforms, boots, radios and batteries, and even a small salary. The Kenya Police Reservists work alongside Rangers employed by large-scale ranchers to repel cattle raiding. Attacks by Samburu and Isiolo have declined markedly. Because their welfare is well catered for, the Home Guards have not been tempted to use their arms to go raiding, but instead protect the community. The police also have a radio connection with the Home Guards, the government provides daily monitoring of the guns and ammunition issued them. (2008, 152)

The comparative success of the scheme in reducing cattle raids illustrates Mkutu's thesis that a key factor in effective security is good governance, in this case the suitably monitored cooperation of state and community-based security.

Discussion

It will be a long time before most post-conflict states have the resources that can offer state policing and justice services to their rural citizens. For instance, even in Sierra Leone, which has had substantial donor support in its security and justice sector (the police received more than £20 million [US$35 million] from the United Kingdom in 2000–2005, and £17 million [US$30 million] was earmarked for 2005–2010), the formal justice system in 2005 was very small. It could only offer 8,000 police officers (of whom 2,000 were support staff) and courts only in the main towns of Freetown, Bo, Kenema, Port Loko, and Makeni (with just fifteen presiding magistrates and eighteen judges). The paucity of court personnel, court records, and legal reference materials plus the inadequacy of the evidence provided by the police inevitably produced lengthy delays of cases and imprisonment of suspects without formal charge.

The incontrovertible fact is that the formal police and justice systems of post-conflict states will have little to offer the first post-conflict generation of rural citizens. This situation has produced two responses. First are those that argue that therefore states must work with existing local policing groups to strengthen and improve their services. Their case is that, given that these groups are in place in all rural communities, it makes sense to work through these rather than to attempt to build a nationwide state system that not only will be expensive to establish but also will be near impossible to sustain. As Schärf observed, "Western models of justice have resource assumptions that no African country can afford" (2003, 17). Such "pragmatists" reason that where, for instance, customary structures dominate the territory and their dispute resolution and arbitration are generally regarded as effective, they are "the optimal way for putting in place the best performing delivery system" (Mullen 2005, 2). At the very least, such contend, before condemning and dismantling old forms of social control and policing, it is wise to have new state substitutes available. This is not to deny the value of facing up to the clashes between customary law and liberal constitutions but to recognize that resolving those issues necessitates a long and patient dialogue. Before criminalizing, says Schärf, it is worth first asking the question: What contribution can local justice policing make to safety and problem solving (Schärf 2003)?

Others only see in rural local policing systems rough justice for women and the exploitation of the local systems by unaccountable rural elites. Odinkalu is unequivocal:

> The assertion that powerful men are liable to and do in fact get a better deal out of the application of customary law is obvious. This is particularly the case in disputes concerning personal status, marital rights in customary law, and ancestral land ... using customary law mechanisms to grab ancestral lands in rural communities. These rural lands are then taken into the orbit of statutory law through the cynical manipulation of complex rules of conflict, of laws that are unintelligible to local people poorly equipped to defend themselves with the law against abuse of power. (2005)

At the very least, such critics would strictly regulate, educate, and monitor such systems. Many would ban them outright. This seemed to be the position of the Human Rights Committee of UN General Assembly in 2005, when they were examining Madagascar's report on its compliance with the International Covenant on Civil and Political Rights. One expert told the Madagascar representatives that "a modern State which had its prescriptive law and which had signed up to many international commitments and instruments could not use customary law and tradition as an excuse for human rights violations." He noted critically that there were clearly times in Madagascar when the customary structure "was being used as the court system, and however serious the offence, the judges or people acting as judges were viewed as equal in status to judges. ... The Committee could not tolerate any breach of article 3 of the Covenant." It was the duty of the state and the state alone to ensure compliance with the articles of the covenant, and no local-specific conditions could ever be used to justify a government not fulfilling its obligations under the covenant (Human Rights Committee of UN General Assembly 2005).

The "abolitionists" would have everything under formal control, but in their defense of the right of state monopoly they come dangerously close at times to disregarding reality and thus, ultimately, justice. Such unreality, I suggest, is found in the words of the president of the High First Instance Court in Bunia, eastern DRC, on Interactive Radio for Justice in 2006:

> Customary jurisdictions are finally in a transition phase. They are temporary. As soon as a *Tribunal de Paix* is set up in a Territory, such as in Aru and Mahagi, we can no longer talk of collaboration between these *Tribunaux de Paix* and these customary jurisdictions. Customary courts simply disappear, because the *Tribunaux de Paix* automatically adopt the competence the law maintains concerning customary courts. ... What we have to remember is that we have to completely eliminate the idea of collaboration, only the *Tribunal de Paix* has mandate to act in lieu of these customary courts.[9]

If everyone must use a formal court, what, asks the radio host, about the fact that, "There are so few lawyers or public defenders; in fact in Aru there is only one?" The president of the High First Instance Court replied:

> The defense of accused or suspects does not necessarily have to be ensured by defenders or lawyers. Someone can seek the assistance of a lawyer or a public defender to ensure his defense, but generally, everyone in fact ensures his or her own defense. The problem that must be addressed is whether the rights of the defense are respected or not. If the rights of the defense are respected in compliance with the law, someone who is prosecuted and must defend him or herself, he or she takes the stand to ensure his or her own defense ... for grave infractions, these infractions are of the competence of the High First Instance Court. There we commit public defenders or lawyers to assist suspects who cannot properly present their defense. But the suspect is free to accept a public defender or not.[10]

Even if it means self-defense because of the absence of a lawyer, the formal court system must prevail over customary. I suggest that injustice will result from this attempt in the DRC to uphold formal justice. Ironically, many customary courts are accused of denying the opportunity of a fair trial because they forbid legal representation (e.g., Sudan, Sierra Leone, South Africa) and insist on the court being conducted in accessible language without being subject to professional oratory and expertise. I agree with Bennett (2006) that the customary courts thus underscore the right of access to justice and set this as above the right to legal representation.

In Chapter 3, I argued that an assessment of whether a group was reformable seemed a sensible place to start before criminalizing all local policing. An approach that would help in rural areas would be to link local policing groups with either the state or reliable human rights NGOs. The Ugandan and Rwandan cases of local or informal local government structures are clear examples. Many other countries have pursued the linking of customary courts to formal courts through an appeal procedure. And, I mentioned the links between the communities and the police in antirustling in Kenya and between chiefs acting as "people's vigilance" in Mozambique and the police.

The degree to which links already exist and offer the opportunity of further strengthening can be illustrated from the case of southern Sudan. To a considerable degree, the southern Sudanese judicial system mixes statutory state structures with customary, local ones, blurring the distinction between statutory court and local justice mechanisms. The chiefs' courts are as local government structures; state courts officially supervise customary court's execution of judicial power and accept appeals from the chiefs' courts. Local justice networks act with state authority when they issue warrants, which, if not answered, entitle the customary court to imprison the nonresponsive recipient in a state prison. Court clerks, who record the minutes and decisions of customary courts, often receive salaries from their respective ministries of local government. In some states within southern Sudan, the fees and fines assessed and collected by the local justice networks are shared with the state local administration as the Government of Southern Sudan and the local networks split the proceeds. It is also not uncommon for a state magistrate's court to refer a case to a customary court. For example, I observed cases referred to the county customary court of "fighting" between an "Arab northerner" and a "southern Sudanese." According to observers, since the case was politically delicate, the customary court was better suited than the magistrate's court to resolve the conflict according to the values of the complainants and involved communities. There was also a traffic violation case that, when it came before the magistrate's court, was transferred to the county customary court to be resolved more speedily. Sometimes, a customary court's activities in southern Sudan are, strictly speaking, illegal, as when they act outside their mandates and jurisdiction, but this often happens with the full consent of the state judicial system, the accused, and the victim, and in the cases witnessed by me, it appeared as if all participants agreed that fair and effective justice was being done. The relationship between the local justice networks and the police is also well developed. The police often seek the assistance of the customary chiefs when attempting to find a person; routinely testify in customary courts; frequently act as prosecutors in customary courts after bringing the case to them; serve in uniform and in official capacities in the customary courthouse to maintain order; and often carry out a sentence of the court by "whipping" the convicted individual (although they may be "off duty" at the time).

Of course, much more could be done in most post-conflict countries to strengthen these links. One thinks of shared training between magistrates and customary chiefs or between policing forum and antirustling group members and the police. Again links may improve the process by which remedies are ascertained for those cases for which fairness and equity do not prevail. They may provide a reliable method within the local justice system of rectifying miscarriages of justice or, conversely, a means by which appropriate oversight of the rural policing and justice can be exercised. The general point, however, is that links with human rights and justice standard bearers may well be more effective than legislation per se.

Close links between rural local providers of policing and the state do raise, however, some issues of concern. Links that are exploited by the state to establish its sovereignty at the expense of perceived rivals will only create local resentment in rural communities, not a beneficial partnership. Second, there is a concern about using links for state surveillance. Security is obviously a prime concern for post-conflict states, especially in rural areas, because rebellion often originated in those areas where people were most disillusioned with the state as a provider of services. Where there is particular regime anxiety, rural security links can easily become not only a gathering of criminal intelligence but also an all-pervasive surveillance of citizens, including their political activities, such as Mozambique's vigilance groups. Again, in the case of Rwanda, detailed information is recorded about individual citizens through the informal local government (and through the militia [Local Defense Force, LDF]; area security committees; and student, youth, and women's organization security committees). The *nyumbakumi, chef de zone,* and *résponsable* all make weekly reports that detail people "known for trouble": those who drink, fight, stay out beyond the unofficial curfew, children who do not behave or listen to their parents, and strangers in the area. Such an intelligence system obviously raises questions of civil liberties. If it is not to be seen as a spy network or as a system open to abuse, there is a case for greater transparency regarding what is recorded, about whom and for whom. It is currently possible that misunderstandings or inaccuracies can be placed on the files of individuals and be used as a basis of judgment by others in authority—a situation not conducive to fostering state–nonstate relations.

Notes

1. http://go.worldbank.org/c9gr27wrj0.
2. Secretary-General Kofi Annan at the opening meeting of the G-8 Contact Group on Food Security in Africa in New York, March 5, 2003. http://www.unis.unvienna.org/unis/pressrels/2003/sgsm8623.html.
3. The following paragraph is based on the International Fund for Agricultural Development's fact sheet, *Enabling the Rural Poor to Overcome Poverty in Angola* (IFAD 2008a).
4. IRIN, March 31, 2008.
5. IRIN, March 31, 2008, http://www.irinnews.org/report.aspx?ReportID=77530.

6. Although there is no crime of "witchcraft" in Sierra Leonean state law, it is still handled by chiefs. For example, in 2005 a woman in a village near Makeni, Sierra Leone, whose 13-year-old son suffered from epilepsy, was accused of bewitching her child. Her husband brought the charge before the chief, who found her guilty and required a payment to him of five gallons of palm oil, 50,000 leones (US$15), one goat, and a twenty-foot pan of straw rice. Because she could not pay that, she was sent to the tribal prison until she had paid bail money of 12,000 leones (US$4). After payment of bail, she sought money for the fine. Finally, she approached an NGO human rights lawyer, who wrote to the chief. The chief dropped the witchcraft charge and all the fines (Amnesty International 2006).

7. This is the argument against codification.

8. *The Monitor* (Kampala), June 18, 2008.

9. www.irfj.org/Programs/DFJ_prog06/DFJ_prog06_english.doc.

10. Ibid.

Policing the Workplace 6

Introduction

Through work associations of market traders, taxi drivers, money lenders, woodworkers, and others crafts and professions, many of the economic activities in Africa organize much of their own policing. They settle disputes between traders and between traders and the public, and they protect their members from crime. These policing agencies, authorized by formal and informal commercial interests, tend to have the state's approval.

Workplace policing in itself is not so surprising until it is recalled that it can be conducted in the most difficult areas of all to police. No public spaces are so crowded, chaotic, and prone to crime as the markets and taxi parks. Large numbers are crammed into small spaces, with goods open to unprotected display. Yet, it is precisely in these crime hot spots that people have organized effective policing with a minimum of resources and where they do their best to keep the police out. Put another way, workplace policing is not an example of the professional police leaving it to the willing amateurs to oversee relatively quiet, crime-free environments. This is policing precisely where one might think the professionals are needed most; yet, in fact it turns out to be where they are absent and not required. How is it that ordinary people are able to organize their own effective policing in such difficult environments? This chapter looks at the work of some that function in post-conflict Africa.

Market Traders' Associations

Markets flourish in Africa and still predominate over shops for most people's source of goods. In Liberia alone, there are at least 1,000 large markets in the country, and in the center of Monrovia there are three large ones. In those Monrovian markets, there are some 100,000 registered traders, although as the president of the Liberia Markets Association told me in 2007: "It fluctuates. At Christmas everyone is a marketeer!" And, at Nakasero Market, Kampala, perhaps the biggest open market in Uganda, the Market Vendors Association told me there were 5,000 members, about 6,000 stalls, and 370 lockups. In other words, these urban markets are large commercial concerns, and of course, with the open display of goods and the large crowds, they are vulnerable to theft. "We have numerous problems! Theft; street-smart boys— we are ideally located for them!" said the president of the Liberia Markets Association. Further, the very nature of the stalls and street displays creates problems with demarcation between vendors and, from the police point of view, between wares and the public pavement or roads. There is thus plenty of opportunity for conflict even before disputes arise about payment and credit.

Markets invariably have a vendors' association run by an elected committee that is recognized by the local council. In addition, there are often associations that link market associations across the country. A variation of this voluntary association pattern is in Uganda and Rwanda, where the informal local government acts as the market association; in other words, the market is treated as a small residential area.

The work-based associations assume responsibility for the control of the conduct of vendors and customers. They fine antisocial behavior, such as smoking cannabis, spitting, abusive language, drunkenness, and "pickpocketing," while in the case of more serious matters, such as fighting and large unpaid debt, they seek to mediate a settlement between the parties. If that is unsuccessful, it may lead to the suspension of the trader for weeks or months in addition to a fine. Regarding pickpocketing and petty theft by visitors to the markets, this is dealt with in the time-honored manner of shout and chase, and if a thief is caught by the traders, the thief is usually beaten on the spot. Only serious problems will be referred to the police. For the most part, the police tend to leave the markets alone, and according to a market leader in Fort Portal, Uganda, if they want to make an arrest, "They can't without going through our office."

Most vendors have a low estimation of the state police as protectors of their markets. In fact, their absence from the markets may be seen as an advantage. At Kiseka market in Kampala, Uganda, they claimed that "police don't come at all" and were not missed since they were seen as corrupt and unwilling to help unless bribed. Similarly, one chairlady of a large Freetown market, "abhorred" their presence: "If they come here, it is because they want money." Certainly, in the center of Monrovia in 2007 police officers could be seen openly moving through the markets taking what they wanted or demanding money for its return. Most vendors regard going to the police as "a waste of time." In the case of Freetown vendors, the criticisms are the following: "There is no response from the police unless you pay money. We are on our own"; "They will not act, they refer incidents back to the market committee for adjudication, or they release the thieves straightaway" (a sign to many of collusion). In southern Sudan, there were even more serious accusations. According to a female restaurant owner in the main Juba market, the "police patrols … take women at night in some parts of the market—take money and sexually harass them. When one tries to call the police for help, they don't come."

Traders, therefore, see their market association as the primary source of protection from crime and of exercising punishment for crime, although they sometimes hire guards to supplement their work, especially at night. A market women's leader in Kono, Sierra Leone, said: "Discipline is done by the market women [rather than the police] because we know their problems and know native customary law." The market vendors' association of the biggest market in Kampala claimed they "rarely" called the police for they could handle all but the most serious disputes and disorder without them.

The largest markets may actually provide a specific security team. This is what the Liberia Market Association has done for all the main markets in the country. When the newly elected association president took over in 2006, she made safety and protection of the markets a priority. Finding a poorly trained security team, she "employed a man who had worked 27 years as a police officer to train that unit so that market vendors and their goods would be protected." She insisted that they be trained, uniformed (not accomplished by 2007), carry IDs, and be the sole security providers "for some leaseholders were bringing in their own security guards." Some carry a baton. By 2007, there were thirty-six security men for the four main markets of Monrovia. Their role is to check that vendors are authorized to trade; enforce the locations of stalls (where road/pavement ends and private property begins); protect vendors; intervene if there is conflict; or with serious cases, call the police. Intervention by the security team normally leads to the case going to the association committee. According to the president:

> We deal with our problems ourselves. Every market has an investigator to resolve the problem. Here at Central, we have Mr. Ramsey. Mr. Ramsey is like a judge! He sends his finding to me. ... We don't expel them—that just removes the trouble to out there. We find a solution and who is wrong. If goods have been destroyed, there must be payment [compensation]. Fines are possible but rare—when there has been deliberate trouble—then we must take action if it is deliberate. Criminal cases have to go to the police.

Naturally, there are variations. Another Monrovian market association said of misbehaving members who came before the committee: "We give them a warning, and then we suspend them or fine them. We expelled two last month who wouldn't take authority." Here, then, in the center of urban commerce, self-policing has carved out for itself a space largely autonomous of the state police.

Drivers' Associations

Public transport, whether taxis (minibuses) or motorbikes, is the principal means of transport throughout Africa. In the center of most towns are bus and coach stations where large numbers of people and vehicles crowd together in confusion and competition. The main taxi park in Kigali, for instance, has at any time between 600 and 1,000 taxis present.

National taxi drivers' associations control many of the commercial vehicle and minibus parking areas in the main towns. Commercial users have to pay a service fee to their association. For its part, the elected management committees of the associations deal with problems relating to drivers, passengers, and pickpockets. For instance, they check owners' particulars, including driving license and insurance, and they may organize car park marshals to oversee loading and protect passengers. They claim to resolve problems between drivers and between drivers and passengers with mediation and to discipline members who drive irresponsibly with fines or potential banning from the park for a set period. What constitutes irresponsible driving, however, is variously defined. The bus drivers' association in Rwanda claimed: "The most frequent faults that are found are speeding and drinking." If drivers are "driving too fast or drinking or smoking [marijuana] on duty," then they are first given a serious warning, then a fine, and finally the police are asked to take away their license. The Bo Bike Rental Association in Sierra Leone was clear: "We stop speeding and carrying pregnant women or a woman with a child. We are against recklessness." They did not confine themselves to the parking areas. They claimed a task force that oversaw drivers' conduct night and day anywhere in the town and resolved disputes. In Makeni, Sierra Leone, the drivers' association responds seriously to dangerous driving: "We give them lashes."

There are also problems with dangerous passengers. Two Rwandan motorbike taxi drivers were shot in the period 2004–2006. The motor bike association reported that they faced "people stealing their motorbikes—not a lot—and people sometimes being killed" and "before [we wore] vests we had a big problem with people saying 'give me the money first so that I can get petrol' and then going off." A group of thirty motorbike taxi drivers in Monrovia told me the following: "We keep our money in two pockets—if the thief takes one, the other is left"; "Stealing of bikes is common. You can't see the man on your back what he is doing"; "Some areas round here are not safe at night—passengers cut your neck [from behind they are threatened with a knife to hand over bike and money]"; "We stay on the main road." The last responses made one sympathetic with the unarmed police who would also not patrol the very same areas at night.

The drivers' associations are surprisingly large. In Liberia, there are 25,000 registered with the Federation of Road Transport Union (although only ten to fifteen thousand paid-up members). But, the members do include garage owners and petrol station owners as well as drivers and vehicle owners. Two hundred members are women. It is estimated by the association that the 25,000 represent about 50 percent of all drivers. The Uganda Taxi Operators' and Drivers' Association has 60,000 members (30,000 in Kampala) with 10,000 taxis. The Motor Drivers' and General Transport Workers Union of Sierra Leone has a membership of about 5,000 (including thirty women). *Assetamorwa*, the Rwanda motor bike taxi association, has 2,050 members in Kigali (with just three women drivers). The bus drivers' association in Rwanda (which has turned itself into a private company, ATRACO [Association pour le Developpement de l'Artisanat du Rwanda]), has 3,000 to 4,000 drivers nationwide in its association.

The size and economic significance of these associations gives them considerable political leverage within local politics. This is well illustrated by Uganda. The Uganda Taxi Operators' and Drivers' Association had experienced a history of conflict between drivers and the police, especially over roadblocks where police demanded money. After the war, however, the association made a concerted effort to improve the relationship. By 2004, they could claim that they had a good working relationship with the police and a definition of respective roles. Slowly, they have been able to establish themselves as a managing and policing authority of taxis. By 2004, the association had secured a contract with the Kampala City Council to run the taxi parks and had 100 traffic wardens who worked with the Uganda Police in enforcing traffic regulations by taxi drivers, in directing traffic in rush hour congestion, and in providing wardens for children's crossings. In addition, a law enforcement department, trained by the police and local council (LC), arrested thieves and other criminals operating in the taxi park. (In Chapter 4, the training of taxi drivers and others in policing their own through the crime preventers program was described.)

In Rwanda, there also was evidence of cooperation with the police. The areas of responsibility were clearly demarcated in the minds of ATRACO: "We work alongside the police and with their ideals, but they don't do what we do. We are responsible for security, but if there is something beyond us we call the police."

In Liberia and southern Sudan, however, there were still problems in the aftermath of the war in 2007. Taxi drivers in Malakal in 2007 accused the police of demanding separate fees to come to the scene of an alleged crime, to open the file, to investigate the case, and to remand a suspect into custody. Things were only a little better in Liberia. Traffic police in Monrovia still openly ask for bribes from taxi drivers as they seek to set down passengers at busy junctions in the center of Monrovia. The secretary general of the Federation of Road Transport Union admitted that problems were on both sides:

> The war had a serious negative impact on drivers and the police. Some of the LNP [Liberia National Police] are not living up to the expectations people had after the war. Likewise some of the [union] membership were involved in factions in the war and need to be reintegrated. They lack education. So there is not a cordial relationship with the LNP. Drivers tend to think of them as "enemies." ... Bribery is getting less by the police. They used to beat drivers and steal their money. The police need training concerning the way they approach drivers. They should not be aggressive but polite.

They were making headway with police cooperation, however. In 2007, they were having monthly meetings with them to cover driving issues and together were developing a program of driver training. Although there was no official driving test from 2005 to 2007, they planned free training on traffic regulations for all drivers.

Commercial Security Companies

The commercial security sector escalated rapidly across Africa in the early 1990s as a result of a conjunction of factors. First, African state policy, which had been fiercely monopolistic in its hold on policing, softened in the face of structural adjustment and the additional demands of conflict and post-conflict security. Whatever principles they had held concerning universal provision of a public good, they were faced with costs of state policing that they could not meet. Thus, the apartheid South African regime actively encouraged the commercial sector in the 1980s to defend their "key" strategic installations and factories (Philip 1989, 213–14; Irish 1999, 12). In the case of Uganda, the government made a strategic decision in 1992 to withdraw state policing from guarding duties.

Second, although faced with increased insecurity during and after war, the state police were reduced in numbers and were not up to protecting businesses or international humanitarian actors. For instance, during the civil war in Sierra Leone approximately 900 Sierra Leone Police (SLP) officers were killed, and a considerable number suffered amputation. As a result, the size of the SLP was reduced from 9,317 to 6,600 (Malan, Rakate, and McIntyre 2002, 65). As the general manager of Exsecon, Liberia, explained: "The company formed in 1993 when we could not find hardly any police. VIPs wanted protection for themselves and their property. So we began with residential property and then after 2003 moved into commercial security." Likewise, the rise in the private security industry in Mozambique was to fill the policing gap in the civil war when the police were no longer able to keep pace with rising crime. Enabling legislation was therefore passed in 1990 while the civil war was still ongoing.

Of course, even commercial security can be adversely affected by conflict. The diamond industry has been a motivator for many security companies to become involved in Angola. According to Schreier and Caparini (2005, 76): "There are cases where some commercial military and security activity has been paid for through the granting of mineral or oil concessions or other non-monetary methods." The managing supervisor of FAITH[1] Security Systems, Liberia, pointed out: "We were badly hit by the war. We had to close down many contracts because people couldn't pay or had closed down themselves." Yet, generally, in the fluid conditions of the immediate post-conflict environment, commercial security is well positioned to offer organizations, businesses, and persons immediate protection.

Third, many argue that commercial security has taken advantage of the sudden postwar crime wave or at least the perception of it. Some argue that private security companies have actively promoted fear and vulnerability as part of their promotion of their services. By 2005, there were already thirty-one private security companies in Mozambique. In Uganda in 2004, there were about eighty-seven commercial security companies, reflecting eighteen years of commercial activity in a growing urban economy. In Sierra Leone, before the war there were only two companies; in 2005, three years after the war, there were thirty licensed companies, twenty of them medium to large in size, employing more than 3,000 guards. Angola's private security industry has flourished particularly since the early 1990s. The number of private security companies operating in Angola in 1993 was about five in 1993. By 2000, estimates ranged from 90 to 150, and in 2004 there were 307 registered or being registered, employing 35,715 and holding 12,087 light arms and weapons (Joras and Schuster 2008, 46). Angola's diamond and oil industries have, in particular, contributed to the growth of the industry, considering that the government has required that foreign investors provide their own security. But, there are exceptions. Only Rwanda has seen relatively limited growth. Of Rwanda's five main commercial security companies in 2006, one was begun before the genocide (1991), two as it ended (1994), and one in 2000. There are suggestions that the small numbers in Rwanda were due not only to the smallness of the country and its economy but also to restrictions by the regime, which was sponsoring or closely linked with at least two of the commercial security operators.

Finally, the presence of many international nongovernmental organizations (NGOs) and transnational corporations in post-conflict Africa requiring security for their staff has certainly benefited commercial security operators. The internationalization of both commercial and development organizations has brought with it a demand for security provision that meets standards deemed appropriate for staff from the West. Increasingly aware of real security risks to staff and operations (and perhaps subject to increasing perceptions of risk), they turn to commercial security, particularly those with international presence, to provide them a consistent quality of security across all their global operations.

> The increasingly global needs of transnational corporations provide a competitive advantage to PSCs [private security companies] that can offer a complete and integrated spectrum of services—from intelligence and risk analysis, to satellite tracking and multiple forms of response services—that is, to those companies that can claim a capacity as global providers to global clients. (Abrahamsen and Williams 2008, 549)

Such global security companies include Group4Securicor (500,000 employees, operating in over 115 countries; 82,000 of its employees work in 20 African countries); Securitas (250,000 employees operating in 30 countries); Chubb; and ADT Security Systems. In UN-led peace operations, for instance, private security companies are increasingly used for installation guarding, logistics, evacuation support, and security sector reform (SSR) work (e.g., in Liberia DynCorp International is training and equipping the 500-strong Emergency Response Unit of the LNP). In unstable conditions, there has not only been an increase in the presence of government armed forces, but also "the role of private security companies has also grown. ... Donors are making funds available to private security companies to undertake assistance activities, without uniforms, often with guns and relatively unregulated" (Luff 2008, unnumbered). In Liberia, while several aid agencies rely on UNMIL (UN Mission in Liberia) assets for the delivery of aid, a number of NGOs complain about the lack of readiness and availability on the part of UNMIL troops to assist with providing security for humanitarian assets and staff (Bashua 2005, 143; Spearin 2008). Other examples of development organizations turning to commercial security include the International Rescue Committee in the Central African Republic (CAR; Boggero 2008, 18) and the World Wildlife Fund in the Democratic Republic of the Congo (DRC; Avant 2004, 153).

The relationship of security companies with conflict can be complex. Thus, in Niger the security of Areva, the state-owned French nuclear power company that held a de facto monopoly of uranium mining until 2007, has been accused by the rebel *Mouvement des Nigeriens pour la Justice* (Nigerien Movement for Justice/MNJ) of providing financial backing to the Niger government and therefore constituting itself as a legitimate target. On the other hand, the Niger government accused Areva's security of backing the rebels to deter competitor companies and has expelled Areva's security advisor and declared its country manager *persona non grata* (Consultancy Africa Intelligence 2007).

Once commercial security enters the security market and is seen to prosper, their numbers invariably increase. Hence, the number of companies operating in a post-conflict country is closely related to length of time since the conflict ceased as well as factors such as the size of the economy. Yet, the number of companies does not by itself reveal their significance in terms of numbers of personnel and in comparison to the state police. The largest private security sector in Africa is in South Africa, where in 2007 there were 4,898 registered security companies employing 307,343 security officers as against 173,241 officers in the South African Police Services (SAPS) (Private Security Industry Regulatory Authority [PSIRA] 2007; Minnaar 2004). Elsewhere, the numbers of employees often nearly equals the number in the state police within a short period after war. Sierra Leone in 2005 had at least 5,000 guards compared with a police force of 8,000 (2,000 of whom were support staff). The five main commercial security companies of Rwanda in 2006 employed about 4,300 guards, compared with 5,800 officers in the Rwanda National Police. In Uganda in 2004, just the largest two companies employed some 2,000 guards between them, compared with the 13,000 available to the Uganda police. In Liberia in 2007, there were an estimated 3,000 to 4,000 security guards, compared with the 3,500 officers in the LNP.

Their economic significance, of course, outweighs their size. It is the commercial security companies that are invariably guarding the chief remaining economic and strategic assets of post-conflict countries. It is they that are found protecting government offices, international agency premises, banks, hotels, embassies, large mines, plantations, factories, warehouses, seaports, airports, and the principal businesses. In South Africa, even police stations are guarded by private security guards. For these reasons, private security tends to be urban and especially capital based. However, the span of the activities is wider than guarding. There are two ends of the market. First, there are those larger companies (often foreign-owned internationals such as Group4Securicor, Securitas, Chubb, and ADT Security Systems) that offer a range of security services. Besides guarding, they undertake VIP protection, risk assessment, and corporate protection. I even found one large company in Kampala that investigated theft and stock loss in companies by using a polygraph on the employees to determine their honesty. At the other end of the market are smaller local companies that focus on providing guards for individual properties and businesses. Again, the urban bias is apparent.

The commercial security sector has assets that could be put to good use if shared with the police. Yet, cooperation between private and state security is spasmodic and poor. This is an opportunity missed. Exchange of information, if regularized and enhanced, could improve the effectiveness of both sides of the partnership, and there is potential in combining resources to undertake joint operations. Yet in Liberia, according to security managers, there is little cooperation with the police; with the exception of the Firestone plantation, which is faced with serious illicit tapper violence, there are no joint operations with the police. And, even in the case of Firestone, cooperation does not extend beyond patrols. On the contrary, it concerns the company that the government has said publicly that whatever happens on the plantation was "Firestone's worry," not the government's (despite the fact that of the 90,000 who live on the plantations, only 7,000 are company employees). However, in 2007 it was agreed that meetings would be held between the commercial security and the Ministry of Justice officials to recommend industry standards. Elsewhere, I have found that the relationship varies considerably depending on personal ties. Thus, in Rwanda, company managers, asked whether companies cooperated with the police, often replied negatively: "Not really. But we report to the police what has happened. Nothing else"; "We do not share. Actually exchange of information is zero." Yet another manager claimed:

> We have asked the police to appoint a judicial police officer [to work in the company office] to deal just with our cases as they arise. This saves going to the police station. And they can take it through to the court. They are paid by the police, and the company adds an allowance. Then we also gave a walkie-talkie to the Criminal Investigation Unit so that they can follow our communications. If they hear there is an incident on it they come to the incident.

In Uganda in 2004, there was the same importance on personal ties. Whereas one manager said, "The police see us as a rival. There is no cooperation between us. No exchange of information," others said, "We do joint-ops. They call us in for backup. And we exchange security information. They vet recruits for criminal records and do fingerprinting"; "We have a good relationship. We take suspects to them. Exchange of information [EOI] is both ways, and we do joint operations if we have a tip off of an imminent robbery. Our guards stake out the place with them"; "We cooperate with them. And sometimes there are joint ventures—ambushes when we have a tip off that there is going to be an armed robbery." One manager, an ex-policeman, even claimed:

> We have a good relationship with the police. They appreciate that we are part and parcel of the criminal justice system. We work together. On important functions such as National Independence Day, we help them as a public service. And we give them help at rallies and joint operations when there are robberies.

The truth is that the police themselves are typically ambivalent in their attitude toward commercial security companies in the workplace. On the one hand, they recognize that their activity relieves the police of work pressure or at times offers them partnership in certain areas, such as exchange of information, joint operations to ambush armed robbers, and policing of large public functions. Yet, on the other hand they are envious of their income and resources. In an effort to tap into the perceived available income, the police in the DRC have set up a brigade that offers police officers for hire in Kinshasa; the LNP and the SLP have exploited the monopoly of armed personnel that their armed wings have to provide inter alia security to companies for an additional premium. In 2008 Liberia set up the QRU, the Quick Response Unit, as its armed wing, trained by DynCorp. For its part, Sierra Leone's armed police wing, known as the OSD (Operational Support Division) is 2,500 strong, and its activities include providing security alongside unarmed security guards at diamond mines, banks, and some diplomatic missions and for some rapid response teams. Commercial operators work alongside the OSD to provide a mix of armed and unarmed guards, with security companies paying a premium to the individual OSD officers above the standard wages. The irony does not go unnoticed among the general public that government revenue is spent sending SLP personnel to guard commercial rather than citizen interests.

Discussion

As discussed in the previous chapters on policing urban and rural areas, policing the workplace involves nonstate security actors often operating alongside the state police. Commercial security companies, like the trade associations, operate in the workplace with the authorization of the state and sometimes on behalf of the state. Having said that, on the ground the relationship between agents of state policing and workplace policing agencies is a complex mixture of cooperation and competition. It demonstrates again that nonstate policing is not simply a case of filling the security vacuum left by a failing state. As Abrahamsen and Williams observed: "Instead of a simple decline or retreat of state power, we see the contours of a changing public-private relationship, where this very distinction is being reconfigured, gradually losing its conceptual and empirical validity" (2008, 44).

Most businesses perceive private providers of security as the most effective way of protecting their property and their assets and responding to criminal activity. As a result, the principal part of the economy, formal and informal, is protected by private, not public, security. For private businesses vulnerable to crime and occupying central city and populous locations, private (not public) policing undertakes the security provision. It might be assumed that by private businesses I mean only larger commercial operations since private security is often portrayed as the prerogative of the wealthy. Although this may have some validity in residential areas, in the workplace private security is as much the chosen provider of small business as large ones. Few shopkeepers in the main towns are without a security company guard or watchman of their own or shared with other neighboring premises. And, they are happy with that service. Interviewing shopkeepers in Kampala who used hired guards to protect their shops day and night, the responses were invariably: "They do a good job at night. … They are respectful." As the chapter has shown, even market vendors and drivers have managed, through the cooperative efforts of their trade associations, to pay for the security of their workplace. In the workplace, therefore, it is not possible to generalize that crime and insecurity follow the lines of wealth or that crime is displaced from wealthy business areas to poor business areas. The charge that only the relatively well-off can afford the services of private security, leaving the rest to the state police or no policing, is not irrefutable. On the contrary, one could make the case that the general disinterest or abandonment by the police of guarding and patrolling commercial property, whether market stall, factory, or mine, for the most part acts as a "force multiplier" to increase security for all sections of society.

Beyond questions of equality, some would raise the issue of legitimacy, which looks particularly crucial in the face of substantial numbers of well-equipped guards and possibly armed security companies, based abroad and answerable only to foreign shareholders and their customers in-country. If they are authorized by an elected government under national legislation, the issue becomes one of ensuring standards of guard recruitment, training, and supervision and of inspection of accounts and, if relevant, armories. In other words, the private control of security is not legitimate if its activities are removed from public scrutiny and oversight. Although they do have contractual accountability to clients, they must also have lines of accountability to the representatives of the people. This applies to market associations and taxi drivers' associations, just as it does to those large security organizations with armed guards, as for instance in Uganda, Rwanda, Mozambique, and Angola. Although democracy may not necessitate a state monopoly of workplace security, it does necessitate accountability to the state of all workplace policing. It is precisely in this area that post-conflict states, with their under-resourced and inexperienced oversight institutions and practices, are weak.

With the presence of large numbers of often-armed guards in public places, the commercial security sector requires legislation or at least close working relationships with the police to ensure it is not a source of insecurity. Such insecurity has indeed happened in Liberia, for instance. There, the private security of the rubber company Firestone, known as the Plant Protection Division (PPD), is accused of acting illegally at times: "There is a recurring problem on the plantations concerning illegal detention and arrest by private security officers without the knowledge of the LNP."[2] It is therefore vital that private security as much as state security be incorporated into the national security policy and be regulated. Yet, in fact specific legislation in post-conflict Africa is rare. If private security is to be legitimate, legislation needs to control standards of recruitment and training to ensure that criminals and former rebels/soldiers with records of human rights abuses are not being employed, and that those who do join know how and when to use a weapon if they are armed. Other areas to tackle include clear engagement rules when a suspect of a serious crime is resisting arrest; the level of public indemnity insurance required; the quality of police criminal records vetting for would-be company employees (given that most police data are not computerized and limited in scope and that fingerprints are inspected manually); the use of communications equipment and shared wavebands; and protection of information and privacy. Legislation could make it an offense to employ an unregistered person and company, meaning that the client can also be prosecuted. An independent security officers board, like that used in South Africa, could also be considered. The greatest challenge, however, for any post-conflict state is to produce a national integrated security policy that incorporates the security companies as active partners.

Even where there is basic legislation, there is a problem with inexact terminology and poor enforcement. In Uganda in 2004, for example, companies were licensed and supervised by the police, with operating licenses liable to be renewed each year, subject to satisfactory inspection of the company armory and the suitability of its guards. Yet, the regulations were broad enough to allow wide discretion. For example, only "appropriate" insurance coverage of employees was required; personnel were simply to have "proper and regular training"; and organizations could be deregistered if companies were "below the acceptable standard." Although some firms indeed had their operational licenses withdrawn, elsewhere there had been problems with security guards aiding criminal activity.

Similar problems are found in Mozambique. Legislation makes private security accountable to the Ministry of Interior. Companies are not allowed to undertake criminal investigations. Guards must be Mozambican citizens, have no criminal record, and have attained a minimum level of education. However, as Berg pointed out, the legislation allows a broad interpretation: "For instance, not only are security companies given discretion as to the training of their guards, but each company is responsible for the control of their firearms and is not required to prove competency in owning firearms" (2005, 18). And, although the police are to inspect the companies' armories on a monthly basis, this is not often carried out.

In Rwanda in 2006, security companies were licensed and officially supervised by the police. Operating licenses had to be renewed each year, subject to satisfactory inspection by the police of the company, including the armory and the suitability of the guards. There was no specific law regulating commercial security, although one was anticipated. What was surprising was that security managers claimed to know nothing about its details:

"We haven't seen it yet!" said a manager, "It was framed without any input from us. We don't have a clue about it!" For Liberia in 2007, the Ministry of Justice required all private security agencies to register and be certified. Yet, the Ministry's Public Safety Division, responsible for its supervision, had no clear idea of their number (forty-five were registered, but there were probably at least one hundred); did very little inspection; and did not enforce the Ministry of Justice "guidelines." Thus, as one manager put it: "We register every year. They don't check our guards. There are no inspections. They only come to see we have paid." There appeared to be no legislation to control private security, and no criminal records checks were made on those employed.

Enacting legislation is relatively easy, but without the ability to enforce it, it is worthless. Whether it is the inspection of premises, armories, accounts, or training, if the police or Ministry of Justice inspectors are going to be required to carry this out, they must be given the resources and skills to implement it. Alternatively, it might be thought better to follow the South African pattern of the PSIRA, one that is entrusted with oversight of the security companies. Even the formation of a professional association to regulate companies and to maintain professional standards would help, although these associations are rare at the moment.

Training is varied across the workplace security sector. In the informal sector, it is understandably weak. Yet, the law enforcement section of the taxi drivers' association in Uganda is trained by the police, while the drivers' association in Sierra Leone has had help from a British NGO in safety training. Even the Liberia Market Association employs a former police officer to train its security unit. Most informal security guards, however, have no training. In contrast, commercial companies invariably make stronger claims. Some companies claim two or three months of training in a wide variety of subjects. One Rwandan manager boasted: "The course includes first aid; weapon training; self-defense; observation; civic education; the history of Rwanda; public relations; use of mobile phone; bible study; employment law; social security; salaries; changing from a military mind to a commercial mind; the disciplinary procedures of the company and its leadership." A Ugandan manager said: "It covers social skills, guarding skills, public relations, and personal hygiene. Then they do training for a specific role, whether it is fire fighting, loss control, weapon handling." A Sierra Leonean manager maintained: "We train them for three weeks in loss prevention. And we give them physical training. And if it's UN work, you have to give them human rights training." Yet, individuals in other companies have told me that there is no training offered. A Sierra Leonean manager said: "No initial training is given, but we recruit ex-servicemen, army, prison, police." Likewise, a Uganda manager said: "There is no training. We pick only ex-soldiers, ex-police, ex-prison officers." Training, when provided by the company, sometimes uses ex-police trainers, or it is outsourced to training companies—in one instance in Uganda, I was told: "We use Israelis. They give you mental training—they challenge them: 'Why are you guards?!'" The training diversity calls for standardization. As a Rwandan manager observed: "There is duplication and different standards. We use a Canadian manual with some South African extras; [another company] uses a British manual; others just rely on their military training." Perhaps a single training school for commercial security approved by the police is the answer.

Equipment available to workplace policing is also controversial. Security in the informal sector at most consists of an ID and perhaps a bright-colored bib and a baton. However, most company security guards carry whistles, batons, and handcuffs. Some will, in addition, carry radios, pepper spray, and electric shock batons. Still others carry weapons. The pressure for guards to be armed in a context of violent crime against businesses is increasing in Sierra Leone and Liberia, where it is not allowed at present. Yet, where weapons can be carried, as in Uganda and Rwanda, there is a surprising caution and even doubt among security companies about the value of weapons. In Uganda, although some companies armed all their employees, there were others that only armed some of their guards, and one I researched that armed most of its guards, but with an unloaded shotgun, the bullets being kept in the belt. In Rwanda, I found companies arguing for their increased restriction: "We want to reduce weapons. After the war people felt the need for protection with guns. Nowadays, we are trying to teach them that it is not so necessary." Another indicated that not only were foreign security companies not allowed to use guns, but "the majority of our clients don't like guns—they are ex-pats and foreigners. And it can cause very serious problems for the company. There were three cases where [another company] guard shot people." Another ensured that the police accompanied his security guards on the rapid response team: "We have a rapid response unit that includes two police. We have two police for the day shift and two for the night. They go with our guards, and if there is a need for the use of weapons they are there. But our own guards do not carry guns." The company had chosen an unarmed policy because "I wanted to avoid unnecessary shooting. And many of our customers like the UN have a rule that they must be protected by professional guards who are unarmed. And all our clients are ex-pats." It seems that company policy is under pressure from guards on the one hand, who want weapons to defend themselves, and customers and insurers on the other hand, who would rather that weapons were removed to avoid accidents.

In Liberia, the PPD, Firestone Rubber Company's private security force, used to have arms and gas before the civil war. Now, they have just batons and riot shields. That the guards themselves want arms is hardly surprising given that they are faced on the huge plantation with extreme violence from illegal tappers. In 2007, I was told by the company manager: "Since 2003 we have had one [guard] killed and ten (including the PSU—the police Public Service Unit) have had acid burns [from acid thrown at them]. And two of the [Superintendents'] Team Watch have had their throats slashed." To combat this, they do joint patrols with the armed PSU.

All the issues mentioned only reinforce the point that workplace security is an issue that belongs in the domain of the political. The coercive power, economic responsibility, and sometimes foreign ownership of private security actors have an impact on the political landscape by shaping who is doing the protecting and how and who is protected and how. Governments not only have to decide future standards for the security industry but also have to examine the existing relationships they already have with it. There is much they may not approve of about private workplace security, but they will have to remember that some of the very problems they identify with private security also bedevil their own state policing. The misuse of weapons, inadequate training, the use of ex-combatants, inadequate accountability, poor pay and labor conditions, and collaboration with criminals are all charges that have been laid at the door of the state police as well.

Notes

1. FAITH is an acronym for Faithful, Accurate, Intelligent, Trustworthy, Honest.
2. IRIN. May 11, 2006.

Policing Women

7

Gendered Patterns of Crime

There are very large gender differences in the experience of crime in post-conflict Africa. It is not only that women invariably experience conflict (and authoritarian rule) differently from men, but also that even in so-called democratic peacetime women suffer distinct abuses and rights violations. These gendered patterns apply not only to the nature and frequency of the abuses themselves but also to the policing responses (or lack of them).

The situation is complicated by the fact that laws do not always exist in the statute book against particular abuses, such as domestic violence, domestic rape, and sexual harassment. This lack of legal protection is almost universally true at the everyday level of social interaction, at which women frequently experience offensive attitudes and behavior because of their gender. As a woman I spoke to in a town in Liberia observed: "Men don't respect women. They can talk to them badly." But, beyond the abuses of everyday social interaction, women endure widespread discrimination, exploitation, intimidation, and harassment in the home, the workplace, and their communal life. Discriminatory cultural practices and religious beliefs contribute to human rights abuses, including denying women and girls access to education, economic resources, health and child support payments; forced early marriage; forced female genital mutilation; and parents requiring their daughters to engage in "transactional sex" for food. Or, take land: Increasing land pressures are placing severe constraints on women, who do not have sufficient access to and control over land. Even where there has been land reforms and new legislation, it has often involved utilizing local structures. To prevent the appropriation of customary land by wealthier outsiders, often through unscrupulous means, control of land has been kept within the communities. Customary or local council structures have assumed responsibility for adjudication, registration, titling land, and land dispute resolution. Yet, the downside of localizing land administration has been that elements that subordinate women have been preserved (Wiley 2000).

Many of the discriminatory actions are contrary to state law but are not enforced by the state. In 2004, the head of information, the Uganda Association of Women Lawyers, summarized the complexity for me:

Things can be lawful but unacceptable from a human rights point of view or even from the point of view of a woman. Women want to be comfortable and secure. Yet they are often the object, with children, of abuse, even deaths. But they rarely go to the police and the police themselves don't want to be involved. They say it is not their business if someone else's wife is beaten. And some laws are unjust such as the divorce laws—they have just been changed. Women need property rights and safety and the same rights in marriage as men.

Thus, in addition to the problem of a lack of enforcement, there is a lack of reporting. Further, there is ignorance of the law and rights by many. In Mozambique, for instance, the Family Law of 2005 defined, inter alia, women's legal rights with regard to property and child custody. Yet, a 2007 survey conducted by the nongovernmental organization (NGO) Associação Mulher, Lei e Desenvovimento (MULEIDE) found that approximately 63 percent of women remained uninformed about the law (U.S. Department of State, Country Report 2007).

In the face of the evidence, men still persist in denying that male attitudes and behavior are the main cause of discrimination against women. Some argue that women themselves are partly to blame for their problems. A chief inspector in Rwanda told me in 2006 that the problem of rape "is due to illiteracy [lack of education?]; irresponsible parents who do not protect their children properly or who allow their young girls to go around without any covering below the waist." Another man, a local government leader in Rwanda, insisted that much of the crime and disorder in his area was due to immorality and the condom:

The main problem is family problems. Prostitutes may get pregnant and claim a man was responsible; or boys and girls may have sexual relations, and the girl gets pregnant. The girls want the man to pay. This is a big problem these days. It's the condom. Before girls were neglected and shown no respect if they got pregnant. And bastards were neglected and shown no respect by the family. Now young people play sex. They get used to it. Then one day the boy will forget a condom. And he will say, "Now you are used to sex let's carry on this time." And the girl gets pregnant.

It is customary law, however, not state law and international rights, that prevails in many parts of Africa, particularly rural areas. In this environment, women have limited access to the state judicial system for enforcing state laws and constitutional rights and instead rely on customary law to settle disputes. Under customary law, women are frequently discriminated against. One such gender discrimination is a pervasive denial of the right of women to inherit land and homes. Whatever the statutory law might say, in practice in many areas of Africa, land use, housing, and the transfer of land and housing between generations are regulated by customary law, which largely excludes women from property ownership and inheritance. Land ownership is commonly passed through male heirs. A woman's right to access and to use land is normally defined by her relationship to men. Married, she may enjoy the use of land belonging to her husband; single, she has access to that of her father or guardian; when her husband or father dies, her right to the land is in question. Should she fail to secure the land and property rights, she can potentially be made homeless and without access to adequate food (Richardson 2004). It is true that many ethnic groups have in the past had a social safety net providing for widows and orphans at the death of the male head of household. This required the men who did inherit property to care for the wife or wives of the deceased and all of his dependents as the deceased would have. But, under severe pressure from conflict, population growth, decreasing land plots, and the social upheaval caused by HIV/AIDS, these mechanisms have been breaking down. How the issue of land and inheritance is policed is therefore of no small concern for women and currently rests largely with customary leaders. Yet, as with other issues of abuse, women will weigh carefully the cost of challenging the perpetrators of injustice before chiefs who control access to other rights and benefits.

An account of the crimes and injustices experienced by women does not, however, capture their whole experience. What it neglects is the fear of crime that many women experience on a daily basis. It could be argued that women's sense of threat is a routine aspect of their lives. "The normalization of the presence and gendered nature of threat and fear provokes among women a ubiquitous, vigilant awareness that leads to the avoidance of socially constructed cues of danger" (McLaughlin 2003). This avoidance shapes the structure of daily life of women, restricting their freedom of movement and reinforcing self-perceptions of vulnerability. Note the long-term cumulative strategic adjustments made by a group of three women who spoke to me in Monrovia in 2007:

> We are frightened of armed robbers at night. We can't protect our homes. Gangs of twenty bust the doors. Our only protection is to put pots behind the door. We don't go out at night. We don't go on the road after 8 p.m.

> We are frightened of thieves breaking into our homes and stealing and raping us. We put all the dishes behind the door so we can hear if any break as someone tries to enter. We are abandoned.

To begin to appreciate women's perceptions of everyday crime and disorder, I briefly quote from two discussions with women's groups. The first was in a Rwandan village in 2006. The women identified three matters of current concern. The first concern mentioned was the land grabbing going on in the fertile river valley by wealthy powerful people; the second expressed concern about the drunken behavior associated with the two bars in the center of the settlement; finally, there was talk about child rape, some saying that it had happened and others saying it had happened in nearby areas and they feared it spreading in this area. On a map to portray local crime, they wrote: "We had swamps [common land wetlands to grow food], but those who had money, they took it away, and we have little security"; "The drunk fight"; "The children are taken by force [raped], there are some places where they steal; there is a woman who left her child in the house, she came and found that they had taken her." It is an account of actual and perceived threats from the powerful grabbing vital land; drunk men intimidating (with perhaps a sexual threat); and sexual abuse of their children. This was in what appeared to be a quiet village with a low criminal record: where the male *résponsable* (local government official) of the village, when asked what the main crimes in the area were, replied: "Theft is not common. But there is unauthorized local brew which is prohibited and building illegally without asking permission."

The second discussion group was held in 2004 with twenty women from a fishing village beside Lake Victoria. Asked what life was like for a woman, they replied: "Youth are disrespectful. They use vulgar language about women"; "Bars are a problem for women—if they go near when men are intoxicated"; "It's a difficult place to raise children"; "There are immoral tendencies"; "There's a lot of alcoholism because fishermen are around in the day. They earn good money but spend it on drinking a lot"; "The fishermen earn 30,000 [shillings] a day. Easy come, easy go. They spend it in a day! On women and alcohol"; "The men need to be sensitized as regards their behavior. They don't spend money on children and family"; "And only rarely take the children to school." It is an account of actual and perceived threats from drunk, abusive, immoral (and threatening?) men and irresponsible fathers. This was in a village where eight male leaders, five of whom were Local Council (LC) executive members, told me there was very little disorder: "LC is in charge of good manners. It mediates between husbands and wife"; "More than forty villagers have been trained by the [Crime Prevention] panel"; "Training makes us follow the law"; coming before the LC1 court, we have cases of "fighting after beer, stealing from homes, stealing nets. ... There can be a month without a case." It might be a month without disturbance to female order.

These two women's groups tell us that what women see as crime and disorder men are often blind to. This disparity in views has significant consequences for policing. Although women suffer disproportionately more criminal (as well as moral and social) abuse than men, there is often little understanding or concern of their plight by male-dominated policing agencies, state or nonstate. Indeed, policing agencies can be the perpetrators of these abuses. This unsympathetic policing is just one reason why a large proportion of crimes and abuses against women go unreported. There is also family pressure to preserve honor; fear of stigma and discrimination; reluctance to speak out because the victim lives within the same community as the perpetrator or even depends on the perpetrator for survival; and, of course, the very trauma of the crime experience itself. The situation is therefore one in which those most victimized are those least policed: Those that need policing are ignored or unjustly treated or even subject to criminal abuse by those who have the role of protectors. It is a disturbing situation.

In addition to the ubiquitous discrimination and exploitation, women in Africa also endure widespread sexual abuse and gender violence. According to the United Nations Population Fund (UNFPA), it is estimated that worldwide at least one in every three women has been beaten, coerced into sex, or abused in some other way (2000). Gender-based criminal violence, whether rape, domestic violence, "honor" killings, infanticide, or trafficking in women, is not only a grave violation of human rights but also a major public health concern that exacts a heavy toll on women's mental and physical well-being. The World Health Organization (WHO 2005, 22) reported:

> Violence against women is widespread and deeply ingrained and has a serious impact on women's health and well-being. Its continued existence is morally indefensible, its cost to individuals, to health systems and to society in general is enormous. Yet no other major problem of public health has until relatively recently been so widely ignored and so little understood.

In Africa, the crimes of domestic violence, rape, and other sexual abuse are widespread; tragically, there is extensive evidence that during conflict, levels of domestic and sexual violence increase in both quantity and severity, and that these escalated levels remain high long after the conflict is over. This is related to several factors, including the breakdown of social order during conflict; the availability of weapons to intimidate; the vulnerability of women left alone as men depart to fight; and the fact that sexual abuse is actually used as a weapon of war—used to destabilize and demoralize the community or even sometimes as a tool to reshape the ethnic balance of a community.[1] The next sections seek first to outline the main categories of crime that particularly affect women in post-conflict Africa and then examine how nonstate policing addresses these crimes.

Domestic Violence

Domestic violence covers the whole range of sexually, psychologically, and physically coercive acts used against adult and adolescent women by male intimate partners.

Although both state police and legal aid centers run by NGOs handle large numbers of cases of domestic violence, there is no knowledge of just how large the problem is. All the evidence suggests it is much higher than that reported. For instance, after just a single three-month awareness program in 2007 in a northern Ugandan village, the number of cases reported to the police of violence against women rose from 30 to 315 cases.[2] One survey in rural Uganda of more than 5,000 women of reproductive age in the Rakai District found that 30 percent of women had experienced physical threats or physical abuse from their current partner; 20 percent during the year before the survey. Also, 60 percent of women who reported recent physical threats or abuse reported three or more specific acts of violence during the preceding year, and just under half reported injuries as a result (Koenig et al. 2003). In 2003, interviews with nearly 500 women in Mbale District, eastern Uganda, revealed that the prevalence of lifetime intimate partner violence was 54 percent and of physical violence in the previous year was 14 percent (Karamagi et al. 2007). The same picture emerged from Angola. There, a preliminary study on domestic violence in Luanda indicated that 78 percent of women had experienced some form of violence since the age of fifteen. While 27 percent of the total reported abuse in the twelve months preceding the study, 62 percent of women living in the poorest suburbs of Luanda reported abuse (U.S. Department of State, Country Report 2007). And in Ethiopia, UNFPA reported in 2005 that "between 94 and 91 percent of women between 15 and 49 years have been beaten" (Immigration and Refugee Board of Canada, Ethiopia 2007). The WHO reported in 2005 that 71 percent of Ethiopian women who had been married or otherwise partnered had experienced either physical or sexual violence, and that 35 percent of these women had experienced at least one incident of "severe" physical violence. Another report recorded that more than 65 percent of women in the Asmara area, Eritrea, were the victims of domestic violence during the year 2001 (U.S. Department of State Country Report 2002).

Tragically, levels of domestic violence are often found to increase after war when male ex-combatants return home. They appear to redirect their violence and aggression to their wives and partners, "demanding a return to prewar societal patterns of interaction and responsibilities" (Fitzsimmons 2005, 188).

Many men condone or at least tolerate a certain amount of violence against women. Over much of Africa, men are seen as having a right to discipline their wives by beating or physical intimidation. For example, a Sierra Leone Peoples Party (SLPP) candidate for the chairmanship of a district council in 2008 said: "Domestic violence is not a human right abuse. You can call the United States embassy in Freetown and crosscheck with them. ... I fought my wife, which any man can do. Fighting my wife is not a human rights abuse."[3] Even some women view a certain amount of physical abuse as justified under certain conditions. The survey I mentioned in Rakai District, Uganda, revealed that 70 percent of men and 90 percent of women viewed beating of the wife or female partner as justifiable in some circumstances (Koenig et al. 2003). Justification for violence rests on particular views about the roles and responsibilities of men and women in relationships. Events that trigger violent responses are typically the following: not obeying the husband; talking back; refusing sex; not having food ready on time; failing to care for the children or home; questioning the man about money or girlfriends; or going somewhere without the man's permission. And, in Sierra Leone 85 percent of women felt that domestic beating was justified for actions such as going out without telling a husband, neglecting the children, arguing with a husband, refusing sex, or burning food, according to the UN Children's Fund (quoted in U.S. Department of State, Country Report 2007 for Sierra Leone).

In my interviews with senior police officers, local community leaders, and those in NGOs across post-conflict Africa, domestic violence has been commonly raised as prevalent. In Sierra Leone, both the police and women's organizations reported in 2005 that there had been steep rises since the war in reported domestic violence, although they attributed it largely to the sensitization programs among the public and police and hence the greater willingness to report such cases. In Rwanda in 2006, senior police officers said that after rape, the next major challenge the police faced was domestic violence. Likewise, the Liberia police in 2007 said that domestic violence was one of the main crimes they faced. According to an Ethiopian study, 39 percent of the women "had never talked to anyone about the physical violence." Women who did seek help tended to approach local leaders most often, then sought medical assistance, and, far less frequently, approached the police and the courts. Those who did not look for assistance indicated that "they feared the consequences or had been threatened" or that they considered the violence to be "normal" or not "serious" (WHO 2005).

The frustration of women having nowhere to turn to for help is captured in an interview I undertook with five women in their twenties and thirties in a village in Liberia in 2007.

Q: Do men treat women well in this village?
A: Husbands beat women. They say they are lazy and can do nothing.
Q: Do women call the police if they are beaten?
A: No because the husband will have to give permission [for her to call the police]. We advise them to settle it.
Q: And you can't go to the clan court?
A: We are afraid of the expenses.
Q: Do you feel there is no one to protect you from domestic violence?
A: Nobody.
Q: Have you heard of the Community Police Forum?

A: A woman was beaten by her husband and he broke her sewing machine and she went to the Community Forum depot, but the man wanted payment and she said she might as well go to the police.

In domestic violence against women, therefore, we have a serious crime that, despite its frequency, is scarcely policed.

Sexual Abuse and Rape

War only greatly increases what is already a widespread serious crime against women. Rape is committed by both state and nonstate actors, including police, army personnel, and rebels. The trend toward more civil and regional conflicts means civilians are targeted more than ever. It is common in conflicts for women to be the object of sexual mutilation, forced pregnancy, rape, or sexual slavery. The scale of the sexual violence against women in war is appalling. In Rwanda during the 1994 genocide, Tutsi women were subjected to sexual violence on a massive scale, largely by the Hutu militias:

> Although the exact number of women raped will never be known, testimonies from survivors confirm that rape was extremely widespread and that thousands of women were individually raped, gang-raped, raped with objects such as sharpened sticks or gun barrels, held in sexual slavery (either collectively or through forced "marriage") or sexually mutilated. These crimes were frequently part of a pattern in which Tutsi women were raped after they had witnessed the torture and killings of their relatives and the destruction and looting of their homes. According to witnesses, many women were killed immediately after being raped. (Human Rights Watch 1999)

It is estimated by the UNFPA that 60,000 women were raped during the 1994 conflict, two thirds of whom have been infected with HIV/AIDS. In the Democratic Republic of the Congo (DRC), more than 40,000 women and girls were raped by combatants during 2000–2005 (Amnesty International 2004). Women in Burundi suffered widespread rape during the conflict, with an average of 1,346 women a year reporting rape to Médecins sans Frontières between 2004 and 2006 (Amnesty International 2008a). It is thought that in Liberia 60–70 percent of women and girls suffered some form of sexual violence during the conflict (United Nations Division for the Advancement of Women 2006).

It is impossible to calculate the full impact of these crimes. In most contexts, the bearing of a child from rape brings women immense distress and conflict. Sideris (2000, 42) said of women war survivors in Mozambique that "where the social construction of female sexuality places high value on the sexual purity of women, the birth of children conceived by rape is real evidence of violation of their virtue." Similar findings are reported from northern Uganda (Liebling-Kalifani et al. 2007). There is also the issue of damage to women's reproductive ability. The psychological effects and social stigma of not bearing children in Uganda "combine to contribute to the undermining of their sense of self-worth, and the damage to their identity as Baganda women, as well as eradicating from infertile women the power they would normally gain from being mothers" (Liebling-Kalifani 2009). Further, the physical effects of their experiences may also render survivors unable to work due to pain and disability.

The Liberian government has failed to tackle the problem of impunity with regard to the crimes committed during the country's fourteen-year conflict. This is particularly pertinent for those crimes relating to rape and crimes of a sexual nature. Little effort has been made to investigate and document rape and other forms of sexual violence that took place during this time. As a result, there will be no effective basis for eventual prosecution of the alleged perpetrators of those crimes.

The humiliation, pain, and terror inflicted by the perpetrators are meant to degrade not only the individual woman but also the larger group of which she is a part. In some cases, women raped are killed afterward by the perpetrators. Of those who survive rape, some have stated that they were told that they were left alive so that "they might die of sadness." Wars may end, but for women the sadness lives on. For many men, the rape of their wives is a form of humiliation, not only for themselves but also for their ethnic or religious group, leading many husbands and communities to reject the victims and even their children. The stigmatization of victims appears to stem from an attitude that the women must at some level be "responsible" for what happened to them. They are often viewed as shameful or "dirty" because of the type of violence that has been used against them. Women and girls who survive rape are sometimes accused of not having resisted enough, of having somehow consented to sex, or of having cooperated with their attackers. Children who are born from the rape can also face severe discrimination and are often referred to as "the child of the enemy." The consequence of this stigmatization is that the women, having endured sexual brutality and its physical and psychological consequences, in addition find themselves ostracized.

Tragically, protected refugees do not necessarily have freedom from sexual abuse. Government forces commit mass rapes and abuse women in the internally displaced person (IDP) camps, and police regularly rape those in custody. A study carried out by the Uganda government and UNICEF in 2005 in Pabbo, the largest IDP camp in Gulu District, reported that 60 percent of women "are physically and sexually assaulted, threatened and humiliated by the men in whom they have the greatest trust."[4] Survivors speak of the perpetrators of rape, child sexual abuse, and physical assault as ranging from government forces, law enforcement officers, official authorities, local council leaders, spouses, and relatives. Similarly, rapes of women and girls are common in the former buffer zone in western Côte d'Ivoire vacated by international forces after the 2007 peace deal, according to the Truth and Reconciliation Commission (IRC). Women in two towns, Duékoué and Man, complained that they were afraid to go after their attackers because they did not feel supported by law enforcement authorities; the nearest court is 100 kilometers away in Daloa. In response, they had set up neighborhood vigilante groups, although one resident said a recent rape was perpetrated by a youth who belonged to a self-defense group.[5]

As for "normal" life in post-conflict Africa, rape occurs with terrible regularity. Even child rape is widespread, fueled by popular belief that sex with a virgin cures AIDS.[6] Almost 40 percent of Ugandan women aged between fifteen and forty-nine have experienced some form of sexual violence in their lifetime, and 25 percent said their first sexual intercourse was against their will (Uganda Bureau of Statistics [UBOS] 2006). The study also found that rape was often considered a normal part of life. And, the WHO reported in 2005 that in Ethiopia about 17 percent of the women respondents indicated that their first sexual encounter was rape. In Mozambique, a 2006 survey revealed that 54 percent of women admitted suffering an act of physical or sexual violence by a man at some point in their lives, 37 percent in the last five years and 21 percent during the past year (U.S. Department of State, Country Report 2007). The figures suggest, therefore, that nearly one half of all women have experienced sexual violence.

Even allowing for poor police statistics, the figures of reported sexual violence are very high. According to the South African Police Service, in 2000 there were 21,538 rapes and attempted rapes of children under the age of eighteen reported. Children are the victims of 41 percent of all rapes and attempted rapes reported in the country. Over 15 percent of all reported rapes are against children under eleven. In eastern Sierra Leone in 2005, an assistant superintendent of police admitted: "Rape, domestic violence is rampant. It takes supremacy over serious crimes." Across Rwanda in 2006, rape was rising. In Kigali, it had risen to the second-highest category of reported crime, and similar patterns were found in the provinces. Senior police officers described their major challenges as follows: "First the problem of rape" (commander, Kibuye); "Rape and defilement. It is everywhere" (commander, Gitarama Province); "Rape—that is a big thing among the people" (commander, Butare Province); "Our busiest section [in the Central Investigations Department, CID] is gender-based violence. … In other areas there are not high rates of crime, but this is not so for rape and defilement" (deputy head of CID). And, the same story emerges in Liberia. When asked what were the main crime problems they faced in 2007, there was widespread agreement among Liberia National Police

(LNP) commanders that rape was one of them. The NGO Foundation for International Dignity reported that one of the main issues brought to them was "gender violence such as rape." They claimed that although security had improved dramatically since 2005, rape was still a prevalent crime in the east, especially the rape of juveniles.

Whatever the reported statistics, it is certain that there is massive under-reporting of rape. In South Africa, it is reckoned that only one in three rape cases is reported to police.[7] The Lofa County police chief of Liberia says that most incidences of rape and sexual assault are reported to NGOs rather than to the police (Malan 2008, 54). Similarly, although reports from human rights NGOs in Sierra Leone (e.g., Campaign for Good Governance [CfGG] field officers' reports) described rape and domestic violence as very common, the police's nationwide figures for 2004 were only 800 for sexual offenses and 740 for domestic violence.

The bare statistics do not, of course, fully capture the human suffering in every case and the necessity for adequate policing. In all post-conflict societies, women who have endured sexual violence face overwhelming problems because of social stigmatization, poor physical and psychological health, and unwanted pregnancy. In an Integrated Regional Information Networks (IRIN) report from Bujumbura, Burundi, there is an account of women sitting patiently on benches as they wait for assistance at the offices of the League Iteka, a human rights group. Among the ten or so women at the offices, there were the following: There was a young girl "raped by a close family friend—and she is only 13. Now she will have to live with the memory all her life"; an elderly lady "raped by rebel soldiers a few days ago. She is back from hospital to seek more help." A 15-year-old could no longer do basic chores such as washing clothes because a rapist dipped her hands in scalding water. Now pregnant from the rape, she was unable to figure out how she will support her child. A twenty-year-old had been raped, then beaten and left for dead in a gutter. Her body was found by dogs, whose barking attracted the attention of passers-by. Now undergoing psychiatric treatment, she was still traumatized by her ordeal.[8]

What have policing systems got to offer women who have endured discrimination, domestic violence, and sexual abuse in terms of investigation and arrest and punishment of the perpetrators or future protection from a repetition of such abuses?

Nonstate Police Responses to Gender Discrimination

State responses to gender discrimination are weak, either because there is no legislation or because of indifference on the part of a male-dominated police force. But, nonstate policing may not necessarily serve women any better.

Customary chiefs may be the only available policing for many women, yet customary law can be discriminatory, particularly against women. Take the example of Sierra Leone. According to the 2007 U.S. Department of State, Country Report, chiefs in Sierra Leone

> sometimes collude with men to forcibly evict women and children from their homes or subject them to arbitrary detention. In some cases chiefs imposed arbitrary and exorbitant fines, imprisoned women unlawfully in their homes or "chiefdom jails," and expelled them from the community. Their rights and status under customary law varied significantly depending upon the ethnic group to which they belonged, but was routinely inferior to that of men. ... A woman was frequently perceived to be the property of her husband, to be inherited on his death with his other property.

Interviews I conducted in southern Sudan in 2007 revealed that women did not always feel that they were listened to appropriately in all circumstances. They noted that customary courts are presided over overwhelmingly by men, and according to some respondents, those accused of adultery felt judged in advance as guilty. In contrast, it was argued that men could secure divorce on grounds of adultery much more easily than women or if they petitioned for divorce on the grounds of neglect or abuse. In the case of a widow without grown-up male children or one who might object to being inherited by a brother-in-law, there was the real danger of the customary court endorsing the transfer of the property of her deceased husband to members of his family. Generally, little regard is paid to how the woman will be able to raise her children or what is to happen to her. Further, in the outskirts of Juba a group of women complained: "It is all about favoritism. ... They look for one who has money," who is invariably the man. Poor women stonebreakers in Juba agreed that chiefs treat men better: "These things happen; they consider those with money." It is not just the poor who complain. A wealthy woman from Yei acknowledged that in chiefs' courts, "Corruption can intervene. ... Cases die a death after money is given."

Why, then, do customary chiefs still enjoy popular support even among women? Research conducted in Sekhukhune, Northern (now Limpopo) Province, one of the poorest areas of South Africa (Oomen 2002), examined the levels of and reasons for support for customary leaders. It found that people's support is pragmatic, based on the abilities of customary leaders to meet their needs. The research also indicated that people may support and use both customary and civil law structures, depending on their needs.

Despite their obvious weaknesses in policing women regarding discrimination, some customary courts have taken steps to ensure greater justice for women. They have brought women onto court panels, such as in southern Sudan and South Africa. Elsewhere among nonstate policing providers there has been a similar move in recent years to bring forward women into judicial procedures, such as the Ugandan and Rwandan informal local government courts. In Rwanda, these have promoted women members to ensure women are treated equally to men. One *résponsable* claimed in 2006:

> Concerning men who beat their wives: at the *Akarere* level [commune] there is a committee of 10 women who look after the women of that area.

In Uganda, each LC1 has a women's secretary. One such, in a high-density inner suburb of Kampala in 2004, admitted that for a woman to come to the LC1 with a complaint could be difficult: "Some refuse to come. But we press neighbors to come out and tell us. It helps that four of the ten LC members are women." Another in a village said: "Women come to me. My goal is to promote women and to see what can be done as regards development and in home matters. Women have no problem coming to me" concerning "drunkenness—quarrelling with the men who do not buy food or look after the children. I have to tell men their responsibilities—to clothe their children, to take them to school. And HIV is a problem. Promiscuity is high." Asked if the presence of a women's secretary had improved things for women, she responded: "Definitely. Women had no say before. All they could do was go to court."

For their part, NGOs have been active, at least in assisting women to fight discrimination cases and in preventing discrimination through sensitization programs concerning the law.

To take one example, the Uganda Association of Women Lawyers, runs legal aid clinics for women and children. Although they have lawyers available who see clients, they acknowledged to me that

> there may be a relevant law as regards the case, there may not—law doesn't help when a husband has no job to feed his children; when he doesn't pay support. Legally you could jail him, but that would only decrease his helpfulness! So we only go to court as a last resort. Instead we prefer to invite the man complained against to come in and we offer mediation.

Women's groups have been active, not only in cases of sexual violence but also regarding land tenure and challenging customary arrangements that undermine women's status. They argue that although community institutions ideally could improve accountability and efficiency of land law systems,

> the rhetoric about empowering local institutions to administer "customary" land law risks romanticizing or essentializing "community" and "customary" law, assuming the internal politics and hierarchies in communities to be benign, and overlooking potentially inflammatory identity politics and

the sometimes deeply conservative or even reactionary tendencies local communities may contain. (Haugerud 2003, quoted in Tripp 2004, 147)

Women's groups therefore have been active in a variety of land alliances and coalitions that have challenged existing or proposed legislation regarding land tenure laws, such as in Uganda, Mozambique, Eritrea, Namibia, and South Africa (Tripp 2004).

Nonstate Police Responses to Domestic Violence

Despite domestic violence against women being such a widespread and serious problem, the evidence is that post-conflict state criminal justice systems are poorly equipped to respond. Judicial systems are rarely able or willing to handle even the reported cases of abuse. Police often fail to provide women friendly services whenever they fall victims to violence; courts insist unrealistically that victims and witnesses give evidence in public. Police officers also are selective regarding whether they treat a reported case of domestic violence as a criminal offense. Even where state law is clear on domestic violence, it does not necessarily mean that the state police will attend to it unless it has involved serious injury or death. There are male police officers who, confronted with an accusation of wife beating, may not feel it is their business to get involved in another man's "personal affairs." Thus, in Sierra Leone, even as a law was being passed on domestic violence, police statistics for 2006 showed that although 990 women reported domestic violence, in only 153 cases were perpetrators charged, and just 13 of those were convicted (U.S. Department of State, Country Report 2007). As for where the law is not explicit, although there is a clear abuse of human rights, few officers will show an interest. This gendered perspective of state policing has nothing to offer those women who are looking for the provision of care as much as protection.

The good news, however, is that new family support units (FSUs) within police services are beginning to make a difference. For example, in a village in northern Sierra Leone in 2005, although they had their local chief's court "for conflicts between men and women," it had not gone unnoticed that

after the war the police changed. They come to our aid. ... There is an SLP [Sierra Leone Police] officer at the next village. Last week there was a case of domestic violence. The woman came to him, and he sent her to the FSU in Makeni. She had a medical report. Then he brought the husband and wife together!

Likewise, in eastern Sierra Leone, the chairlady of Women's Organizations in Kono, 2005, described a new sympathy among the police toward problems that affect women: "The Family Support Unit handles problems like beating of wives by husbands and rape." Yet, for all their good work in investigating cases of violence against women and children and in community education and sensitization through radio and television programs, the U.S. Department of State Human Rights report for Sierra Leone 2007 still recorded their inadequacy. They lacked "basic infrastructure and communications support, and FSU officers often told female victims of domestic abuse to go back to their families, to the chief, or to simply survive on their own." In Mozambique, also, the police in Maputo operate special women and children's units to provide assistance to victims of sexual abuse and violence and their families. All thirty police squadrons in Maputo had women and children's centers. Outside Maputo, a free phone line ("green line") has been installed to receive complaints of violence against women and children.

How does the response of nonstate policing compare with state policing? The evidence is mixed. In most cases of domestic violence, the woman or her family first tries to reach a settlement with the husband's family. Failing this, it will be taken to the headman of the village or to the state civil law structures if these are perceived to offer in the individual case a better prospect. Chiefs are generally more concerned with finding solutions that will restore peace and harmony to the community than their adversarial counterparts. Their usual practice, in cases of domestic dispute and violence, is to seek reconciliation. Thus, the chief of Po River, in Montserrado County, Liberia, in 2007, faced with cases in his court of "fighting over women; men not satisfied with women; love fears and cheating," did not fine people:

> I advise not fine people ... but normally if I am told a man is beating his wife I go straight to them and tell them stop it! If it's fighting, I address it. If it is aggravated assault, then I have the police informed.

Even if chiefs do hear cases of domestic violence, do they always respond with justice? One rural South African study found that fewer than half of those interviewed felt that customary leaders discriminated against women: 42 percent of women and only 28 percent of men (Oomen 2002, 25). The same study found that although some women thought that customary leaders and customary courts supported them when they experienced violence at the hands of their husbands, others indicated that these institutions did not invariably assist women (2002, 23, 26).

Yet, customary law can be discriminatory, particularly against women. In Sierra Leone, for example, there are regular reports from NGOs like the CGG of serious beatings of wives for which chiefs' courts handed out sentences of small fines or even took no action. With uncertainty over whether the police or customary chiefs will offer justice, many women are faced with a dilemma regarding to whom they should turn. A group of women I spoke to in a village in northern Liberia in 2007 explained that beating women was a problem: "They [husbands] can beat you for nothing"; "Some [women] get beaten hard." As for their redress: "You can complain to the general town chief"; "He will appeal to the man to take the woman to hospital"; "But what is the reason?! It is that women don't respect their husbands!" And, how does this compare with the response of the police? "The police don't investigate"; "They are still beating people to confess!"; "Police brutality is serious."

Having noted some of the weaknesses, it should also be observed that not all customary chiefs are male chauvinists who have no concern about the abuse of women. Indeed, much of their time is taken up with handling "men-women" problems, and it is by no means clear from my observations that male chiefs always side with the male. A village head in northern Sierra Leone told me that one of his village bylaws was "no beating of wives at night." If they did, "It is a 4,000 Leones fine." Chiefs can even be more particular about the statutory law than the police as shown by the following incident that was told to me by a customary chief in Paynesville, a poor suburb of Monrovia in 2007:

> The police use the police station as if it were a court whilst some of the courts are empty! It's better to have less police and have those who are trained, than to have those who will not uphold the law and the Constitution. We have cases where the police mingle with criminals. Yesterday we arrested at 5:45, after the magistrate's court had closed, a man who had threatened his girl-friend. So we took him to the police station to be held in custody until the morning. But he was released in the morning by the commander. Technically he is a fugitive. Then the man went and got a lawyer and sued his girlfriend for theft. The magistrate issued a writ against her to attend a criminal court. I protested that "he is a fugitive!" The commander said I should investigate the girl. I said "no." The police are connected with those who fought the war. The police are falling short of ethics. People should be taught how to protect their rights.

The stereotypical view of chiefs was not true in 2007 in Masvingo Province, southeast Zimbabwe, where they partnered gender activists in a bid to curb domestic violence. It is reported that the Women's Coalition of Zimbabwe has chiefs in all of the province's seven districts actively supporting programs for the eradication of domestic violence.[9] From a village chief's wife, in a village within the Firestone Plantation, Liberia, in 2007, I was told that the chief does not necessarily have the authority to intervene that is imagined. Although it was conceded that one of the main problems that came before the chief's court was of "man beating his wife," she argued that the chief was powerless to act unless "his wife and the man *agree* to come." Even then, "though at times the chief just solves it, some will pay [the fine], some won't."

What about the responses to domestic violence of informal local government policing structures? A female police inspector in Rwanda told me that crimes against women had been:

> a real problem in days gone by. Now it happens but not as much. Problems of fighting occur if the [female] worker is not paid; and domestic violence happens; or a woman is dismissed she may accuse her employer of raping her; or suppose a girl gets pregnant and the boy refuses to accept responsibility, then she may accuse him of rape.

So, why had domestic violence reduced, and who responded when it did occur? "The *nyumbakumi* (lowest level of local government) are expected to do it" unless "a woman is badly beaten, then it goes to the police station." For this, the *nyumbakumi, chef de zones,* and *résponsables* (higher levels of local government) are given training in how to respond. It was clear from the interviews that those local actors took their role seriously. One résponsable reported the following:

> We have tried to use the system of nyumbakumi. If husbands and wives fight, nyumbakumi can try and rescue them. There is a hotline telephone number to deal with these problems. Then they send the police. Such unprovoked crimes are the most serious and are a matter for the police. [And] concerning men who beat their wives: at the Akarere level [commune] there is a committee of ten women who look after the women of that area. A wife [or husband!] can come to them and explain the beating that is going on. It has been put in place in the last two years or so.

Another *résponsable* assured me: "There is a wife beater that I am going to warn that if he continues he will be sent away."

Similarly, NGOs seek to offer help and practical advice to the survivors of domestic violence. An attorney and member of the Association of Female Lawyers of Liberia said in 2007 that besides lobbying for laws that would protect women, they ran a legal aid clinic where women and men could come with their problems: "We try to find an amicable solution; we seek restitution to prevent it going to court." Given that in 2007 there were only 30 or so women lawyers in the country out of a total of 230, this is a sensible policy.

Another NGO that responds to women survivors of domestic violence is the Ethiopian Women Lawyer's Association (EWLA). In addition to advocacy, it provides legal aid in cases of violence against women. It also runs a shelter for women victims of violence—the only shelter for women victims of sexual and domestic violence in Ethiopia. In August 2001, EWLA publicly criticized the Ministry of Justice for its failure to effectively investigate, arrest, and prosecute the known perpetrator in an ongoing case of domestic violence. The response of the minister of justice was to suspend EWLA for allegedly "engaging in activities different from those it was mandated by law" without substantiating its allegations. EWLA's registration and its bank account were frozen. This suspension was finally lifted in October 2001.

Nonstate Police Responses to Sexual Violence

As with domestic violence, sexual violence is a widespread and serious problem that the state criminal justice systems are ill equipped to handle. Even when rape, including spousal rape, is illegal and punishable with imprisonment, successful prosecution is hindered by limited investigative resources, poor forensic capabilities, and an ineffective judicial system. The same police stations and police officers so unsuitable for domestic violence cases are no better for cases of rape. It is no easier for a rape victim than a victim of domestic violence to tell their story in a crowded police station or in a public court. The criminal justice systems offer survivors of sexual violence little in the way of justice, redress, or medical and psychological provision. Police and magistrates regularly demonstrate an unresponsive and uncaring attitude to victims reporting crimes. Further, many prosecutors place a disproportionate emphasis on the completion of a medical report as evidence, while not attempting to secure evidence using other investigatory techniques. Not only is current sexual violence inadequately tackled by state authorities, but also the endemic sexual violence that was committed during the conflict is largely ignored in post-conflict countries, especially when it comes to investigating and prosecuting perpetrators among the state's own security forces. As a result, the rate of successful prosecutions for sexual crimes for current or wartime crimes is very low.

The high level of impunity partly explains survivor's distrust of the state system. As the Ugandan representative of Amnesty International observed: "The vast majority of cases of violence against women are not reported to the police because most victims have lost hope in getting any kind of justice" (2007a). Besides immunity, there are also issues of ignorance of the law and legal procedures and the difficulty of accessing a police station and of finding a police officer to show interest without a bribe. "And adding insult to injury," according to the Amnesty International representative, "the justice system operating in northern Uganda is grossly inadequate in ensuring the protection of these women and girls—almost always allowing the perpetrators to walk free."

Combined, these factors ensure that many victims and their families resort to silence, concluding "it is better to forget the past." In cases, for instance, of incest, in which children are raped by their grandfathers, fathers, and uncles, most are dealt with by the family. In Burundi, for instance, the father will usually settle for something like 60,000 francs (US$60) from the perpetrator to drop the matter of abusing a twelve-year-old. In Kitgum, Uganda, a seventeen-year-old rape victim received 50,000 shillings (US$30) as compensation following a family meeting with the perpetrator and his family (Amnesty International 2007c).

Looking beyond the family, survivors may turn to nonstate policing systems for response if not for protection. Many customary leaders are not willing to handle such serious cases and refer them to the police. Others, however, in disregard of the law, use dispute resolution to negotiate compensation from the perpetrator or the family of the perpetrator. If the victim was previously a virgin, there is a stiff penalty, usually a sum of money, that the perpetrator is supposed to pay to the victim's family and the chief; however, if she was not previously a virgin, a lesser penalty is normally imposed. In some Muslim communities, family pressure is put on the victim to marry the rapist since her chances of getting married are greatly reduced by the fact that she is no longer a virgin. This would seem to further compound the original injustice.

Given the choice between state and customary proceedings, it is little wonder that many rape survivors are uncertain how to proceed. Amnesty International quotes one survivor in Sierra Leone as saying: "I couldn't go to the chief [as] he would not have taken my matter seriously; I didn't go to the local court [as] I had no money. If human rights had not been there I don't know what I would have done. I suppose I would have left it to God" (2005).

If the customary chiefs focus on restitution and compensation, many of the community-based informal policing groups offer retribution of a violent kind. Alleged rapists are summoned to their court or hunted down and then beaten severely. The Ivory Park Peoples Court, Gauteng, South Africa, had a code of punishment that laid down the following penalties: "Rape—Paraded naked before receiving 500 lashes, or execution; … Assault by a man on his wife—50 lashes." This was operating at least until 1998.[10] Other more recent reports demonstrated that such violent retribution continues, and that on occasions, those accused of raping young children have been burned to death by residents or have had their genitals crushed. In a case in KwaMashu, four men had been arrested by the police for serial gang rape and were being taken to be identified by a victim. A mob attacked the police car, dragged these men from it and beat them to death. The latest rape survivor of their crimes said at the scene of the murder: "Thank God he's dead."[11]

Liberian police commanders observed that survivors often prefer to take cases of rape to NGOs rather than the police, and this is true across post-conflict Africa (Malan 2008, 54). For instance, in Bujumbura, Burundi, many women turn to the League Iteka, a human rights group. Located in the city center, the NGO is one of several organizations trying to help victims of sexual abuses. The majority of cases it handles are of sexual violence involving ten- to eighteen-year-old girls. Such NGOs offer legal advice and provide transport if necessary for a public prosecutor to go to the scene of the crime to investigate the case. Others may offer medical and psychosocial services to rape victims. In Angola, the Ministry of Family and the Promotion of Women (MINFAMU) operates a program with the Angolan Bar Association to give free legal assistance to abused women; the ministry also opened counseling centers to help families cope with domestic abuse.

Most NGOs do not handle investigation or prosecution but do work with the police in terms of the provision of medical and psychological help. In Liberia, rape victims are taken to the Christians Children's Fund for medical attention, and the NGO transports them to the Médicin sans Frontières in Monrovia for medical treatment and medical evidence. But, difficulties exist on the ground when trying to follow the law by channeling all rape cases through the state legal system. One NGO in Liberia informed me of the following:

> There is no functional court in Bopolu [county town of Gbarpolu]. There you can't take issues to the court or the police—there is only one police officer. So although issues of rape cannot be mediated [legally], there is no court to go to. So we work with the chiefs. We train chiefs as well. We cannot have two mediation teams. If rape is mediated by them, we report that as unlawful for the rule of law is the basis of stability. … Our concern in reporting it is more to put the spotlight on it so that the state can see the problem. But there are huge issues here.

Again, one sees the problem with criminalizing nonstate policing when there is no state policing to take its place.

Discussion

Although some of the discrimination against women has often been placed at the feet of customary law, women in Africa are not simply passive victims of customary law. They can and do manipulate the relationship between customary law and civil law. "Research indicates that African women very rarely live exclusively in terms of either 'traditional' or 'modern' identities" (Curran and Bonthuys 2004, unnumbered). Rural women who have worked in the cities for a large part of their lives may have multiple perceptions of their identities. Bronstein's argument is that "although culture is integral to the lived reality of people's lives, it does not possess or own its subjects" (1998, 394). These interchangeable traditional and modern identities are also reflected in women's legal strategies. Research from Zimbabwe shows how parents in Zimbabwean community courts "strategically use both 'customary' and 'western' arguments to obtain custody of their children" (Armstrong 1994,

151), using both legal systems interchangeably and pragmatically. Whether women use the civil or the customary mechanisms to claim property or maintenance on divorce or whether they refrain from pursuing any claims often depends on a practical assessment of their positions in the community and the kinds of networks and resources to which they have access (Griffiths 1997, 118–22).

The list of policy recommendations from human rights and feminist NGOs to redress the inadequacies of policing women is long and serious, but there do have to be critical questions about the practicality of their reform strategy. Take Amnesty International's report, *Sierra Leone Women Face Human Rights Abuses in the Informal Legal Sector* (2006). Among other things, it calls on the government of Sierra Leone to end chiefs' abuses and discrimination against women by taking the following actions "without delay":

> Enforce the prohibition of unlawful punishments and other human rights abuses inflicted on women in the name of custom and tradition; Prohibit all violence against women, including "chastisement", as assault and a crime against the person and prosecute the perpetrators; Rape and other sexual violence against women should be treated as offences against the woman … ; Ensure that Family Support Units fulfill their responsibility to protect women against all forms of gender based violence in the family and in the wider community and do not in any way attempt to persuade women to remain in situations where they are subjected to such violence.

Further, it demands that the government

> Ensure that Chiefs, Local Court personnel, the police and formal legal personnel are trained in human rights principles, in particular as they apply to women, including a recognition that VAW [violence against women] is a crime, and that when exercising any mediation functions, they do not use their influence to coerce women to remain in violent or abusive relationships, impose unlawful fees, or attempt to unlawfully adjudicate in matters which should be referred to the police, Magistrates and High courts; Ensure that paralegal and legal aid services are available and accessible on a systematic basis throughout the country, in order to ensure effective access to justice. Strengthen paralegal and legal assistance for women … ; Conduct effective public education throughout society.

Thus, Amnesty International's (2006) whole focus is on the state as the solution to a problem that is largely perceived to be the fault of customary practices—would that it were that simple. Would that discrimination could be willed away by new state legislation.[12] Would that the police would so understand the new and existing statutory law and human rights as to enthusiastically enforce it without favor. Would that governments had the resources to equip and sustain family support units. Would that the discriminating attitudes of male chiefs, police officers, magistrates, and judges could be eradicated by "training." Personally, I am skeptical concerning this faith in state law, state resources, and state training. For post-conflict African states—the poorest in the world—it is a strategy doomed to failure. If every case of discrimination against women and sexual violence against them has to be channeled through the state institutions, they will not be able to cope—either now or in the medium-term future. More fundamentally, if the lives of most women are in practice governed by customary law rather than state law, how can the reform of the latter in Parliament be used to improve the position of women (Armstrong 1995, 5)? We have to find another way of bringing about equity and justice for all rather than relying on the state alone. It has to be a policy that utilizes the resources that already exist in the poorest communities. Somewhere in a practical solution must surely be nonstate policing of women.

The issue of crimes against women brings to prominence what has not been discussed in this book: post-conflict responses to conflict crimes. It is clear that women often experience atrocity and conflict to a far greater degree than men and are left with serious long-term consequences in the post-conflict era. Yet, transitional justice that is established to deal with conflict abuses often neglects women's experience of conflict sexual violence. Far too often, truth commission mandates, judicial opinions, and reparation schemes are written and implemented with little regard for what women have suffered in the conflict. The neglect of the gendered patterns of abuse seriously affects women's access to justice. It does so by limiting the reach of reparations programs, entrenching impunity, distorting the historical record, and undermining the legitimacy of transitional justice initiatives. A policing response to conflict abuses is particularly critical to women's struggles for justice in the post-conflict era (Rubio-Marín 2006a). Reparations are probably the most tangible manifestation to remedy the harms victims have suffered. Yet, official reparation programs will only perpetuate injustice and inequality for women if they fail to insist on prosecuting perpetrators; documenting and acknowledging violations through nonjudicial means such as truth commissions; reforming such abusive institutions as the police and army; and providing reparations to victims. Thus far, official reparations programs have been accused of not being designed with an explicit gender dimension in mind. The issue is not helped by the fact that, as Rubio-Marín pointed out (2006b, 3), the notion of reparation has competing meanings: the compensation of victims for harms endured; the rehabilitation of victims and facilitating a sense of closure on their part; the public recognition to victims for what they have endured or for their condition as equal citizens and rights holders; the reassurance to victims that they will no longer have to face similar violations in the future, including measures to contribute to prevention.[13] The uncertain meaning has led to variable programs. And, which would women want of these alternatives? The contributors to Rubio-Marín's edited collection indicated that, when consulted in the aftermath of conflict about the form of redress that they would favor, many female victims expressed preference for services to meet the basic needs (including medical and psychological provision for themselves, education for children, housing assistance for families) over restitution of lost property or monetary compensation in proportion to the harm experienced. Perceptively, Rubio-Marín framed the question differently. Namely, what are the reasons that may account for differences in expressed preferences? She suggested several competing interpretations: It may be an indicator of women's overall levels of poverty and their seizing of whatever opportunity is provided to meet their basic needs, or it may be an expression of their ignorance concerning their rights of entitlement to compensation and the like (2006b, 4). All the authors, however, agreed that procedural aspects may be just as important as substantive ones in determining whether female victims actually access reparation benefits. Forcing women to "come out" as victims (and to bring with them adequate evidence) to qualify for reparations may have a largely inhibiting effect, especially for victims of sexual violence who hold back because of shame or fear.

Notes

1. It was only in 1998 that rape was recognized as a war crime and a crime against humanity.
2. http://www.actionaid.org/uganda/index.aspx?PageID=1762.
3. *Concord Times,* Freetown, July 1, 2008.
4. Quoted in http://www.crin.org/resources/infoDetail.asp?ID=14554. See UNICEF, 2005, *Suffering in Silence: A Study of Sexual and Gender-based Violence in Pabbo IPD Camp.*
5. IRIN, October 21, 2008, http://www.irinnews.org/Report.aspx?Report Id=81038.
6. Largely unreported is the large number of men who are also victims of sexual violence. Some men in conflict have been subjected to rape in the presence of their wives or children. In the DRC, for instance, although male rape is reported much less frequently than the rape of women, one Congolese activist noted that "the rape of men is much more frequent than you might think. However, it is very difficult for the victims to speak out and condemn the violence to which they have been subjected" (Amnesty International 2004).
7. *Business Day,* Johannesburg, September 23, 2003.
8. IRIN, June 4, 2008.
9. See http://www.wluml.org/english/newsfulltxt.shtml?cmd[157]=x-157-557361.
10. *Sunday Times,* Johannesburg, July 5, 1998.
11. *The Mercury,* October 27, 2006.

12. Since 2007 in Sierra Leone, there have been laws passed outlawing domestic violence and marital rape law; governing intestate succession so that the surviving spouses of either gender are entitled to remain in the family home until they die—husbands and wives inherit property from each other equally, and male and female children inherit equally when a parent dies without a will; prohibiting the ejection of a widow from the home she shared with her husband during marriage; requiring the consent of both parties for a marriage to be lawful; providing for reasonable spousal and child maintenance; removing any necessity for a dowry to be returned on divorce.

13. See Human Rights Resolution 2005/35, Basic *Principles and Guidelines on the Right to a Remedy and Reparation for Victims of Gross Violations of International Human Rights Law and Serious Violations of International Humanitarian Law*, E/CN.4/2005/L.48, April 13, 2005.

Fitting Nonstate Policing into Security Reform

8

Introduction

Security sector reform (SSR), or security system reform, is an approach that is widely used in assisting countries to make the transition from conflict to sustainable development. Its focus is all those institutions, groups, organizations, and individuals, whether state or nonstate, that have a stake in the security provision. In general terms, SSR aims to ensure that the security providers respect human rights; that they are responsive to the security concerns of citizens; that public safety is enhanced by raising the effectiveness of the security services; and that all citizens, including the most vulnerable, are served (Nathan 2007, 37). Put another way, its intention is that the security sector will be managed and operated in a manner that is consistent with democratic norms and principles of good governance. In terms of policing in particular, the aim is to provide security to citizens in a manner consistent with human rights and the rule of law and an effective system of democratic regulation and oversight of policing providers.

In most post-conflict countries, "SSR has been forced on states by external forces, either as part of the process of rebuilding societies torn by conflict, or as part of a process of fiscal reform (or both)" (Hutchful and 'Kayode Fayemi 2005, 71). Exceptions would be Mali and the largely indigenous SSR programs of Ethiopia, Eritrea, and South Africa.

One of the major international players engaged in SSR in post conflict Africa is the United Nations due to its international legitimacy, neutrality, and peacekeeping mandates. Its multidimensional peacekeeping missions now commonly have an explicit role to undertake reconstruction and reform of the security and justice sector (see Table 8.1). In particular, the United Nations is well established in police reform, with a specific headquarters (Department of Peacekeeping Operations, Police Division) and field resources (UN Police, UNPOL) available for UN support to police reform. According to Hänggi and Scherrer:

> Police reform constitutes the most substantive SSR-related activity assisted by UN integrated missions. Reforming or restructuring the police is one of the most consistent roles attributed to the UN, present in all peace operations which are implicitly or explicitly mandated to carry out SSR related activities. (2008, 17)

Table 8.1   UN Security Council Africa Mission Mandates

UNAMSIL: United Nations Mission in Sierra Leone

Security Council Resolution (SCR) 1436 (September 2002): "To strengthen the operational effectiveness of the security Sector"

MONUC: United Nations Mission in the Democratic Republic of Congo

SCR 1493 (August 2003): "Reform of security forces"

UNMIL: United Nations Mission in Liberia

SCR 1509 (September 2003): "Support for security reform"

ONUB: United Nations Operation in Burundi

SCR 1545 (May 2004): "Provide advice and assistance to the Government to contribute to their efforts to carry out institutional reforms as well as the constitution of the integrated national defence and internal security forces"; "to complete implementation of the reform of the judiciary and corrections system"

MONUC: United Nations Mission in the Democratic Republic of Congo

SCR 1565 (October 2004): Assist with "security sector reform, including the integration of national defence and internal security forces together with disarmament, demobilization and reintegration and, in particular, the training and monitoring of the police, while ensuring that they are democratic and fully respect human rights and fundamental freedoms"

UNIOSIL." United Nation's Integrated Office in Sierra Leone

SCR 1620 (August 2005): "Strengthening the Sierra Leonean security sector"; "to liaise with the Sierra Leonean security sector and other partners"

BINUB: United Nations Integrated Office in Burundi

SCR 1719 (October 2006): "Support for the development of a national plan for reform of the security sector"

UNOCI: United Nations Operation in Côte d'Ivoire

SCR 1721 (November 2006): "Seminars on security sector reform"

MONUC: United Nations Mission in the Democratic Republic of Congo

SCR 1756 (May 2007): "Importance of urgently carrying out security sector reform"

Source: Based on Hänggi and Scherrer, 2008, 9.

UNPOL (together with the United Nations Development Programme [UNDP]) provides police training and advises governments and senior police management on police management structures; operating procedures, vetting, and certification of personnel; and monitoring and mentoring police officers. In some cases, police equipment is provided through UNDP, and in some missions UN police officers work alongside national police on patrols, such as UNMIL (UN Mission in Liberia).

State Building

Security sector reform rests on the assumption that post-conflict states in Africa are weak and fragile and therefore unable to offer development to their own citizens and, more importantly for the international community, unable to protect others from the terrorists they might harbor.[1] The near-universal solution offered to the problems of fragile states is the state-building agenda, which focuses on strengthening state institutions, particularly security institutions. State building is about enhancing the capacities of state actors for control, regulation, and implementation, particularly in the core fields of statehood, namely, internal security, basic social services, the rule of law, and legitimacy of government (Call and Wyeth 2008; Fukuyama 2004; Chesterman, Ignatieff, and Thakur 2005; United Nations Development Programme/United States Agency for International Development [UNDP/USAID] 2007). State building, said the Organization for Economic Cooperation and Development (OECD), "is the central objective of international engagement in fragile states" (2008, 7). Likewise, Lakhdar Brahimi, former special adviser to the UN secretary general, asserted: "Statebuilding is unapologetically seen as the central objective of any peace operation" and "all international protagonists" should "serve that objective" (2007, 4). The intensity of their argument is due to the belief that state building is the way to legitimate the state. And, given that they see justice, security, and policing as foundational state activities, they cannot conceive a legitimate state other than one that is performing these functions. "In the new millennium," noted Fritz and Menocal, "state-building has become a leading priority for the international development community" (2006, 4). Thus, the Department for International Development (DFID) spoke of "the centrality of states within development" (2008, 3) and of the donor's role as being to "enhance their ability to function" (2008, 4). Similarly, the OECD said that the overall aim must be to support the building of "effective and legitimate states able to fulfill key international responsibilities and to provide core public goods and services, including security" (2008, 3). It is hard to disagree with the conclusion that "the generally accepted view" is that the "re-establishment of a strong government is essential to rebuilding failed states" (François and Sud 2006, 153).

By state building, of course, advocates mean building a state along the lines of the Western OECD state model (Hameiri 2007, 138). It is this model that is seen as the best means of sustainable development and peace. Yet, this goal is easier to set down on paper than to achieve. It means nothing less than to build a form of statehood that hardly exists in reality beyond the OECD world.

> Most African states have never had effective institutions, relying instead on the personalized networks of patronage. ... They have more often been instruments of predation and extraction than tools for the pursuit of public goods. In vast parts of Africa, state failure is less an objective condition than a permanent mode of political operation. (Englebert and Tull 2008, 110)

In these circumstances, the value of considering post-conflict African states as being "not yet properly built" or as "having failed to deliver core state services" has to be questioned. "Failure," "weakness," and "fragility" are normative statements, based on the view that OECD states represent the required standard. Yet, the "healthy" Western version "has little relevance to most of the states in question because it has simply never existed there" (Boas and Jennings 2005, 388).

Is it any surprise, therefore, that the almost universal conclusion of studies and reports on post-conflict state building in the security and justice sector is that little has been achieved? Call and Cousens admitted that efforts to build security institutions have not been "especially encouraging" (2007, 8–9). Englebert and Tull argued that the results of UN peace operations in Africa "have been paltry, particularly as regards the establishment of self-sustaining state institutions" (2008, 106). Despite large investment of resources, the World Bank admitted that "the numerous rule of law assistance programs in post-conflict or fragile countries have so far resulted in few lasting consequences" (Samuels 2006, 15).

State-building programs and the security and justice sector reform within them have, then, "tended to focus on the state itself ... [on] helping build the capacity of state institutions to provide the core functions" (Eyben and Ladbury 2006, 4). They rarely take into account the main players in the sector, namely, nonstate ones. "The tendency of reconstruction programs to dismiss the contributions of indigenous institutions—such as self-help associations, churches, NGOs [nongovernmental organizations], and other grassroots organizations—alienates citizens from the rebuilding of their states and undermines democratic accountability" (François and Sud 2006, 148). Consequently, SSR has rarely been able to "create change in social organization at grass roots level" (Chandler 2006, 76). While programs have struggled to build new institutions, they have ignored local policing structures. "Yet, traditional and local authorities may be key channels for public service delivery as well as critical actors in re-establishing post-war stability and social reconciliation" (Call and Cousens 2007, 9).

Take, for example, SSR in Burundi. Both the UN Security Council and the Peacebuilding Commission wanted improved internal security in the country and pinned their hopes on the United Nations Operation in Burundi (ONUB) undertaking a reform, inter alia, of the police services. The Arusha peace agreement and the subsequent cease-fire agreements stipulated that a national police service should be created through the integration of (1) former rebels; (2) former members of the policing services (the 2,500 within the prosecutorial judicial police under the Ministry of Justice; the public security police under the Public Security Ministry; and the Police of the Air, Borders, and Foreigners under the Public Security Ministry; (3) the former Burundi Armed Forces (FAB); (4) and the 5,000-strong gendarmerie. This integrated force was to come under the Ministry of the Interior and Public Security.

Hindered by inadequate resources, ONUB focused on the reestablishment of institutional structures and capacities. The newly created national police (Police National du Burundi, PNB) grew to 17,000, but training proved difficult since not only was it brief, but also the Burundian officers lacked basic education and spoke only Kirundi and some French (whereas the majority of UNPOL officers were Anglophone). In addition, trainers were internationals with police experience rather than pedagogic skills. For all their claims that by December 2006 "progress had been made," Banal and Scherrer admitted that "it is questionable whether they can be considered viable security forces in the sense of a public service provider that provides equal access to all" (2008, 33). They described a national police that is

> less efficient, coherent and reliable than the FAB. The police lack core funds for uniforms and training centres, and rely on weapons recovered from the former FAB, thus contributing to its loss of credibility in the eyes of the population. The police force is also regularly accused by the local population and human rights organisations of perpetrating acts of torture and frequent human rights violations, and of being distinctly corrupt. (2008, 39)

These failures of reform in the new Burundi police force are blamed on the United Nation's "lack of a comprehensive SSR concept and strategy" and its "limited human and financial resources" (Banal and Scherrer 2008, 46)[2] together with a Burundian government that never accepted local ownership (it did "not want to approach SSR holistically") (2008, 54). Nowhere in Banal and Scherrer's account is there an acknowledgment of the customary structures, the *bashingantahe* (customary courts), which provide most of the safety and security in Burundi. Indeed, they are not part of the security sector in the Burundian SSR view of things, even though half of all returnees who have sought outside assistance in disputes have approached and used their customary dispute resolution institution (Huggins et al. 2005).

Burundi only too clearly illustrates the ineffectiveness of state-centric policies. In their defense, SSR advisers are only following expert prescriptions. Etannibi Alemika is a respected police researcher in Africa. He is in no doubt that security is related to democratic transition and economic development in Africa. Yet, as many other experts, his hope rests entirely on the state police to provide this security:

> Without effective, efficient, responsive, representative and accountable police forces, democratic transition and economic development in African nations may stagnate or regress. African countries need to develop and implement comprehensive police reform measures that will promote democracy, good governance, economic development, safety and security. (Quoted in Geyer 2008, 1)

Alemika, of course, faces a dilemma. Although he asserts the need for "citizens to go back to basics to understand and construct security systems appropriate to their needs and to constitute them within a rights framework," he admits that governments are in no financial position "to provide the necessary services to citizens."[3] Yet, his dilemma is of his own making. It is because he is locked into a state-centric view of policing that he cannot see how the priority of citizens for security can be met. Another respected African researcher, Nicole Ball, set out her desire as to increase "a country's ability to meet the security and justice needs of its people in a manner consistent with democratic norms and sound principles of governance, transparency and the rule of law," yet her solution is the reform of the state security services (IDASA 2007).

Hybrid Governance

An alternative approach to viewing African states as failing and in need of state building would be to view them as following a very different governance model. It would recognize that across much of postcolonial Africa it is nonstate authorities that are those primarily responsible for the distribution of public goods. As Boege et al. argue, "It might be theoretically and practically more fruitful to think in terms of hybrid political orders" (Boege et al. 2008, 2); "hybrid" not only implying parallel state and nonstate forms of order and governance arising from different societal sources and following different logics but also recognizing a mutual influence that creates a distinct political order of its own. Chabal similarly speaks of the postcolonial state in Africa as one with a structure that is composed of "overlapping layers of formal and informal spheres of power ... [with a] clientelistic" and neopatrimonial foundations (Chabal 2006, 1).

In other words, "the processes and institutions freely associated with Western experiences of democracy may easily co-exist with social and political relations and practices which may continue much as before" (Roberts 2008, 71). It is one, says Scheye (unpublished manuscript), that "blurs distinctions between public and private, state institution and civil society, public good and private benefit, all of which underpin the foundations of the Western state-building agenda." Many postcolonial states have retained "indigenous mechanisms of socio-legal and political organization from their own historical experiences" since these "are considered more appropriate" than those offered by international donors (Roberts 2008, 79). This understanding that there exists in much of the postcolonial world a very different political order compared to the Western experience, one that is a clientelistic state based on a hybrid form of government, has a long history (Ekeh 1975; Clapham 1982;

R. Jackson and Rosberg 1982; P. Lewis 1992; Sklar 1993; Bratton and van de Walle 1997; Sandbrook 1998; Boone 2003; Engel and Erdmann 2007).

In this postcolonial context, it is not just the institutions that are different:

> People do not perceive themselves as citizens or nationals (at least not in the first place). They define themselves instead as members of particular sub- or trans-national social entities (kin group, tribe, village). This is particularly true where state agencies are not present on the ground and the state does not deliver any services with regard to education, health, infrastructure or security. Rather, it is the community that provides the nexus of order, security and basic social services. People have confidence in their community and its leaders, but they have no trust in the government and state performance. "The state" is perceived as an alien external force, far away not only physically (in the capital city), but also psychologically. Individuals are loyal to "their" group (whatever that may be), not the state. As members of traditional communities, people are tied into a network of social relations and a web of mutual obligations, and these obligations are much more powerful than obligations as a "citizen". People do not obey the rules of the state, but the rules of their group. Legitimacy rests with the leaders of that group, not with the state authorities—or only with state authorities insofar as they are at the same time leaders in a traditional societal context, e.g. a minister who is also a tribal chief (and warlord), and who became a minister in the first place because of being a tribal chief (and warlord). (Boege et al. 2008, 10)

As this book has sought to demonstrate, there are many orders at the substate level in post-conflict Africa, each enforced by its own policing. The state does not have a privileged position as the political framework that provides security. It has to share authority, legitimacy, and capacity with other structures. Those orders may overlap in cooperation and competition. It may be that the state has hardly penetrated society. But even where there are parts of country with minimal state policing presence, there will be a social order that is policed to some degree. It should not be imagined that the lack of the state means anarchy; rather, it means different institutions that set and police order.

The strategy required, in my opinion, is not a state-building one that presumes the state to be the only actor but a strategy that recognizes the postcolonial diversity and hybrid nature of political power. In this historical context, I argue that the only way to deliver policing is through utilizing the existing providers at the nonstate level, whether they be customary, community based, commercial, or informal. Such mediation of security services through nonstate providers does not follow the ideal type of "proper" state institutions. To persist in holding to the state-centric paradigm and its normative position about the necessity for a state monopoly of violence will only bring disappointment. It is to build SSR on two false assumptions: that the

African state is able to deliver policing to a majority of its population and that it is even the principal actor in policing provision.

A sense of the impossibility of the task being undertaken by the state single-handedly resonates in the words of General Antoine Gambi, who leads SSR in the Central African Republic (CAR). He argued in 2008 that highway bandits (*zaraguina*) could not be tackled because the state security forces "aren't strong enough to provide security across the country." For the job to be done by his few urban-based forces, he would need helicopters to drop troops into zones where the *zaraguina* were active. Even as he said this, the UN humanitarian coordinator in CAR was saying: "What you need to do is empower the police, the gendarmerie and army as well as the justice system so that the country can be controlled within the letter of the law."[4] More helicopters, more police training, more law enforcement? How long will these requirements take to achieve, and how will the enlarged state police service be sustained? The truth is that the CAR security forces are not going to be able to tackle banditry in the short or medium term by themselves. Yet, if "fragile" post-conflict states are reconceptualized as "hybrid" political orders, new options for governance can be envisaged—ones in which security is not the sole prerogative of the state, ones that are multilayered. These would recognize not only the layer of the state but also that of the commercial, community based, customary, and informal provision.

Multilayered Policing Governance

Rather than trying to eradicate hybrid political orders, it would be more appropriate, in my view, to work with the reality of multiple authorities and maximize their strengths and minimize their weaknesses. I believe, therefore, that the starting point of reform should not be who *should* be providing policing so much as who *is* providing it, and not how state capacity can be built, but discerning what sort of service is actually being provided. In other words, the first step is an audit of security providers to understand what is available, how good are they, and is there any support that can be given to improve and strengthen them? The focus on actual providers, whatever their relationship to the state, goes with the proviso that they are reformable. Hutchful and 'Kayode Fayemi made the pertinent point that "the intent behind some approaches to SSR seems, consistent with the term 'reform', to be a re-engineering of often decrepit and discredited institutions and a re-centering of the state in the security system" (2005, 86). Their principle of not reforming the unreformable should be applied to all.

Security reform is surely right to emphasize a "people-centered and locally owned" point of view, with the actual experience of the citizen in mind. If that is treated seriously, then the range of available policing providers immediately broadens. Looking beyond state policing to nonstate as well offers at least the possibility for states actually to deliver effective safety and security to all their citizens, rich and poor, urban and rural. The evidence provided in other chapters shows that according to the crime and disorder that threatens them and the location in which they find themselves, people look to different policing agencies for protection and response. In post-conflict states and indeed most developing states, their choices, inasmuch as they have them, are based on "what is available," "what works best," "what supports my personal values," and "what can I afford" more than issues of who controls the agency and to whom are they accountable. People shop around for the type of policing they want. From the perspective of the users of policing providers, *public* and *private* do not exist as straightforward terms. Public does not mean to them what SSR program managers mean for public policing in practice very often fails to serve all equally and it is not (bribe) free (Clapham 1999). I have not found in my research evidence of a presumption by people that public policing must be better than the private (contra Goldsmith 2003, 9).

The everyday policing experience of people in post-conflict states, therefore, is of a degree of alternative and overlapping networks. Yet, it cannot be assumed that these networks are cooperative networks or that the state police are the dominant node within them. It may be that the relationships are competitive rather than cooperative, and that the state police are marginal in particular contexts and geographic spaces. What is true is that in any situation there are often a number of policing agencies, nonstate and state, offering localized protection of different levels of legality, effectiveness, availability, methods, and services.

Moving from the perspective of people to the perspective of security sector reformers, it would transform the approach if the program were to recognize the multiple layering of policing providers that form a continuum that only toward the margins of the range can be readily delineated as state or nonstate. Equally significant would be the recognition of the existent and potential linkages between state and nonstate nodes of security provision. In Africa, there is frequently found a "systemic balance and linkage between the sovereign state authority and the 'second state' through constitutional dispensations, which define specific modes of incorporation" (Düsing 2002, 36). From this foundation, a multilayered approach to the support of policing providers can be designed. The approach identifies at least four layers of policing providers below the state: commercial, customary, NGO, and informal sector policing providers. All can be considered as potential providers and partners worthy of support.

The realization of the need for a multilayered approach is just beginning to penetrate practitioners' articles and handbooks, although it has yet to be implemented on any significant scale. In 2004, Abrahamsen and Williams were still being told by the DFID that commercial security "is not integrated into SSR in Sierra Leone" (2006, 10), and in Liberia in 2007 I was being told by the government adviser to the SSR review that, as regards the customary structures, "they have not even featured in the SSR debate. The donors don't want to consider it." Evidence of change back at headquarters, however, is manifest. Thus, the OECD *Handbook on SSR* argues that SSR will be enhanced if SSR programs

> consider the need for a multi-layered or multi-stakeholder approach. This helps target donor assistance to state and non-state justice and security providers simultaneously, at the multiple points at which actual day-to-day service delivery occurs. A multi-layered strategy helps respond to the short-term needs of enhanced security and justice service delivery. ... Evidence suggesting that in sub-Saharan Africa at least 80 per cent of justice services are delivered by non-state providers should guide donors, encouraging them to take a balanced approach to supporting state and non-state provision, while understanding and respecting the context in which these services are being supplied. (2007, 17)

Likewise, according to DFID's *Safety, Security and Access to Justice Programmes*: "The approach to the security sector has to be comprehensive in nature, taking into account the main actors of the security sector and their functions; namely, all jurisdictions with a capacity to use force, both statutory and nonstatutory" (Law 2006, 2). Again, the World Bank's Conflict Prevention and Reconstruction Unit has argued that "in post-conflict countries where the formal mechanisms have completely disappeared or been discredited ... informal mechanisms may be crucial to restoring some degree of law and order" (Samuels 2006, 18). Such a multilayered strategy, based on an understanding that the post-conflict state may not be the majority provider of justice and security, is not a strategy of abandoning support for the state providers of policing. Instead, it is one that offers to support both them and the nonstate layers of security provision. Programs that support "either state or non-state institutions, one to the exclusion of the other, are unlikely to be effective" (OECD 2007, 17). It appears misguided to focus the *majority* of SSR effort on reforming the police when the concern is to improve the experience of policing of all citizens. Prioritizing state and capacity building ahead of the provision of safety, security, and justice when the post-conflict state is incapable of delivering justice and security to a majority of its population seems bound to end in failure. Instead of impossible dreams regarding the policing that the state's security agencies can provide and ill-founded dismissals of nonstate security systems, it is wiser to begin actively developing an entire spectrum of unique partnerships and associations between state and nonstate systems. What is needed is for a security model in which the emphasis rests on the quality and efficacy of the policing received by the end user regardless of who delivers that policing. Experience shows, said Boege et al.,

> that attempts at state-building which ignore or oppose hybridity will encounter considerable difficulty in generating effective and legitimate outcomes. Strengthening central state institutions is unquestionably important, but if this becomes the main or only focus it threatens to further alienate local societies by rendering them passive, thereby weakening both a sense of local responsibility for overcoming problems and local ownership of solutions. (2008, 11)

Once we understand exactly *who* it is that provides the majority of safety, security, justice, and policing; *what* most Africans in post-conflict states want; and *how* it is beyond the resources of post-conflict states to provide a monopoly of policing nationwide, the state-centric approach becomes untenable. For the sake of ensuring that SSR has local ownership, organizational attainability, financial affordability, long-term sustainability, and effective security accomplishments, it needs to be inclusive of state *and* nonstate. SSR cannot afford to remain confined to the state policing services alone.

The Value of Nonstate Policing to SSR

Local Ownership

As every handbook on SSR says (OECD 2007; Nathan 2007) and as every donor policy statement on the subject reiterates (OECD 2005b; DFID 2004, 2006, 11–14), for SSR to be effective there has to be in-country support or "local ownership." The purpose of police reform, according to the conference delegates at the annual IDASA conference in 2008, is that it should

> create an institution that is owned by the citizens of that state and serves their dreams and desires for a safe society that can enable development and improve the lives of the people who live in that country in real terms. (Geyer 2008, 2)

Yet, according to many (Nathan 2007; OECD 2005b; Scheye and Peake 2005), a major problem in SSR in Africa has been the *lack* of local ownership. In practice:

> The principle is often very difficult to apply, it is frequently breached by donor governments and it has not been translated into a set of donor strategies and methods of working in the field. As currently conceived, local ownership is more of a rhetorical device than a guide to donor officials engaged in SSR. (Nathan 2007, 4)

For instance, donor influence in, or oversight of, SSR "has been almost total, directly so in the case of Sierra Leone or indirectly in the case of Guinea-Bissau" (Hutchful and 'Kayode Fayemi 2005, 82).

Local ownership as a concept is usually limited in practice to the ownership of the government, national politicians, and national civil society. It often ignores citizen ownership and overlooks countrywide diversity. Too often, as reported in Afghanistan, "local ownership clearly means 'their' ownership of 'our' ideas" (Suhrke 2007, 1292). It rarely spends much time concerned with local ownership at the level of delivery. Yet, as Nathan perceptively observed, local ownership of SSR

> is misconstrued if it is understood to mean that there must be a high level of domestic support for donor activities. *What is required is not local support for donor programmes and projects but rather donor support for programmes and projects initiated by local actors.* The actual reform of the security sector must be shaped and driven by local actors. (Nathan 2007, 8; italics in the original).

The intent is to win consent at the strategic decision-making level rather than at the grassroots level of implementation (e.g., OECD 2007, 73). The aim is to reach consensus among those who will drive it forward, namely, the executive branch of governments and donors.

Whatever the dynamics of acknowledged failure of local ownership at this national state level,[5] at the grassroots level there are two reasons why a state-centric SSR program fails to secure local ownership. First, a program that ignores local and preferred security networks and promotes the state police based in the main cities is seen as domination and paternalism. It is something imposed by external actors—and the capital-based state is as much external as a "foreign" donor in most of rural Africa. Externality "generates resentment, resistance and inertia among local actors. Local actors have little commitment to externally imposed products; these products do not adequately reflect local needs, dynamics and resources" (Nathan 2007, 5). Second, in post-conflict Africa it may well be that the state has little legitimacy, and it is very likely that the police have none. If, as the Commonwealth Human Rights Initiative argued, the Ugandan government "has used illegitimate influence to militarise the police, shoring up its own power, and ensuring that the police are an extension of its partisan politics" (2006, 43), then the police stand or fall with that government. Neither may have a track record for providing security; indeed, they may be known for the *in*security they have caused. That being so, a security sector program that is implemented by the state using the police alone is not guaranteed a welcome in many communities. Neither elections for the state nor reforms for the police will necessarily have removed the suspicion and fear of these powerful organizations in the minds of the poor.

However extensive the reform of a policing institution, if there are questions about its legitimacy in the eyes of the people, it is always going to struggle to offer effective policing. This is precisely the problem that many post-conflict state police services face. Carothers's comments on state law are pertinent: "Law is a normative system that relies on the understanding and support of the citizens and its strength depends on how citizens value and use the law" (2003, 8). If a significant number regard their justice and security system as alien, contrary to their cultural values, there is little likelihood of the system being regarded as legitimate. It will take a long time to win back the support of a citizenry that has a well-grounded suspicion based on half a century of abuse. Far from being the obvious solution to post-conflict Africa's security needs, many would say that the *state* police are unsuited for the task. This is certainly true as long as their culture remains one of existing to protect the regime and where the notion of the police as an agency responsible for even-handed service delivery to a wider citizenry is incomprehensible to that organization.

In the light of this discussion, it should be obvious how valuable local nonstate policing could be in a program of reform in the security sector. It offers the opportunity for an SSR program to support and enhance policing services that are actually functioning locally and that people know and use. Ironically, many recipient governments and donors are reluctant to provide support to these local policing networks on the grounds that they are deemed culpable of abuses and corruption and inadequately accountable. Yet, there is little point offering SSR if all the actors in the sector are already operating full democratic policing. There would be nothing to reform. Policing reform is allegedly part of a democratizing project; it should hardly expect the recipients to be already democratic in all their actions and processes (Nathan 2007, 17). As Neild argues, "Police reforms are dependent on and not a determinant of democracy" (2000, 35). It is the *failings* of the state police that are used to garner support for reforming them; there is no reason, therefore, why the same argument should not be valid for supporting the reform of the actual policing providers—nonstate police. As long as support for such local organizations is not strengthening repressive and abusive policing but moving them toward more democratic policing, then the case for including them within the SSR process is irresistible. Further, they actually add to the likelihood of the reform process being successful by providing locally owned policing. Any assistance and improvement offered to them will almost certainly be locally supported.

Organizational Attainability

Another concern of states and donors is that SSR programs be organizationally attainable, as opposed to being so complex that they falter amid the other pressing tasks of post-conflict reconstruction. Yet, SSR is anything but simple, especially when finance and skills are in short supply and the task involves not only management change but also culture change. Turning around the security sector is akin to turning round a huge oil tanker. It includes, at the very least, the transformation (or construction from scratch) of management structures, financial flows and accounting practices, behavioral patterns, training courses, equipment, oversight bodies, and the habit of political interference—and this at every level and across competing and diverse internal security organizations. It may well be true that in the long term the most effective SSR frameworks "should be multi-sectoral, combining a broad range of diplomatic, legal, social, economic, security and political instruments" (OECD 2007, 67), but did the authors of this prescription consider the immensity of carrying this out? In the final analysis, complex police reform has to be accomplished in post-conflict Africa using personnel with high degrees of illiteracy, who are undertrained, who have little computing or communications equipment, and whose only experience may have been in an abusive police force or rebel army. SSR is a massively complex task (Geyer 2008, 19). Not only will a large number of policies have to be transformed (perhaps radically), but many of these policies will have to be changed simultaneously. Managing such complex transformation can be overwhelming to a new government with little or no experience in running a state, with limited resources, faced with volatile transitional politics, and operating in a country where the penetration of the state into society is minimal. Is it any wonder that a post-conflict government may lack a comprehensive national policing strategy, let alone a realistic plan of action for the implementation of police reform? Reform of the state police is a worthy cause and a necessary cause, but it is not a simple and fast solution to the security needs of Africa's post-conflict peoples. Far from police reform being the obvious or even a quick route to internal security provision, weak states and short-term donors are faced with a raft of issues to address before the state police will be suitable even in small numbers for public service. While a long-term strategy is pursued, who will provide policing for the current generation and probably the next?

For the sake of ensuring that SSR is organizationally attainable, I would argue that it needs to include local nonstate policing as well. In the name of realism, the skills and resources of some of the existing nonstate policing networks need to be utilized.

Here are networks that are already in every village and township and around every economically valuable location; here are structures that do not need funding; here are organizations with people in place with experience. Building on what currently exists, even if the intention is in time to replace them with something provided by the state, makes practical sense.

Financial Sustainability

Finance inevitably looms large over schemes to provide enhanced security for citizens through the reform of the state police. Post-conflict states have severe fiscal restraints. Their finances are overcommitted and dependent on uncertain revenue streams. Hence, setting up new police forces with the implications in terms of training, equipment, and accommodation, let alone sustaining the new force at those levels, is extremely problematic, as was found in Haiti (Mendelson-Forman 2006). Financial auditing of police forces also is not a very transparent process in Africa. Taxpayers are invariably left uncertain regarding where the substantial money spent on the police service has gone. What is clear, from the regularity of bribes demanded by many police in post-conflict Africa, is that salaries are very low and not always paid. Cost-effectiveness is not a widespread characteristic of most African police services. It might be thought that SSR programs in Africa will simply be largely paid for by the donors promoting it, but on the contrary, a survey found that underfunding was "true of virtually all instances" of SSR programs (Hutchful and 'Kayode Fayemi 2005, 84).

The scale of the financial problem is sometimes overwhelming because, with their limited receipts and donor assistance, states are faced not only with restoring or reconstructing state policing structures after conflict but also with establishing a new state system. In the case of southern Sudan, public finances are severely restricted since revenues from oil, which comprise over 90 percent of the government income, are currently significantly lower than anticipated. Here, as elsewhere, there is serious doubt about whether the finances can be found to support a state policing system that will provide a national network available to all the population in the current generation or the next. Despite the justice sector development programs they have devised, the international community working in southern Sudan knows the design is "unsustainable." A police advisor with years of experience in southern Sudan told me that it was unrealistic to attempt to establish a police service that would "cover south Sudan. ... [It] would be impossible. You couldn't do it." In his opinion, the best that can be achieved, after thirty years, is the establishment of a state police service working primarily in the former "garrison towns," leaving most of "the population of southern Sudan with no contact with the [state] police." The accuracy of his assertion was reflected in the 2007 estimated budget of approximately $50 million of the southern Sudan Police Service (SPSS). Salaries for the twenty thousand strong (some say ten thousand) service consume nearly 88 percent. Operating and capital costs are both projected to be 6 percent, with only 1 percent allocated for fuel and vehicle maintenance, restricting the police to urban centers. In such circumstances, the police service will remain undertrained, underequipped, and essentially paralyzed because of the lack of operating funds.

For southern Sudan and elsewhere, there do not appear to be the financial resources from the government and donors to put a state system in place in the foreseeable future. Matters also have not been helped by reduced public spending under pressure from structural adjustment programs. This has affected not only social welfare, education, and capital investment but also public security provision. There is, therefore, considerable reason to be uncertain regarding whether the security systems being installed will be sustainable or have an appreciable effect on enhancing security delivery (Sedra 2007). Against this financial background, it is surely in the interests of all to look again at the nonstate sector, which requires minimal financial support. As Samuels observed, nonstate providers "may be more effective and less costly" (2006, 18). In other words, there is a need to evaluate the contribution that the existing policing providers might make since they will remain sustainable after the donors have reached donor fatigue and disappeared. SSR literally cannot afford to remain confined to the state policing services alone.

Human Resources Capacity

Too often, SSR miscalculates the human resources available to post-conflict states to design and implement police reform programs. Governments in post-conflict countries usually lack the people with the requisite knowledge, expertise, and skills and the required equipment to staff all the security institutions and agencies. The state's political instability, extreme poverty, and war-torn economy and social fabric make policing crucial and, at the same time, elusive. Few would presume that their fragility is only a short-term condition. A DFID-sponsored study suggested that sectorwide approaches to justice and security programs were not yet achievable in fragile states, partly due to serious shortfalls of human capital (Stone 2005, 20). For some, the answer to low numbers is simply that SSR "may have to be accompanied by increases in the costs of at least some types of uniformed forces" (Brzoska and Heinemann-Gruber 2004, 10). Yet, simply increasing numbers raises again the issue of sustainability of staff and equipment levels. In these circumstances, existing networks of nonstate policing organizations have their attractions. They offer the opportunity of the focus of SSR to shift from building state policing institutions to creating the conditions that will make effective policing possible.

Yet, human resources are not simply a matter of professional training and experience. The role of local communities can be easily undervalued, just as the importance of professionalization can be exaggerated. When the peace committees of South Africa first began, their organizers talked with local people about leadership and asked what qualities were needed. The reply was that the most important quality was not technique but respect. As a result, the code of practice that was drawn up stated that members would, inter alia, respect the Constitution, work within the law, would not use violence or take sides, would not gossip, and would heal not hurt. The success of the program is that it built civility and created social capital through bringing (nonprofessional) people together to create safer communities.

Accountability

Nonstate policing is frequently dismissed for its lack of accountability. Yet, Law's (2006) worldwide study of SSR programs found that donor plans for the security sector have done little for state systems in this respect themselves. It is true that accountability can be formally enhanced relatively easily by the appropriate legislation; internal institutional disciplinary and auditing mechanisms; and external oversight mechanisms. But, implementation is another matter. States struggle to control the use of force by their own police and to coordinate their own interior security agencies. Besides, accountability is broader than institution building. Accountability combines various processes, including being open regarding policies, decisions, and operations; providing information willingly; explaining and justifying actions; responding to public concerns, needs, and complaints; investigating alleged abuses and publishing the findings; accepting imposed sanctions for illegal conduct; allowing a right to redress of abuses committed; and showing responsibility for the impact of actions on individuals' safety, security, privacy, and livelihoods. Accountability therefore is primarily about holding values concerning how the relationship is to be conducted between policing agencies and those policed (Goetz and Jenkins 2005). This degree of accountability is only developed in a culture over time rather than being decreed. The complex web of institutional and social practices by which one section of power holders examines the other and the public examine the whole and one another necessitates a public demand that everyone, but particularly power holders, be held to account; a willingness by everyone, including power holders, to be held to account; constitutional powers to affect that accountability; freedom to use those powers effectively; and the necessary abilities to make use of those powers (Goetz and Jenkins 2005). The complexity of developing accountability means that institutional structures are not enough on their own.

Consequently, it is no surprise to read that donors have

> tended to concentrate on the efficiency of security actors as opposed to their accountability. They have favoured strengthening statutory security sector actors, as opposed to bringing under control the ever more important non-statutory ones. ... Building capacity for the civil management authorities ... has tended to figure more prominently than the building of parliamentary, judicial and civil society institutions capable of overseeing and monitoring

the security sector, and keeping it in check. The brunt of foreign intervention has thus fallen on security forces and the public part of the security sector at the expense of private actors, and governance and management bodies. The potential for the failure of security sector reconstruction programmes is substantial. (Law 2006, 17)

As a normative position, it is possible to say that the state has "a viable and justifiable role to play in the delivery or governance of security" in a pluralized world of policing (Loader and Walker 2001, 11). But, as a practical program for African post-conflict states it is a long way from realization. There also should not be any generalized presumption that accountability and protection of human rights is best achieved through state systems. The dismissal of nonstate policing as unaccountable or at best, in the case of commercial security, as only accountable to their paying clients is too sweeping. It may in fact be the case that nonstate systems, as they are closest to their clients, are more "people centered," and "locally owned," may be more amenable to the preservation of human rights and the delivery of an accountable service, for they more accurately reflect local beliefs and needs and are regarded by local people to be more legitimate.

Bringing nonstate actors into SSR may not necessarily enhance rights accountability, but it may make an important difference to performance accountability. With limited resources, it may be better to focus on the area where initiatives are most likely to lead to short-term improvements in effective policing, namely, performance accountability, as desired by local populations. This is vital in post-conflict states, where the provision of policing is skewed toward the powerful, wealthy, male regime clients and the urban population. The key to this form of accountability is the responsiveness of the policy maker and policing provider to local needs. This entails answerability (providing information or a decision), enforcement (strengthening achievement of policing norms), and organizational change (changing the way policing is delivered).

Effectiveness

Security reform has as its goal increased effectiveness. The outcome must be that people perceive that they are more secure and are more effectively policed. There is little point in rearranging the institutional furniture if there are no measurable improvements in policing to the population. Yet, one of the handicaps of SSR is that, being donor driven, their programs rely on external staff and professionals that rarely have any background and expertise in the country, its politics, its culture, and its security. Even if they have a security background, donor governments tend to use serving (or former) police officers from their own countries to support their SSR programs (OECD 2007, 23).

Also compromising effectiveness is the state penchant for centralization. Yet, focusing on creating an effective centralized, coordinated, state-provided security when the state has limited capacity, legitimacy, and even sovereign authority is not straightforward. Many post-conflict states have artificial borders, heterogeneous populations, and personalized structures of kinship, religion, and community that may matter more than nationality. Further, centralization tends to be concerned with institution building. But, is the priority to build capacity, or is it to ensure that an effective service is provided? If it is the latter, then the central question becomes how we can work with the existing actors as opposed to how can new structures be built where they do not exist.

The fact is that local needs for protection from and response to crime and disorder are often better served by local security systems. The OECD argued that "an understanding of how poor and vulnerable people experience safety, security and justice is required in order to determine priorities for external assistance aimed at helping ... without such knowledge, external interventions are likely to be ineffectual and counterproductive" (2007, 41). But, this caution is aimed at external professionals. The intention of the OECD is that externals secure local knowledge to be effective, but a better strategy is to employ those with local knowledge in the first place. Those most likely to be aware of the dangers facing local people and to be in a position to protect them are local security providers. Likewise, those best equipped to track down the perpetrators of crime are those with local knowledge. For all their failures, few would question that the most effective policing agents are those nonstate actors closest to the people. This is why the police already link with nonstate policing leaders as they seek fugitives and suspects. It is these linkages that need to be recognized and strengthened in SSR to ensure that the new and reformed institutions of state are effective in practice. In a context where most of the policing is delivered by nonstate providers, SSR programs that are either state or nonstate institutions are unlikely to be effective (OECD 2007, 17). Effective SSR has to be inclusive. One of the main facets of SSR, says Law (2006, 2), is that the approach has to be "comprehensive in nature, taking into account the main actors of the security sector and their functions; namely, all jurisdictions with a capacity to use force, both statutory and nonstatutory."

The Implications of a Multilayered Policing Governance

Integrating the diverse state and nonstate policing agencies into a single policing governance network would be a daunting task, but there are positive gains to be had as well as potential problems to confront. On the plus side, because nonstate systems operate at the local level, they can actually fulfill decentralization strategies and be readily responsive to local needs. They may not only be more "locally owned" but also likely more adaptable to the changing needs of the local populace and thus more capable of modification during periods of transition. Further, supporting local nonstate systems may be the best means of realizing short-term, sustainable gains in policing provision for with their local knowledge and support they can be highly effective. Other attractions are that they are cost-effective: cheap to support and cheap to end users. And, as has been noted, they may be linked already (formally and informally) with the police in shared activities and information and with state police functions delegated to nonstate systems. These nonstate systems are also often more resilient than state systems, enduring throughout conflicts and deteriorating environments. In this sense, nonstate systems may be the most productive vehicles for the reconstruction of social capital and social efficacy. Where a central government with limited penetration and capacity relies on local policing actors to execute what in the West are seen as the core functions of security, state institutions are typically regarded as weak and fragile. But, as Boege et al. observed:

> this very weakness may become a strength as the state gains legitimacy in the eyes of the people, because it acknowledges the strengths of local institutions and does not attempt to impose its supremacy, and because state authorities do not try to displace local orders of governance, but work with them, providing a co-ordinating or harmonising framework ... it is important to stress the positive potential rather than the negative features of so-called fragile states—de-emphasising weakness, fragility, failure and collapse, and focusing on hybridity, generative processes, innovative adaptation and ingenuity. This also entails perceiving community resilience and customary institutions not so much as "spoilers" and problems, but as assets and sources of solutions that can be drawn upon in order to forge constructive relationships between communities and governments, and between customary and introduced political and social institutions. (2008, 15)

Local institutions generally have greater legitimacy than a distant predatory or indifferent central state. Their familiarity with the history and the root causes of a dispute or disorder facilitates their role in mediating between the aggrieved parties. For all these reasons, it is understandable that the OECD called for states to work with local forms of governance when they "perform the same functions and generate the same outputs as formal state institutions" (2008, 36) and urged donors to "focus on supporting dialogue aimed at better integration of state institutions and customary or other nonstatutory systems" (2008, 38).

However, there are, of course, a number of potential difficulties associated with nonstate policing systems. Typically, groups within post-conflict societies that are capable of taking local ownership of a transformation process are either difficult to find or have a limited capacity to participate. The world of nonstate policing is complex and dynamic, making a common national strategy problematic. Anything run by volunteers can be unreliable and unsustainable, and nonstate policing is not immune to corruption, abuse of power, and manipulation by local elites. Further, no one is under any illusions about the fact that they may breach international human rights standards. And, besides the problems with the nonstate groups themselves, any multilayered approach will inevitably face resistance and obstruction from certain elements of the local and national elites together with the state police, who will regard support for those that they do not control as a threat to their interests. Interestingly, Nathan regarded opposition from conservative groups and others whose values and interests are threatened as a problem with reform of the police as well. Beyond personal antagonism, he rightly noted the following:

> Substantial policy and organizational transformation is intrinsically threatening and gives rise to resistance and conflict in all circumstances. Resistance, inertia and confusion are inevitable when security officers are expected to implement (and sometimes design) new policies that are completely at odds with their training, experience and worldview. (2007, 42)

This will apply to nonstate as well as state providers.

These inadequacies are serious and mean that there is no certainty that nonstate policing will progress in a liberal direction. Yet, however valid the fears about using nonstate policing, it must not be assumed that their difficulties are any more severe than those encountered in the state system. Both, after all, share the same or similar indigenous cultures. The failures of nonstate policing are not any less reformable than those perpetuated by state policing systems. The argument is weak that when the overall aim is to create policing within a framework of democratic governance, agencies with poor democratic records cannot be considered for development. The issue is not whether agencies *need* reforming, but whether they are *willing to be reformed.*

The question of who delivers policing services and how, from a development point of view, is about the quality and efficacy of the policing received by citizens, regardless of who delivers that policing.[6] However, ultimately the question is a political and normative one, dependent on local contexts, institutional capacities, popular demands, leadership, national trajectory, and dominant ideology. It cannot be answered generically, and, similarly, SSR should abandon any a priori state-centric bias. Instead, it requires in-depth analysis of the post-conflict state and its political terrain, its capabilities, functions, and cultural legacies. The analysis may reveal that the cornerstones of the post-conflict state little resemble those of Western models. My argument is that the most appropriate developmental approach to the delivery of policing in post-conflict conditions is one that recognizes the differing nature of states and the presence of multiple providers whose services are layered to meet differing contingencies.

Yet, recognizing multiple providers is not the same as integrating them. Listing the benefits and noting the difficulties of utilizing nonstate actors are not the same as actually achieving a holistic approach that brings all policing agencies together in one policing governance network. Is it realistic to imagine the post-conflict African state having the capacity to undertake a steering function of ensuring the quality, efficacy, and accountability of all policing agencies? Could it really fulfill the key functions of a network regulator, namely, to license, vet, monitor, and regulate the delivery of policing; to ensure that effective policing is equally accessible to all; to protect and preserve civil rights and human rights; and to establish the parameters within which nonstate policing is provided? For post-conflict states, fulfilling these functions will prove "either problematic or inoperative" (Meagher 2005, 7).

Perhaps, then, a multilayered approach that uses nonstate policing is utopian dreaming. Or, is it that the dreaming belongs to those who seek to reconstruct public control over security by seeking to reestablish the *state* monopoly of force? If the state is deemed unable to provide that in the medium term, even with donor aid, then it is a logical step to take a different approach. It may be that integrating the existing multiple layers of authority into a system of shared authority over the monopoly of force is a step too far at present. Another way forward has been suggested by Wulf. To fully do justice to the reality of a "globalized world, with hybrid political societies, with porous or non-existent nation-state borders" (2007, 19), Wulf says that we should actually be looking not only at the nonstate and state levels but also at the regional or subregional level and the global level. However "beyond the state" as a category is specified, he correctly identifies two conceptual problems facing multilayered policing. The first is the problem of legitimizing the different levels given the competitive nature of legitimation. Second, there is the problem of apportioning authority at the different levels to avoid disputed sovereignties and yet to achieve a clarity of functions. His solution is to hold fast to two functional principles, namely, subsidiarity for practice and supremacy for norms. He states (2007, 20) that "the monopoly of violence should be exercised according to the *subsidiarity principle*, that is, the lowest level should be the starting point," and only when one level is not capable or cannot be tasked with exercising the monopoly of force should the next higher level undertake the task. Concerning supremacy in norm setting, he argues for it to be top-down so that norms of a higher level prevail over those of a lower level. Of course, none of the levels will function perfectly at all times, but in the multilevel approach it is anticipated that where one of the levels is lacking or incompetent, another takes over. Wulf's is but one attempt to sketch in the nature of a framework to create a public monopoly of force by looking beyond and below the state level. Its vision of "a legitimate multi-level public monopoly of force, with a division of labor between the different levels and acceptable and agreed norms for the application of force" (Wulf 2007, 29) at least offers an alternative paradigm.

Of course, there are doubts regarding the political will to formally abandon the claim of the state to be the sole provider of policing. The state in the developing world does not look willing yet to cede an authority it never had and to work in partnerships with nonstate policing organizations or even to promote them. Neoliberalism has opened up many state monopolies, but security looks likely to be held as a "core" state function to the last. Even everyday policing events such as order maintenance, protection, investigation, and dispute resolution retain a mystique that makes many think only the state can provide it and should provide it. Will even the demonstration of effective, sustainable, and locally accountable everyday policing by nonstate providers overcome the doubts? And, will effective local partnerships convince advisers that hybrid and multilayered governance can work? Even asking these questions raised antagonism among some SSR advisers in DRC in 2008. Support for nonstate policing will "undermine the state," they protested. Yes, it will divert some resources that would otherwise go to the state police. Yet, although they would only support the state, they could not even tell me how many police there were "out there" beyond Kinshasa and off the road, let alone give me a timescale regarding when the 66 million people of DRC spread over 2,345,410 square kilometers were going to be served by the reformed state police. One wonders what sort of state I was supposed to be undermining, but it was clear that for some a rethink on the policy of state building was not about to happen.

The Unanswered Questions

As I reach the end of this book, I am conscious of the questions that I have *not* answered, questions I would have liked to address but lacked the research answers. By concentrating my fieldwork since 2000 on African countries, I do not feel in a position to answer whether what has been written is true only of Africa. I have read excellent accounts of post-conflict policing from Timor-Leste, Afghanistan, Iraq, Solomon Islands, Serbia, Bosnia, Kosovo, Colombia, Haiti, and the like, but not having done research there, I do not feel confident to determine on African exceptionalism. It may be the poorest continent and the most conflict-ridden continent, but is its nonstate policing so different? I suspect not, but others must decide on the evidence.

Another key question is determining the variables that account for differences between African post-conflict countries. I am fairly well acquainted with eight post-conflict countries, but as I have indicated throughout the account, the length of intensity of the conflict and the period since the majority of the conflict ceased is so variable that I still do not feel that there are enough countries in each category to make solid comparisons. At this stage in my research, the uniqueness of each situation is more apparent to me than the similarities, so I have avoided this key issue.

I have suggested that perhaps eighteen African countries can be counted as post-conflict countries since 1980, but that still leaves twenty-seven sub-Saharan countries that are not in that category. Is their nonstate policing the same as in post-conflict countries? Again, although I have done policing research in such, I have not yet enough evidence to pronounce with confidence. It is perhaps hard to grasp just how little research has been done on state and nonstate African policing. Until the research is gathered, there is still a large degree of uncertainty about comparisons between peaceful and post-conflict states.

Given my argument for supporting and reforming nonstate policing within a national security framework, what evidence can I produce of success in strengthening the links between state and nonstate and of reforming nonstate policing? Sadly, so little has been done in this regard that I have to admit that much of what I propose is largely untested. Just two cases come to mind of beginnings in this area. One attempt at reforming nonstate policing and linking it to the state has been undertaken in Malawi, although unaccountably it has never been published in academic literature. In the late 1990s, DFID realized that police reform in isolation would not guarantee safety, security, and access to justice for the poor and vulnerable people of Malawi. As a result, it supported the Malawi government's Safety, Security and Access to Justice (MaSSAJ) program, which aimed to bring all government agencies and ministries working in the security sector together with nonstate actors such as customary chiefs, NGOs, and faith groups. In particular, chiefs have undergone training to enhance the effectiveness and acceptability of their customary "justice forums" and likewise the NGOs and faith groups for their mediation agencies. It began in 2001 and so far has shown encouraging signs of success in terms of creating a range of locally available structures to which poor people can turn (DFID 2003). Malawi, however, is not a post-conflict country.

From that post-conflict category, Boege et al. (2008) proposed the de facto state of Somaliland as the best example of multilayered security governance. From about 1995, Somaliland has created a political order that combines customary institutions (councils of elders; *guurti*) and Western democratic state institutions. The success of peace building in Somaliland was, to a large extent, due to the involvement of clan elders and their councils using customary mechanisms of conflict resolution. As a result of their success, they were appointed by the state as key actors in governance, including security governance. The government, therefore, "does not hold the monopoly of violence. ... Security in Somaliland is dealt with in a decentralized manner and is largely guaranteed by local politicians and elders" (Hagmann and Hoehne 2007, 24). The multilayered approach combines state, customary, and Islamic norms and practices and enjoys high levels of popular legitimacy.

Beyond state recognition of customary courts, I am aware of only these two cases that constitute the nationwide programs that deliberately and broadly link state and nonstate policing in post-conflict Africa, although I am sure others will be appearing shortly, such as in southern Sudan.

Although I have ended on my failures, the purpose for highlighting them is to encourage others to do the research and the policy implementation that will provide us with the answers. I firmly believe that for the security of Africans it is important to find out more about the current and potential future role of nonstate policing in post-conflict Africa. "State-building strategies need to appreciate that states are comprised of more than formal institutions" (OECD 2008, 14). Post-conflict Africa should not ignore nonstate policing. When spider webs unite, they can tie up a lion.[7]

Notes

1. The "top ten" in the Foreign Policy/Fund for Peace 2007 *Failed States Index Rankings* included the African states of Sudan, Somalia, Zimbabwe, Chad, Côte d'Ivoire, Democratic Republic of the Congo (DRC), Guinea, and Central African Republic (*The Failed States Index* 2008; available at http://www.foreignpolicy. com). The most fragile states according to the *State Fragility Index and Matrix* included the African states of the DRC, Sierra Leone, Somalia, Chad, Sudan, Burundi, Côte d'Ivoire, Ethiopia, Liberia, and Nigeria (Marshall and Goldstone 2007, 15–19). The CIFP (Country Indicators for Foreign Policy) group's index has Burundi at the top of its list, followed by the African states of DRC, Somalia, and Liberia (Carment, Prest, and Samy 2007, 18).
2. UNPOL faced difficulties in convincing Burundian police officers to attend UN workshops when no per diem compensation could be offered by ONUB, and at times the UN police officers themselves reportedly put money aside from their own salaries to contribute to these basic costs (Banal and Scherrer 2008, 51).
3. In the DRC, for instance, 80 percent of the police budget is provided by external actors (Geyer 2008, 3). Human Rights Watch has obtained figures that suggest that Australian assistance to Papua New Guinea constituted more than 20 percent of the police force's operational budget in 2004 and nearly all of the police force's development budget from 2000 to 2005 (http://www.hrw.org/ reports/2005/png0905/10.htm).

4. IRIN, http://www.irinnews.org/report.aspx?ReportID=77530.
5. "Reforms that are not shaped and driven by local actors [governments] are unlikely to be implemented properly and sustained. In the absence of local ownership, SSR is bound to fail" (Nathan 2007, 5). It is true that SSR programs often have a mandate from the international community or even the United Nations Security Council, but the first is a nebulous unaccountable subset of rich nations, while the latter is distinguished by being undemocratic, poorly accountable, and dominated by the main nuclear powers.
6. Cf. with the point emphasized by the Mapping the Security Environment project commissioned by the UK NGO Military Contact Group (NMCG), namely, that "local communities were more concerned that aid was delivered and less concerned about who delivered it."
7. Ethiopian proverb, http://www.princetonol.com/groups/iad/lessons/middle/af-prov2.htm.

Bibliography

Abrahams, R. 2007. Afterword: Some thoughts on the comparative study of Vigilantism. In *Global vigilantes*, Eds. D. Pratten and A. Sen. London: Hurst, 419–42.

Abrahamsen, R., and M. Williams. 2006. Privatisation, globalisation and the politics of protection in South Africa. In *The politics of protection: Sites of insecurity and political agency*, Eds. J. Huysmans, A. Dobson, and R. Prokhovnik. London: Routledge.

Abrahamsen, R., and M. Williams. 2008. Public/private, global/local: The changing contours of Africa's security governance. *Review of African Political Economy* 35(118): 539–53.

Academia de Ciências Policiais (ACIPOL). 2006. *Policiamento comunitário em Moçambique: Lições e desafios*. Maputo, Mozambique: ACIPOL.

Adamu, F. 2008. Gender, Hisba and the enforcement of morality in northern Nigeria. *Africa* 78(1): 136–52.

Adu-Mireku, S. 2002. Fear of crime among residents of three communities in Accra, Ghana. *International Journal of Contemporary Sociology* 43(2): 153–68.

African Commission on Human and Peoples Rights (African Commission). 2002. *Report of the fact-finding mission to Zimbabwe*. Banjul, The Gambia: ACHPR.

African Development Bank Group (ADB). 2004. *Bank group post-conflict assistance policy guidelines. Arrears clearance framework*. Tunis-Belvedère, Tunis: ADB.

Agnew, R. 1990. Adolescent resources and delinquency. *Criminology* 28: 535–66.

Alemika, E., and I. Chukwuma. 2004. *A report on poor peoples' perceptions and priorities on safety, security and informal policing in A2J focal states in Nigeria*. Lagos: Center for Law Enforcement Education (CLEEN).

Altbeker, A., and J. Rauch. 1998. *Community participation workshop*, report for Business Against Crime. Gauteng, South Africa: Business Against Crime.

Amnesty International. 1998. *Mozambique: Human rights and the police*. AI Index AFR 41/01/98. London: AI.

Amnesty International. 2004. *Democratic Republic of Congo: Mass rape—time for remedies*. AI Index AFR 62/018/2004. London: AI.

Amnesty International. 2005. *Sierra Leone. No one to turn to: Women's lack of access to justice in rural Sierra Leone*. AI Index 20051/011/2005.5. http://www.amnesty.org.ru/library/Index/ENGAFR510112005?open&of=ENG-SLE. London: AI.

Amnesty International. 2006. *Sierra Leone women face human rights abuses in the informal legal sector*. AI Index AFR 51/002/2006. London: AI.

Amnesty International. 2007a. *Above the law: Police accountability in Angola*. AI Index AFR 12/005/2007. London: AI.

Amnesty International. 2007b. Report details culture of impunity in sexual violence against women and girls in northern Uganda, press release, November 29, 2007. London: AI.

Amnesty International. 2007c. *Uganda. Doubly traumatised. Lack of access to justice for female victims of sexual and gender based violence in northern Uganda.* http://www.amnestyusa.org/document.php?lang=e&id=ENGAFR590052007. London: AI.

Amnesty International. 2008a. *Burundi: No protection from rape in war and peace.* http://www.amnesty.org.uk/actions_details.asp?ActionID=412. London: AI.

Amnesty International. 2008b. *Police accountability in Mozambique.* AI Index AFR 41/001/2008. London: AI.

AMOPROC (Associação Moçambicana para Promoção da Cidadania). 2006. *As Próprias Mãos. O Cidadão.* Vol. 8, October/December. Maputo, Mozambique: AMOPROC.

Anderson, L. 2004. West Africa and Islamic fundamentalism. Series of articles in *Chicago Tribune,* December 2004, quoted in http://www.danieldrezner.com/archives/001796.html.

Anderson, L. 2007. What to do? The dilemmas of international engagement in fragile states. In *Fragile states and insecure people?: Violence, security, and statehood in the twenty-first century,* Eds. L. Andersen, B. Møller, and F. Stepputat. Houndsmill, UK: Palgrave Macmillan.

Annan, K. 2005. *In larger freedom: Towards development, security and human rights for all.* New York: United Nations.

Armstrong, A. 1994. School and Sadza: Custody and the best interests of the child in Zimbabwe. *International Journal of Law and the Family* 151: 162–67.

Armstrong, A. 1995. Rethinking customary law in Southern Africa: What relevance for action? *Women and Law in Southern Africa Research Project Newsletter* 7(2).

Avant, D. 2004. The privatization of security and change in the control of force. *International Studies Perspectives* 5(2): 153–57.

Axworthy, L. 2001. Human security and global governance: Putting people first. *Global Governance* 7(1): 19–23.

Baker, B. 2002. Living with non-state policing in South Africa: The issues and dilemmas. *Journal of Modern African Studies* 40(1): 29–53.

Baker, B. 2003. Policing and the rule of law in Mozambique. *Policing and Society* 13(2): 139–58.

Baker, B. 2004. Popular justice and policing from Bush war to democracy: Uganda 1981–2004. *International Journal of the Sociology of Law* 32: 333–48.

Baker, B. 2005a. Multi-choice policing in Uganda. *Policing and Society* 15(1): 19–41.

Baker, B. 2005b. Who do people turn to for policing in Sierra Leone? *Journal of Contemporary African Studies* 23(3): 371–90.

Baker, B. 2006. The African post-conflict policing agenda in Sierra Leone. *Conflict, Security and Development* 6(1): 25–50.

Baker, B. 2007a. Community policing in Freetown, Sierra Leone: Foreign import or local solution? *Journal of Intervention and Statebuilding* 2(1): 23–42.

Baker, B. 2007b. How civil war altered policing in Sierra Leone and Uganda. *Commonwealth and Comparative Politics* 45(3): 367–87.

Baker, B. 2007c. *Multi-choice policing in Africa.* Uppsala: Nordic African Institute.

Baker, B. 2007d. Reconstructing a policing system out of the ashes: Rwanda's solution. *Policing and Society* 17(4): 1–23.

Baker, B., and E. Scheye. 2007. Multi-layered justice and security delivery in post-conflict and fragile states. *Conflict, Security and Development* 7(4): 503–28.

Baker, B., and E. Scheye. 2009. Access to justice in a post-conflict state: Donor-supported multi-dimensional peacekeeping in southern Sudan. *International Peacekeeping* 16(2): 171–85.

Ball, N., P. Biesheuval, and F. Olanisakin. 2007. *Security and justice sector reform programming in Africa*. Evaluation Working Paper 23, : DFID, London.

Banal, L., and V. Scherrer. 2008. ONUB and the importance of local ownership: The case of Burundi. In *Security sector reform and UN integrated missions: Experience from Burundi, the Democratic Republic of Congo, Haiti, and Kosovo*, Eds. H. Hänggi and V. Scherrer. Geneva: LIT/DCAF.

Barya, J., and J. Oloka-Onyango. 1994. *Popular justice and resistance committee courts in Uganda*. Kampala: Friedrich-Ebert-Stiftung and New Vision Publishing.

Basedau, M., A. Mehler, and J. Smith-Hoehn. 2007. Public perceptions of security in post-conflict urban Liberia and Sierra Leone, Part I: Liberia—Caught between inter-national, state and non-state actors. *Journal of Peacebuilding and Development* 3(2): 84–89.

Bashua, A. 2005. The mechanics of rebuilding a failed state. The governance challenge in Liberia. In *A tortuous road to peace: The dynamics of regional, UN and international humanitarian interventions in Liberia*, Eds. F. Aboagye and A. Bah. London: Institute for Security Studies.

Bayley, D. 1997. Who are we kidding?, or Developing democracy through police reform. In *Policing in emerging democracies: Workshop papers and highlights*. Washington, DC: National Institute of Justice.

Bayley, D. 2001. *Democratizing the police abroad: What to do and how to do it*. Washington, DC: National Institute of Justice.

Bearpark, A., and S. Schulz. 2007. The private security challenge in Africa: Problems and options for regulation. In *Security in Africa: Manifestation, challenges and regulation*, Ed. Sabelo Gumedze. ISS, Monograph 139. Pretoria: ISS.

Belton, R. 2005. Competing definitions of the Rule of Law: Implications for practitioners. Carnegie Endowment for International Peace, Democracy and Rule of Law Project, No. 55.

Benit-Gbaffou, C. 2008. Community policing and disputed norms for local social control in post-apartheid Johannesburg. *Journal of Southern African Studies* 34(1): 93–108.

Bennett, T. 1985. *The application of customary law in southern Africa: The conflict of personal laws*. Cape Town: Juta.

Bennett, T. 2004. *Customary law in South Africa*. Landsdowne, South Africa: Juta.

Bennett, T. 2006. Traditional courts and fundamental rights. In *The shade of new leaves (Governance in traditional authority: A southern African perspective)*, Eds. M. Hinz and H. Pattemann. Berlin: Lit Verlag.

Berdal, M., and D. Malone, Eds. 2000. *Greed and grievance: Economic agendas in civil wars*. Boulder, CO: Lynne Rienner.

Berg, J. 2005. *Overview of plural policing oversight in select Southern African Development Community (SADC) countries*. Cape Town: Institute of Criminology, University of Cape Town. http://www.policeaccountability.co.za/File_Uploads/docs/File_Download.asp?ThisFile=SADCpolicingoversight2005.doc.

Bierschenk, T., and J. Olivier de Sardan. 2003. Powers in the village: Rural Benin between democratisation and decentralisation. *Africa* 73(2): 145–73.

Bigo, D. 2000. When two become one. In *International relation theory and the politics of European integration, power, security and community*, Eds. M. Kelstrup and M. Willimas. London: Routledge.

Boas, M., and K. Jennings. 2005. Insecurity and development: The rhetoric of the "failed state." *The European Journal of Development Research* 17(3): 385–95.

Boege, V., A. Brown, K. Clements, and A. Nolan. 2008. *On hybrid political orders and emerging states: State formation in the context of "fragility."* Berghof Research Center for Constructive Conflict Management. http://www.berghof-handbook. net/uploads/download/boege_etal_handbook.pdf.

Boggero, M. 2008. Local dynamics of security in Africa: The Central African Republic and private security. *African Security Review* 17(2): 15–27.

Boone, C. 2003. *Political topographies of the African state: Territorial authority and institutional choice.* Cambridge: Cambridge University Press.

Brahimi, L. 2007. State building in crisis and post-conflict countries. Paper presented at 7th Global Forum on Reinventing Government Building Trust in Government. June 26–29, Vienna. http://unpan1.un.org/intradoc/groups/public/documents/UN/UNPAN026305.pdf

Brahimi Panel. 2005. *Report of the Panel on United Nations Peace Operations.* A/55/305. New York: United Nations.

Braima Koroma. 2006. *Nationwide perception survey of the SLP: Public and police perceptions.* Freetown: SLP.

Brantingham, P., and P. Brantingham. 1984. *Patterns in crime.* New York: Macmillan.

Brantingham, P., and P. Brantingham. 1993. Environment, routine and situation: Toward a pattern theory of crime. In *Routine activity and rational choice: Advances in criminological theory*, vol. 5, Eds. R. Clarke and M. Felson, 259–93. New Brunswick: Transaction.

Bratton, M., and N. van de Walle. 1997. *Democratic experiments in Africa, regime transitions in comparative perspective.* Cambridge: Cambridge University Press.

Broer, H., and M. Emery. 1998. Civilian police in U.N. peacekeeping operations. In *Policing the new world disorder peace operations and public security*, Eds. R. Oakley, M. Dziedzic, and E. Goldberg. Washington: Institute for National Strategic Studies (INSS), the National Defense University. http://www.ndu.edu/inss/books/Books_1998/Policing%20the%20New%20World%20Disorder%20-%20May%2098/chapter10.html.

Brogden, M. 2004. Commentary: Community policing: A panacea from the West. *African Affairs* 103(413): 635–49.

Brogden, M. 2005. "Horses for courses" and "Thin blue lines": Community policing in transitional society. *Police Quarterly* 8(1): 64–98.

Brogden, M., and P. Nijar. 2005. *Community policing: National and international models and approaches.* Cullompton, UK: Willan.

Bronstein, V. 1998. Reconceptualizing the customary law debate in South Africa. *South African Journal on Human Rights* 14: 388–403.

Brzoska, M. 2007. *Collective violence beyond the standard definition of armed conflict.* http://yearbook2007.sipri.org/chap2/app2C.

Brzoska, M., and A. Heinemann-Gruber. 2004. Security sector reform and post-conflict reconstruction under international auspices. In *Sourcebook on security sector reform*, Eds. P. Furi and M. Hadžić. Geneva: DCAF and Centre for Civil-Military Relations.

Burris, S. 2004. Governance, microgovernance and health. *Temple Law Review* 77: 335–59.

Buur, L. 2005. Sovereignty and democratic exclusion in the new South Africa. *Review of African Political Economy* 104(5): 253–68.

Buur, L. 2006. Reordering society: Vigilantism and sovereign expressions in Port Elizabeth's townships. *Development and Change* 37(4): 735–57.

Buur, L. 2006. Democracy and its discontents. Vigilantism, sovereignty and human rights in South Africa. Paper presented at Security Beyond the State? Aberystwyth University. April 19-21.

Buur, L., and S. Jensen. 2004. Vigilantism and the policing of everyday life in South Africa. *African Studies* 63(2): 139–52.

Buzan, B., O. Waever, and J. de Wilde. 1998. *Security: A new framework for analysis.* Boulder, CO: Lynne Rienner.

Call, C. 2002. Competing donor approaches to post-conflict police reform. *Conflict, Security and Development,* 2(1): 99–120.

Call, C. 2007. Introduction: What we know and don't know about postconflict justice and security reforms. In *Constructing justice and security after war,* Ed. C. Call. Washington, DC: United States Institute of Peace.

Call, C., and M. Barnett. 1999. Looking for a few good cops. *International Peacekeeping* 6(4): 48–64.

Call, C., and E. Cousens. 2007. *Ending wars and building peace: Coping with crisis.* New York: International Peace Academy.

Call, C., and V. Wyeth, Eds. 2008. *Building states to build peace.* Boulder, CO: Lynn Rienner.

Canada. 2000. *Human security.* Ottawa: DFAIT. Canadian Department of Foreign Affairs & International Trade.

Caparini, M. 2006. Applying a security governance perspective to the privatisation of security. In *Private actors and security governance,* Eds. A. Bryden and M. Caparini. Geneva: LIT/DCAF.

Carment, D., S. Prest and Y. Samy. 2007. Assessing fragility: Theory, evidence and policy. *Politorbis* 42: 13–19.

Carothers, T. 1998. The rule of law revival. *Foreign Affairs* 77(2): 95–106.

Carothers, T. 2003. Promoting the rule of law abroad: The problem of knowledge. Rule of Law Series, Democracy and Rule of Law Project, *Carnegie Working Papers,* January. Washington, DC: CEIP.

Carrier, R. 1999. Dissolving boundaries: Private security and policing in South Africa. *African Security Review,* 8(6), http://www.iss.co.za/pubs/ASR/8No6/DissolvingBoundaries.html.

Casey, C. 2007. Policing through violence: Fear, vigilantism and the politics of Islam in northern Nigeria. In *Global Vigilantes,* Eds. D. Pratten and A. Sen. London: Hurst.

Cawthra, G. 1993. *Policing South Africa.* London: Zed Books.

Center for Strategic and International Studies (CSIS) and the Association of the United States Army (AUSA). 2002. May. *Post-conflict reconstruction: Task framework.* Washington DC: CSIS and Arlington, VA: AUSA.

Chabal, P. 2006. States and societies: Why is state formation so difficult? Presentation for ODI Seminar Series: (Re)building Developmental States: From Theory to Practice. London, March 1. http://www.odi.org.uk/events.

Chandler, D. 2006. *Empire in denial: The politics of state-building.* London: Pluto.

Chesterman, S., M. Ignatieff, and R. Thakur, Eds. 2005. *Making states work*. Tokyo: UN University Press.

Chirayath, L., C. Sage, and M. Woolcock. 2005. Customary law and policy reform: Engaging with the plurality of justice systems. Prepared as a background paper for the *World Development Report 2006: Equity and Development*. Washington, DC: World Bank.

Clapham, C., Ed. 1982. *Private patronage and public power: Political clientelism in the modern state*. London: Pinter.

Clapham, C. 1999. African security systems: Privatisation and the scope for mercenary activity. In *The Privatisation of Security in Africa*, Eds. G. Mills and J. Stremlau. Johannesburg: South African Institute of International Affairs.

Clark, T., and T. Moon. 2001. Interoperability for joint and coalition operations. *Australian Defence Force Journal* 151 Nov-Dec: 23–56.

CLEEN Foundation. 2005. *Criminal victimization, Safety and policing in Nigeria*. Lagos: CLEEN Foundation.

Collier, P., and A. Hoeffler. 2001. *Greed and grievance in civil war*. Washington, DC: World Bank. http://www.worldbank.org/research/conflict.

Commission on Human Security. 2003. *Final report*. New York: United Nations Commission on Human Security.

Commonwealth Human Rights Initiative. 2006. *The police, the people, the politics: Police accountability in Uganda*. New Delhi: CHRI. http://www.humanrightsinitiative.org/publications/police/uganda_country_report_2006.pdf.

Consultancy Africa Intelligence. 2007. *Uranium in Niger: The battle begins*. September 6. http://www.consultancyafrica.com/files/Consultancy%20Africa%20Intelligence%20-%20Situational%20Spotlight%20-%20Uranium%20in%20Niger%20-%20September%202007.pdf.

Crawford, A. 1999. *Crime prevention and community safety: Politics, policies and practices*. London: Longman.

Curran, E., and E. Bonthuys. 2004. *Customary law and domestic violence in rural South African communities*. Johannesburg: Centre for the Study of Violence and Reconciliation. http://www.csvr.org.za/wits/papers/papclaw.htm#note157#note157.

Cutter, S. 2009. Sierra Leonean grassroots perspectives of peacebuilding, 1991–2006. PhD thesis, Coventry University.

Day, G., and C. Freeman. 2005. Operationalizing the responsibility to protect—The policekeeping approach. *Global Governance*, 11: 139–46.

Deepa, N., with R. Patel, K. Schafft, A. Rademacher, and S. Koch-Schulte. 2000. *Voices of the poor: Can anyone hear us?* New York: Oxford University Press for the World Bank.

Department for International Development (DFID). 2002. *Understanding and supporting security sector reform*. London: DFID. http://www.dfid.gov.uk/pubs/files/supportingsecurity.pdf.

Department for International Development (DFID). 2003. *Malawi safety, security and access to justice programme output-to-purpose review*. September/October. http://www.dfid.gov.uk/aboutdfid/foi/disclosures/malawi-justice-opr.pdf.

Department for International Development (DFID). 2004. *Non-state justice and security systems*. London: DFID.

Department for International Development (DFID). 2006. *Safety, security and access to justice programmes. Practical lessons from experience*, final report. London: DFID.

Department for International Development (DFID). 2008. States in development: Understanding state-building. DFID working paper. http://www.dfid.gov.uk/pubs/files/State-in-Development-Wkg-Paper.pdf.

Dixon, B., and L. Johns. 2001. *Gangs, Pagad and the state: Vigilantism and revenge violence in the western Cape*, vol. 2. Johannesburg: Centre for the Study of Violence and Reconciliation, Violence and Transition Series.

Duffield, M. 2001. *Global governance and the new wars*. London: Zed Books.

Dupont, B. 2006. Power struggles in the field of security: Implications for democratic transformation. In *Democracy, society and the governance of security*, Eds. B. Dupont and J. Woods. Cambridge: Cambridge University Press.

Düsing, S. 2002. *Traditional leadership and democratization in southern Africa: A comparative study of Botswana, Namibia and South Africa*. Münster: LIT Verlag.

Eaton, D. 2008. The business of peace: Raiding and peace work along the Kenya-Uganda border (part II). *African Affairs* 107(427): 243–59.

Egal, F., A. Valstar, and S. Meershoek. 2003. *Urban agriculture, household food security and nutrition in southern Africa*. Rome: Plant Production and Protection Division (AGP) of FAO. ftp://ftp.fao.org/es/esn/nutrition/urban/stellenbosch.pdf.

Ekeh, P. 1975. Colonialism and the two publics in Africa: A theoretical statement. *Comparative Studies in Society and History* 17(1): 91–112.

Engel, U., and G. Erdmann. 2007. Neopatrimonialism reconsidered: Critical review and elaboration of an elusive concept. *Commonwealth and Comparative Politics* 45(1): 95–119.

Englebert, P., and D. Tull. 2008. Postconflict reconstruction in Africa: Flawed ideas about failed states. *International Security* 32(4): 106–39.

Eyben, R., and S. Ladbury. 2006. *Building effective states: Taking a citizen's perspective*. Brighton, UK: Institute of Development Studies.

Fanthorpe, R. 2006. On the limits of liberal peace: Chiefs and democratic decentralization in post-war Sierra Leone. *African Affairs* 105(418): 27–49.

Finnegan, L., C. Hickson, and S. Rai, Eds. 2008. *Implementing community-based policing in Kenya*. London: Saferworld.

Fitzsimmons, T. 2005. The postconflict postscript: Gender and policing in peace operations. In *Gender, conflict and peacekeeping*, Eds. D. Mazurana, A. Raven-Roberts, and J. Parpart. Lanham, MD: Rowman and Littlefield.

FOMICRES (Mozambican Force for Crime Investigation and Solid Reinsertion). 2008. *Estratégia Comunitária de prevenção e combate ao crime aplicando modelo triangular em apoio a reforma do sistema de justiça, legalidade e segurança pública*. Maputo, Mozambique: FOMICRES.

Forcese, C. 2001. Militarised commerce in Sudan's oilfields: Lessons for Canadian foreign policy. *Canadian Foreign Policy* 8(3): 37–56.

Fourchard, L. 2008. A new name for an old practice: Vigilantes in south-west Nigeria. *Africa* 78(1): 16–40.

François, M., and I. Sud. 2006. Promoting stability and development in fragile and failed states. *Development Policy Review* 24(2): 141–60.

Fritz, V., and A. Menocal. 2006. (Re)building developmental states: From theory to practice. ODI Working Paper 274, Overseas Development Institute (ODI), London.

Fukuyama, F. 2004. *State-building: Governance and world order in the 21st century*. Ithaca, NY: Cornell University Press.

Gastrow, P. 1995. *Bargaining for peace, South Africa and the National Peace accord.* New York: US Institute of Peace Press (has full text of the 1991 Accord).

Geyer, Y. 2008. Post conflict police reform in South Africa and other African countries. Paper presented at IDASA Conference, National Security Agenda, Sandton Convention Centre, June 26, 2008. http://www.idasa.org.za/gbOutputFiles.asp? WriteContent=Y&RID=2282.

Goetz, A., and R. Jenkins. 2005., *Reinventing accountability: Making democracy work for human development.* Houndsmill, UK: Palgrave Macmillan.

Goldsmith, A. 2003. Policing weak states: Citizen safety and state responsibility. *Policing and Society* 13(1): 3–21.

Golooba-Mutebi, F., and A. Mapuor. 2005. *Traditional authorities in South Sudan: Chieftainship in the Bahr el Ghazal region.* Juba: UNDP/SPLM.

Graham, P. 2007. Creating a civil society—The role of civil society organizations in security sector reform during political transitions. Paper presented at Interpol Heads of Training Symposium, Johannesburg, March 6, 2007. http://www.idasa. org.za/gbOutputFiles.asp?WriteContent=Y&RID=1790.

Griffiths, A. 1997. *In the shadow of marriage: Gender and justice in an African community.* Chicago: University of Chicago Press.

Groenewald, H., and G. Peake. 2004. *Police reform through community-based policing: Philosophy and guidelines for implementation.* New York: International Peace Academy/Saferworld.

Hagmann, T., and M. Hoehne. 2007. Failed state or failed debate? Multiple Somali political orders within and beyond the nation-state. *Politorbis. Zeitschrift zur Aussenpolitik* 42: 20–26.

Hameiri, S. 2007. Failed states or a failed paradigm? State capacity and the limits of institutionalism. *Journal of International Relations and Development* 10: 122–49.

Hänggi, H., and V. Scherrer. 2008. Recent experience of UN integrated missions in security sector reform. In *Security sector reform and UN integrated missions: Experience from Burundi, the Democratic Republic of Congo, Haiti, and Kosovo,* Eds. H. Hänggi and V. Scherrer. Geneva: LIT/DCAF. http://www.dcaf.ch/publications/kms/details.cfm?lng=en&id=49473&nav1=4.

Hanlon, J. 1991. *Mozambique: Who calls the shots?* London: James Currey.

Hansen, H., and M. Twaddle, Eds. 1994. *From chaos to order: The politics of constitution-making in Uganda.* London: James Currey.

Harris, B. 2001. *As for violent crime that's our daily bread: Vigilante violence during South Africa's period of transition.* Violence and Transition Series, 1. Johannesburg: Centre for the Study of Violence and Reconciliation.

Haugerud, A. 2003. Kenya's agrarian visions: Land tenure, modernity and the state. Paper presented at Annual Meeting of the African Studies Association, Boston.

Head, S., and I. Brigada. 2006. *Philosophy and principles of community-based policing.* Belgrade: SEESAC, South Eastern and Eastern Europe Clearinghouse for the Control of Small Arms and Light Weapons. http://www.seesac.org.

Heald, S. 2006. State, law and vigilantism in northern Tanzania. *African Affairs* 105(419): 265–83.

Heald, S. 2007. Controlling crime and corruption from below: Sungusungu in Kenya. *International Relations* 21: 183–99.

Helgason A., G. Pálsson, H. Sloth Petersen, E. Angulalik, D. Gunnarsdóttir, B. Yngvadóttir, and K. Stefánsson. 2006. mtDNA variation in Inuit populations of Greenland and Canada: Migration history and population structure. *American Journal of Physical Anthropology* 130: 123–34.

Hills, A. 2000. *Policing in Africa: Internal security and the limits of liberalization.* Boulder, CO: Lynne Rienner.

Hills, A. 2008. The dialectic of police reform in Nigeria. *Journal of Modern African Studies* 46(2): 215–34.

Holm, T., and E. Eide. 2000. *Peacebuilding and police reform.* London: Frank Cass.

Howe, H. 2001. *Ambiguous order: Military forces in African states.* Boulder, CO: Lynne Rienner.

Howell, N. 2000. *Demography of the Dobe !Kung.* 2nd ed. Edison, NJ: Aldine Transaction.

Huggins, C., H. Musahara, P. Kamungi, J. Oketch, and K. Vlassenroot. 2005. *Conflict in the Great Lakes region—How is it linked with land and migration?* Natural Resource Perspectives, no. 96, March. London: Overseas Development Institute. http://www.odi.org.uk/publications/nrp/96-conflict-great-lakes-land-migration.pdf.

Human Rights Committee of UN General Assembly (2424th and 2425th meetings). 2005. http://www.un.org/News/Press/docs/2007/hrct682.doc.htm.

Human Rights Watch. 1999. *Leave: Genocide in Rwanda.* New York: HRW.

Human Rights Watch. 2007a. Nigeria: Investigate widespread killings by police— Police chief boasts of 785 killings in 90 days, press statement, November 18.

Human Rights Watch. 2007b. *There will be no trial. Police killings of detainees and the imposition of collective punishments,* 19(10A). New York: HRW.

Humphries, R. 2000. Crime and confidence: Voters' perceptions of crime. *Needbank ISS Crime Index* 4(2): 1–6.

Hutchful, E., and J. 'Kayode Fayemi. 2005. Security system reform in Africa. In *Security system reform and governance: Policy and good practice,* OECD/DAC. Paris: OECD, Annex 4.A1.

IANSA (International Action Network on Small Arms), Oxfam, and Saferworld. 2007. *Africa's Missing Billions.* Oxford, London: IANSA, Oxfam, Saferworld.

IDASA. 2007. Conference summary report, Police Reform and Democratisation Conference. http://www.idasa.org.za/index.asp?page=topics_details.asp%3FRID%3D11.

Igbinovia, P. 2000. The future of the Nigeria police. *Policing* 23(4): 538–54.

Immigration and Refugee Board of Canada, Ethiopia. 2007. *Protection services and legal recourse available to women who are victims of domestic violence (2005–2006).* ETH102157.E. UNHCR. http://www.unhcr.org/refworld/docid/47d6544fc.html.

International Crisis Group (ICG). 2006. *Liberia: Resurrecting the justice system.* IGG, Africa Report 107. Brussels: ICG.

International Crisis Group (ICG). 2007. *Central African Republic: Anatomy of a phantom state.* IGG, Africa Report 136. Brussels: ICG.

International Fund for Agricultural Development (IFAD). 2008a. *Enabling the rural poor to overcome poverty in Angola.* Rome: IFAD. http://www.ifad.org/operations/projects/regions/Pf/factsheets/angola.pdf

International Fund for Agricultural Development (IFAD). 2008b. *Enabling the rural poor to overcome poverty in Mozambique.* Rome: IFAD. http://www.ifad.org/operations/projects/regions/Pf/factsheets/mozambique.pdf

Irish, J. 1999. *Policing for profit: The future of South Africa's private security industry.* Monograph 39. Pretoria: ISS Studies.

Isaacman, B., and A. Isaacman. 1982. A Socialist legal system in the making: Mozambique before and after independence. In *The politics of informal justice,* Ed. R. Abel. New York: Academic Press.

Jackson, P. 2005. Chiefs, money and politicians: Rebuilding local government in post-war Sierra Leone. *Public Administration and Development* 25(1): 49–58.

Jackson, R., and C. Rosberg. 1982. *Personal rule in black Africa: Prince, autocrat, prophet, tyrant.* Berkeley: University of California Press.

Jensen, S. 2003. Through the lens of crime: Land claims and contestations of citizenship on the frontier of the South African state. wwwserver.law.wits.ac.za/ workshop/workshop03/WWLSJensen.doc.

Johnson, D. 2003. *The root causes of Sudan's civil wars.* London: International African Institute; Oxford: James Currey.

Johnston, L. 1992. *The rebirth of private policing.* London: Routledge.

Johnston, L., and C. Shearing. 2003. *Governing security: Explorations in policing and justice.* London: Routledge.

Joras, U., and A. Schuster. 2008. Private security companies and local populations: An exploratory study of Afghanistan and Angola. Swiss Peace Working Papers 1. http://www.swisspeace.ch/typo3/fileadmin/user_upload/pdf/Working_Paper/WP_1_2008.pdf.

Junne, G., and W. Verkoren. 2005. The challenges of postconflict development. In *Postconflict development: Meeting new challenges,* Eds. G. Junne and W. Verkoren. Boulder, CO: Lynne Rienner.

Justice Africa. 2004. Prospects for peace in Sudan: August–September. http://www.justiceafrica.org/blog/2004/09/03/prospects-for-peace-in-sudan-august-septemebr-2004/.

Kabwegyere, T. 1995. *The politics of state formation and destruction in Uganda.* Kampala: Fountain.

Kane, M., K. MacKiggan, C. Mburu, I. Gassama, E. Morley, and C. Eldon. 2002. *Sierra Leone: Report on preliminary review of justice sector: Joint DFID/World Bank Visit.* London and Washington, DC: DFID and World Bank.

Kanyeihamba, G. 2002. *Constitutional and political history of Uganda: From 1894 to the present.* Kampala: Centenary.

Karamagi, C., J. Tumwine, T. Tylleskar, and K. Heggenhougen. 2007. Intimate partner violence against women in eastern Uganda: Implications for HIV prevention. *BMC Public Health.* http://www.medscape.com/viewarticle/548848.

Kennedy, L., and D. Forde. 1990. Routine activities and crime: An analysis of victimization in Canada. *Criminology* 28: 137–69.

Kenya National Commission on Human Rights. 2007. Arbitrary arrest and illegal detention by the police of alleged terror suspects, press statement, January 31.

Koenig, M., T. Lutalo, F. Zhao1, F. Nalugoda, F. Wabwire-Mangen, N. Kiwanuka, J. Wagman, D. Serwadda, M. Wawer, and R. Gray. 2003. Domestic violence in rural Uganda: Evidence from a community-based study. *Bulletin of the World Health Organization* 81: 53–60.

Koyana, D., and J. Bekker. 1998. *Judicial process in the customary courts of southern Africa.* Umtata, South Africa: University of Transkei.

Kyed, H. M. 2007. The politics of policing: Re-capturing "zones of confusion" in rural post-war Mozambique. In *The security development nexus. Expressions of sovereignty and securitization in southern Africa*, Eds. L. Buur, S. Jensen, and F. Stepputat. Uppsala: Nordic Africa Institute and Pretoria: HSRC Press.

Kyed, H.M. Unpublished manuscript. Community policing in post-war Mozambique. *Policing and Society.*

Last, M. 2008. The search for security in Muslim northern Nigeria. *Africa* 78(1): 41–63.

Law, D. 2006. *The post-conflict security sector.* Policy Paper 14. Geneva: Centre for the Democratic Control of Armed Forces (DCAF).

Leitch, R., and C. Vandewint. 2004. *A study of customary law in contemporary southern Sudan.* World Vision International and South Sudan Secretariat of Legal and Constitutional Affairs. http://www.gurtong.org/ResourceCenter/laws/Customary%20Law%20Overview%20in%20South%20Sudan.

Lewis, I. 2004. As the Kenyan Somali "Peace" Conference falls apart in confusion, recognition of Somaliland's independence is overdue. http://www.somaliland.org/archives/?ID=04032004.

Lewis, P. 1992. Political transition and the dilemma of civil society in Africa. *Journal of International Affairs* 46(1): 31–54.

Liebling-Kalifani, H. 2009. Research and interviews with women war survivors in Uganda: Resilience and suffering as the consequence of war. In *War medicine and gender: The sociology and anthropology of structural suffering*, Eds. H. Bradbt and G. Lewando-Hundt. Aldershot, UK: Ashgate.

Liebling-Kalifani, H., A. Marshall, R. Ojiambo-Ochieng, and N. Kakembo. 2007. Experiences of women war-torture survivors in Uganda: Implications for health and human rights. *Journal of International Women's Studies* 8(4): 1–17.

Loader, I., and N. Walker. 2001. Policing as a public good: Reconstituting the connections between policing and the state. *Theoretical Criminology* 5(1): 9–35.

Loader, I., and N. Walker. 2006. Necessary virtues: The legitimate place of the state in the production of security. In *Democracy, society and the governance of security*, Eds. J. Wood and B. Dupont. Cambridge: Cambridge University Press.

Louw, A., M. Shaw, L. Camerer, and R. Robertshaw. 1998. *Crime in Johannesburg: Results of a city victim study.* Monograph 18. Pretoria: ISS.

Luckham, R., with I. Ahmed, R. Muggah, and S. White. 2001. Conflict and poverty in sub-Saharan Africa: An assessment of the issues and evidence. Working Paper 128, Institute of Development Studies, Brighton, UK.

Luff, R. 2008. Encroachment and efficiency: Armed actors in the relief market place. *Humanitarian Exchange Magazine* 39. http://www.odihpn.org/report.asp?id=2912.

Lund, C. 2001. Precarious democratization and local dynamics in Niger. *Development and Change* 32(5): 845–69.

Lutz, G., and W. Linder. 2004. *Traditional structures in local governance for local development.* World Bank Institute and Swiss Agency for Development Co-operation. Washington, DC and Berne: World Bank and SDC.

Lyons, W. 1999. *The politics of community policing.* Ann Arbor: University of Michigan.

MacLean, S., and T. Shaw. 2001. Canada and new "global" strategic alliances: Prospects for human security at start of the twenty-first century. *Canadian Foreign Policy* 8(3): 17–36.

MacRae, R., and D. Hubert, Eds. 2001. *Human security and the new diplomacy.* Kingston, ON, Canada: McGill-Queens University Press.

Malan, M. 2008. *Security sector reform in Liberia: Mixed results from humble beginnings.* http://www.strategicstudiesinstitute.army.mil/pdffiles/pub855.pdf.

Malan, M., P. Rakate, and A. McIntyre. 2002. *Peacekeeping in Sierra Leone: UNAMSIL hits the home straight.* Monograph 68. Pretoria: ISS.

Mamdani, M. 1996. *Citizen and subject, contemporary Africa and the legacy of late colonialism.* Kampala: Fountain.

Mani, R. 2002. *Beyond retribution: Seeking justice in the shadows of war.* Malden, MA: Polity.

Marenin, O. 1982. Parking tickets and the class repression: The concept of policing in critical theories of criminal justice. *Contemporary Crises* 6: 241–46.

Marenin, O. 1996. *Police change, changing police: International perspectives.* New York: Garland.

Marshall, M., and J. Goldstone. 2007. Global report on conflict, governance, and state fragility 2007: Gauging system performance and fragility in the globalization era. *Foreign Policy Bulletin* 17(1): 3–21.

Massaquoi, J. 1999. Building mechanisms for conflict resolution in south-east Sierra Leone: Sulima fishing community development project. Paper presented at the First Conference on All African Principles of Conflict Resolution and Reconciliation, Addis Ababa. http://www.reliefweb.int.

Mbabazi, P., S. MacLean, and T. Shaw. 2002. Governance for reconstruction in Africa: Challenges for policy communities/coalitions. *Global Networks* 2(1): 31–47.

McLaughlin, A. 2003. Threat and fear in women's daily lives: An examination of social and experiential contexts. Paper presented at the annual meeting of the American Sociological Association, Atlanta, September 15. http://www.allacademic.com/meta/p108018_index.html.

Meagher, P. 2005. *Service delivery in fragile states: Framing the issues.* Washington, DC: University of Maryland.

Meek, S. 2003. Policing Sierra Leone. In *Sierra Leone: Building the road to recovery,* Eds. M. Malan, S. Meek, T. Thusi, J. Ginifer, and P. Coker. Institute for Security Studies, Monograph No. 80. Pretoria: ISS.

Mehler, A., and J. Smith-Hoehn. 2007. The interaction of international, state and non-state security actors in Liberia and Sierra Leone: Roles and perceptions. In *State failure revisited II: Actors of violence and alternative forms of governance,* Eds. T. Debiel and T. Lambach. INEF Report 89. Duisburg, Germany: Institute for Development and Peace, University of Duisburg-Essen.

Mendelson-Forman, J. 2006. Security sector reform in Haiti. *International Peacekeeping* 13(1): 14–27.

Menkhaus, K. 2007. Local security systems in Somali East Africa. In *Fragile states and insecure people: Violence, security, and statehood in the twenty-first century,* Eds. L. Anderson, B. Moller, and F. Steppputat. Houndsmill, UK: Palgrave Macmillan.

Migdal, J., and K. Schlichte. 2005. Rethinking the state. In *The dynamics of states: The formation and crisis of state formation,* Ed. K. Schlichte. Aldershot, UK: Ashgate.

Ministry of Interior (MINT). 2005. *Políciamento comunitário. segurança e ordem pública, seminário nacional dos administradores distritais.* Maputo, Mozambique: MINT.

Minnaar, A. 2004. Private-public partnerships: Private security, crime prevention and policing in South Africa. Unpublished inaugural lecture, University of South Africa.

Mirzeler, M., and C. Young. 2000. Pastoral politics in the northeast periphery in Uganda: AK-47 as change agent. *Journal of Modern African Studies* 38: 407–29.

Mkutu, K. 2008. *Guns and governance in the Rift Valley: Pastoralist conflict and small arms.* Oxford: James Currey.

Mondelane, L. 2000. The growth, extent and causes of crime: Mocambique. Paper presented at the conference Crime and Policing in Transitional Societies, South Africa. http://www.kas.org.za/Publications.

Mullen, J. 2005. *Traditional authorities and local governance in post CPA southern Sudan.* New York: UNDP.

Museveni, Y. 1997. *Sowing the mustard seed: The struggle for freedom and democracy in Uganda.* London: Macmillan.

Narayan, D., R. Chambers, M. Kaul Shah, and P. Petesch. 1999. Global synthesis, consultations with the poor. Paper presented at Global Synthesis Workshop, September 22–23, World Bank, Washington, DC.

Nathan, L. 2007. No ownership, no commitment: A guide to local ownership of security sector reform. Paper commissioned by the Security Sector Reform Strategy of the UK government's Global Conflict Prevention Pool, University of Birmingham, UK.

Neild, R. 2000. Democratic police reforms in war-torn societies. *Conflict Security and Development* 1: 21–43.

Nina, D., and W. Scharf. 2001. Introduction: The other law? In *The other law: Non-state ordering in South Africa*, Eds. W. Scharf and D. Nina. Lansdowne, South Africa: Juta.

Nixon, H. 2008. *Subnational state-building in Afghanistan.* Kabul: Afghanistan Research and Evaluation Unit.

Nolte, I. 2007. Ethnic vigilantes and the state: The Oodua People's Congress in south-western Nigeria. *International Relations* 21: 217–35.

Nyamu-Musembi, C. 2003. *Review of experience in engaging with non-state justice systems in East Africa.* Brighton, UK: Institute of Development Studies.

Oakley, R., M. Dziedzic, and E. Goldberg. 1998. *Policing the new world disorder: Peace operations and public security.* Washington, DC: National Defense University.

Odinkalu, C. 2005. *Pluralism and the fulfillment of justice needs in Africa.* Open Society Justice Initiative. http://www.afrimap.org/english/images/paper/Odinkalu_Pluralism_Justice_ENfin.pdf.

Oomen, B. 2002. Walking in the middle of the road: People's perceptions on the legitimacy of traditional authority in Sekhukhune, South Africa. Paper presented at the research seminar Popular Perspectives on Traditional Authority in South Africa at the African Studies Centre, Leiden, January 17.

Organization for Economic Cooperation and Development (OECD). 2001. *OECD DAC guidelines, helping prevent violent conflict.* Paris: OECD.

Organization for Economic Cooperation and Development (OECD). 2004. *Security system reform and governance: Policy and good practice.* Policy Brief. Paris: OECD. http://www.oecd.org/dataoecd/20/47/31642508.pdf.

Organization for Economic Cooperation and Development (OECD). 2005a. Fuelling the future: Security, stability, development. Paris: OECD. http://www.oecd.org/dataoecd/8/39/31785288.pdf.

Organization for Economic Cooperation and Development (OECD). 2005b. *OECD DAC guidelines, security system, reform and governance.* Paris: OECD.

Organization for Economic Cooperation and Development (OECD). 2006. *DAC guidelines and reference series applying strategic environmental assessment: Good practice guidance for development co-operation.* Paris: OECD.

Organization for Economic Cooperation and Development (OECD). 2007. *OECD DAC handbook on SSR: Supporting security and justice.* Paris: OECD.

Organization for Economic Cooperation and Development (OECD). 2008. Concepts and dilemmas of state building in fragile situations: From fragility to resilience. Paris: OECD. http://www.oecd.org/dataoecd/59/51/41100930.pdf

Orr, R. 2002. Governing when chaos rules: Enhancing governance and participation. *The Washington Quarterly* 25(4): 139–152.

Osborne, D., and T. Gaebler. 1992. *Rethinking government.* Harmondsworth, UK: Penguin.

Paris, R. 2004. *At war's end: Building peace after civil conflict.* Cambridge: Cambridge University Press.

Paulo, M., C. Rosário, and I. Tvedten. 2007. *"Xiculungo" social relations of urban poverty in Maputo, Mozambique.* Bergen, Norway: Chr. Michelsen Institute. http://www.cmi.no/publications/file/?2930=xiculungo-social-relations-of-urban-poverty-maputo.

Peake, G., E. Scheye, and A. Hills eds. 2006. *Managing insecurity: Field experiences of security sector reform.* London: Taylor & Francis.

Pelser, E. 1999. *The challenges of community policing in South Africa.* Monograph 42. Pretoria: ISS. http://www.iss.co.za/Pubs/Papers/42/Paper42.html.

Peters, R. 2001. *The reintroduction of Islamic criminal law in northern Nigeria. A study conducted on behalf of the European Commission.* http://europa.eu.int/comm/europeaid/projects/eidhr/pdf/islamic-criminal-law-nigeria_en.pdf.

Philip, K. 1989. The private sector and the security establishment. In *War and society: The militarisation of South Africa*, Eds. J. Cock and L. Nathan. Cape Town: David Philip.

Plunkett, M. 2005. Reestablishing the rule of law. In *Postconflict development: Meeting new challenges*, Eds. G. Junne and W. Verkoren. Boulder, CO: Lynne Rienner.

Pratten, D. 2008. The thief eats his shame: Practice and power in Nigerian vigilantism. *Africa* 78(1): 64–83.

Pratten, D., and A. Sen, Eds. 2007. *Global vigilantes.* London: Hurst.

Private Security Industry Regulatory Authority (PSIRA). 2007. *Annual report 2006/7.* http://www.psira.co.za/pdfs/annual_report_2007.pdf.

Reno, W. 2000a. Clandestine economies, violence and states in Africa. *Journal of International Affairs* 53(2): 433–59.

Reno, W. 2000b. Internal wars, private enterprise and the shift in strong state-weak state relations. *International Politics* 37(1): 57–74.

Reno, W. 2007. Protectors and predators: Why is there a difference among West African militias? In *Fragile states and insecure people? Violence, security, and statehood in the twenty-first century*, Eds. L. Andersen, B. Møller, and F. Stepputat. Houndsmill, UK: Palgrave Macmillan.

Richards, P. 2005. To fight or to farm? Agrarian dimensions of the Mano River conflicts (Liberia and Sierra Leone). *African Affairs* 104: 571–90.

Richardson, A. 2004. *Women's inheritance rights in Africa: The need to integrate cultural understanding and legal reform.* Human Rights Brief 19, Winter. http://law.lexisnexis.com/webcenters/RuleofLawResourceCenter/.

Robb, C. 1999. *Can the poor influence policy? Participation in the World Bank's poverty assessments.* Washington, DC: World Bank.

Roberts. 2008. Hybrid polities and indigenous pluralities: Advanced lessons in statebuilding from Cambodia. *Journal of Intervention and Statebuilding* 2(1): 63–86.

Roche, D. 2002. Restorative justice and the regulatory state in South African Townships. *British Journal of Criminology* 42: 514–33.

Rubio-Marín, R. 2006a. Gender and reparations: Challenges and opportunities. *International Journal of Transitional Justice.* http://www.ictj.org/static/Gender/0602GenderReparations.eng.pdf.

Rubio-Marín, R., Ed. 2006b. *What happened to the women? Gender and reparations for human rights violations.* New York: Social Science Research Council.

Ruteere, M., and M. Pommerolle. 2003. Democratizing security or decentralizing repression? The ambiguities of community policing in Kenya. *African Affairs* 102: 587–604.

Rweyemamu, R. 1989. Religion and peace: An experience with African traditions. *Studia Missionalia* 38: 377–405.

Salomons, D. 2005. Security: An absolute prerequisite. In *Postconflict development: Meeting new challenges*, Eds. G. Junne and W. Verkoren. Boulder, CO: Lynne Rienner.

Samuels, K. 2006. *Rule of law reform in post-conflict countries: Operational initiatives and lessons learnt.* Washington, DC: Conflict Prevention and Reconstruction, World Bank.

Sandbrook, R. 1998. Patrons, clients, and factions: Explaining conflict in Africa. In *Africa: Dilemmas of development and change*, Ed. P. Lewis, 64–83. Boulder, CO: Westview.

Sawyer, E. 2008. Remove or reform? A case for (restructuring) chiefdom governance in post-conflict Sierra Leone. *African Affairs* 107(428): 387–403.

Schärf, W. 2000. Community justice and community policing in post-apartheid South Africa. How appropriate are the justice systems of Africa? Paper presented at the International Workshop on the Rule of Law and Development: Citizen Security, Rights and Life Choices in Law and Middle Income Countries Institute for Development Studies, University of Sussex, June 1–3.

Schärf, W. 2001. *Police reform and crime prevention in post-conflict transitions. Learning from the South African and Mozambican experience.* http://www.um.dk/upload/english/DP3cScharf.

Schärf, W. 2003. *Non-state justice systems in southern Africa: How should governments respond?* Brighton, UK: IDS.

Schärf, W., and D. Nina. 2001. *The other law: Non-state ordering in South Africa.* Lansdowne, South Africa: Juta.

Scheye, E. Unpublished manuscript. The statebuilding misconception in the fragile and post-conflict state. *Policing and Society.*

Scheye, E., and G. Peake. 2005. Unknotting local ownership. In *Post conflict societies: From intervention to sustainable local ownership*, Eds. A. Ebnöther and P. Fluri. Geneva: DCAF.

Schreier, F., and M. Caparini. 2005. *Privatising security: Law, practice and governance of private military and security companies.* Occasional Paper 6. Geneva: DCAF.

Sedra, M. 2007. Security sector reform in Afghanistan: An instrument of the state-building project. In *Fragile states and insecure people: Violence, security, and statehood in the twenty-first century,* Eds. L. Anderson, B. Moller, and F. Steppputat. Houndsmill, UK: Palgrave Macmillan.

Seekings, J. 2001. Social ordering and control in the African townships of South Africa: An historical overview of extra-state initiatives from the 1940s to the 1990s. In *The other law: Non-state forms of ordering in South Africa,* Eds. W. Schärf and D. Wetton. Landsdowne, South Africa: Juta.

Seesemann, R. 2007. Interview with Rüdiger Seesemann. *Development and Co-operation* 48(10): 372.

Shaw, M., and A. Louw. 1997. *Stolen opportunities: The impact of crime on South Africa's poor.* Monograph Series 14. Pretoria: ISS.

Shearing, C., and J. Wood. 2003. Governing security for common goods. *International Journal of the Sociology of Law* 31(3): 205–25.

Sideris, T. 2000. Rape in war and peace: Some thoughts on social context and gender roles. *Agenda* 43: 41–45.

Sierra Leone Police (SLP). 2004. *An investigative perception survey on the performance of the SLP for the first half of the year 2004: A case study of the western area and the provincial towns of Makeni, Bo and Kenema.* Freetown: SLP.

Sierra Leone Police (SLP). 2005. *The annual crime report for the year 2004.* Freetown: SLP.

Sierra Leone Truth and Reconciliation Commission. 2004. *Provisional report.* Vol. 3a. Freetown: TRC. http://www.usip.org/library/tc/tc_regions/tc_sl.html#rep.

Simone, A. 2002. *Principles and realities of urban governance in Africa.* United Nations Human Settlements Programme (UN-HABITAT). http://www.unhabitat.org/downloads/docs/2112_6752_Principles%20and%20Realities%20of%20Urban%20Gov%20in%20Africa.pdf.

Sklar, R. 1993. The African frontier for political science. In *Africa and the disciplines: The contributions of research in Africa to the social sciences and humanities,* Eds. R. Bates, V. Mudimbe, and J. O'Barr, 83–110. Chicago: University of Chicago Press.

Smillie, I., L. Gberie, and R. Hazelton. 2000. *The heart of the matter: Sierra Leone, diamonds and human security.* Ottawa: Partnership Africa Canada. http://www.partnershipafricacanada.org.

Spearin, C. 2008. Private, armed and humanitarian? States, NGOs, international private security companies and shifting humanitarianism. *Security Dialogue* 39(4): 363–82.

Stone, C. 2005. *Supporting security, justice and development: Lessons for a new era.* New York: Vera Institute of Justice.

Suhrke, A. 2007. Reconstruction as modernisation: The "post-conflict" project in Afghanistan. *Third World Quarterly* 28(7): 1291–1308.

Thomas, C. 2000. *Global governance, development and human security.* London: Pluto.

Thorne, K. 2005. Rule of law through imperfect bodies? The informal justice systems of Burundi and Somalia. Paper presented at Peace and Justice Conference. http://www.peace-justiceconference.info/download/WS6%20Rule%20of%20Law%20through%20imperfect%20bodies-Thorne.pdf.

Titeca, K. 2007. The Masai and Miraa: Public authority, governance and khat in Bwera Town. Paper presented at AEGIS, Leiden, 2007.

Tripp, A. 2004. Women's movements, customary law, and land rights in Africa: The case of Uganda. *African Studies Quarterly* 7(4).

Ubink, J. 2007. Traditional authority revisited: Popular perceptions of chiefs and chieftaincy in peri-urban Kumasi, Ghana. *Journal of Legal Pluralism* 55: 123–61.

Uganda Bureau of Statistics (UBOS). 2006. *Uganda demographic and health survey.* Kampala: UBOS.

United Nations Development Assistance Framework (UNDAF). 2005. *Good practice notes.* http://www.undg.org/archive_docs/6607–2004–2005_UNDAFs_-_Good_Practice__Post-Conflict___Transition_-_Post-Conflict___Transit.doc.

United Nations Development Programme (UNDP). 1994. *Human development report.* New York: Oxford University Press.

United Nations Development Programme (UNDP). 1995. Development assistance to the gendarmerie and communal police force of Rwanda background report to facilitate the elaboration of a final project document, report by Lt.-Col. Cees De Rover for the UNDP, New York.

United Nations Development Programme (UNDP). 1999. *Human development report 1999.* New York: Oxford University Press. http://www.undp.org.

United Nations Development Programme/United States Agency for International Development (UNDP/USAID). 2007. *First steps in post-conflict statebuilding*: Washington, DC: USAID.

United Nations Division for the Advancement of Women. 2006. *Report on the convention on the elimination of all forms of discrimination against women, mission to Liberia, 12–15 June 2006, findings and recommendations of experts.* http://www.un.org/womenwatch/daw/TechnicalCooperation/docs/WRS/report%20liberia2006.

United Nations Human Settlements Programme (UN-HABITAT). 1996. *An urbanizing world—Global report on human settlements.* Nairobi: Safer Cities Programme.

United Nations Human Settlements Programme (UN-HABITAT). 2003. *Global report on human settlements 2003: The challenge of the slums.* Nairobi.

United Nations Interregional Crime and Justice Research Institute (UNICRI). 2003. *Strategic plan of the police of the Republic of Mozambique: Results of surveys on victimisation and police performance.* Maputo, Mozambique: Ministry of the Interior and for Defence and Security; Rome: UNICRI. http://www.unicri.it/PRM/reports_en/StratPlanPRMengl.PDF.

United Nations Office for the Coordination of Humanitarian Affairs (UNOCHA). 2006. *Traditional and informal justice systems: A human rights perspective.*

United Nations Population Fund (UNFPA). 2000. *Gender-based violence in Sierra Leone. A case study.* New York: UNFPA.

U.S. Department of State, Country Report. 2007. Country reports on human rights practices. http://www.state.gov/g/drl/rls/hrrpt/2007/.

Vinck, P., P. Pham, S. Baldo, and R. Shigekane. 2008. *Living with fear: A population-based survey on attitudes about peace, justice, and social reconstruction in eastern Democratic Republic of Congo.* Human Rights Center at The University of California, Berkeley, The Payson Center at Tulane University, and International Center for Transitional Justice. http://www.Reliefweb.Int/Rw/Rwb.Nsf/Db900sid/ASAZ-7HVBFR/$File/Full_Report.Pdf.

von Schnitzler, A., G. Ditlhage, L. Kgalema, T. Maepa, T. Mofokeng, and P. Pigou. 2001. *Guardian or gangster? Mapogo a Mathamaga: A case study.* Violence and Transition Series, 3. Johannesburg: CSVR, Centre for the Study of Violence and Reconciliation. http://www.csvr.org.za/papers/papvtp3.htm.

Wacquant, L. 2001. The penalisation of poverty and the rise of neo-liberalism. *European Journal on Criminal Policy and Research* 9: 401–12.

Wallensteen, P. 2006. *Strategic peacebuilding: Issues and actions.* Paris: Kroc Institute.

Washington Office on Latin America (WOLA). 2002. *From peace to governance: Police reform and the international community.* http://www.wola.org/publications/police_reform_report.pdf.

Wasserman, S., and K. Faust. 1994. *Social network analysis.* Cambridge: Cambridge University Press.

Weber, M. 1948. *From Max Weber: Essays in sociology,* Ed. and trans. H. Geth and C. Wright Mills. London: RKP.

Wiley, L. 2000. *Land tenure reform and the balance of power in eastern and southern Africa.* Natural Resource Perspective, 5. London: Overseas Development Institute.

Wojkowska, E. 2006. *Doing justice: How informal justice systems can contribute.* Oslo: UNDP Oslo Governance Centre.

Wood, J., and C. Shearing. 2007. *Imagining security.* Cullompton, UK: Willan.

Woodman, G. 1996. Legal pluralism and the search for Justice. *Journal of African Law* 40(2): 152–67.

Woodrow Wilson School of Public and International Affairs. 2003. *The missing priority: Post-conflict security and the rule of law.* Prepared for the U.S. National Security Council by Princeton University. http://www.wws.princeton.edu.

World Bank. 1995. *Rwandese Republic emergency recovery project.* Report No. T-6483-Rw, January 12. Washington: World Bank.

World Bank. 2000. *Can Africa claim the twenty-first century?* Washington: IBRD. http://www.worldbank.org/ecommerce.

World Health Organization (WHO). 2005. *Multi-country study on women's health and domestic violence against women.* Geneva: WHO.

Wulf, H. 2007. *Challenging the Weberian concept of the state: The future of the monopoly of violence.* ACPACS Occasional Paper 9. Brisbane: ACPACS.

Wunsch, J., and D. Ottemoeller. 2004. Uganda: Multiple levels of local governance. In *Local governance in Africa: The challenges of democratic decentralization,* Eds. D. Olowu and J. Wunsch J. Boulder, CO: Lynne Rienner.

Zvekic, U., and A. Alvazzi del Frate, Eds. 1995. *Criminal victimisation in the developing world.* UNICRI Publication 55. Rome: United Nations Interregional Crime and Justice Research Institute.

Index

A Call for Authors

Introducing a New Book Series from CRC Pre

Advances in Police Theory and Practice

AIMS AND SCOPE:

This cutting-edge series is designed to promote publication of books on contemporary advances in police theory and practice. We are especially interested in volumes that focus on the nexus between research and practice, with the end goal of disseminating innovations in policing. We will consider collections of expert contributions as well as individually authored works. Books in this series will be marketed internationally to both academic and professional audiences. This series also seeks to —

- Bridge the gap in knowledge about advances in theory and practice regarding who the police are, what they do, and how they maintain order, administer laws, and serve their communities

- Improve cooperation between those who are active in the field and those who are involved in academic research so as to facilitate the application of innovative advances in theory and practice

The series especially encourages the contribution of works coauthored by police practitioners and researc We are also interested in works comparing policing approaches and methods globally, examining such are the policing of transitional states, democratic policing, policing and minorities, preventive policing, inves tion, patrolling and response, terrorism, organized crime and drug enforcement. In fact, every aspect of poli public safety, and security, as well as public order is relevant for the series. Manuscripts should be betweer and 600 printed pages. If you have a proposal for an original work or for a contributed volume, please touch.

Series Editor
Dilip Das, Ph.D.,
Ph: 802-598-3680 E-mail: dilipkd@aol.com

Dr. Das is a professor of criminal justice and Human Rights Consultant to the United Nations. He is a fe chief of police and, founding president of the International Police Executive Symposium, IPES, www.ipes He is also founding editor-in-chief of *Police Practice and Research: An International Journal (*) (Routledge/Taylor & Francis), www.tandf.co.uk/journals. In addition to editing the *World Police Encyclo* (Taylor & Francis, 2006), Dr. Das has published numerous books and articles during his many years of inv ment in police practice, research, writing, and education.

Proposals for the series may be submitted to the series editor or directly to –

Carolyn Spence
Acquisitions Editor • CRC Press / Taylor & Francis Group
561-998-2515 • 561-997-7249 (fax)
carolyn.spence@taylorandfrancis.com • www.crcpress.com
6000 Broken Sound Parkway NW, Suite 300, Boca Raton, FL 33487

CRC Press
Taylor & Francis Group

For Product Safety Concerns and Information please contact our EU
representative GPSR@taylorandfrancis.com Taylor & Francis Verlag GmbH,
Kaufingerstraße 24, 80331 München, Germany

Printed and bound by CPI Group (UK) Ltd, Croydon, CR0 4YY
08/05/2025
01864451-0001